CHARISM AND SACRAMENT

CHARISM AND SACRAMENT

A Theology of Christian Conversion

by
Donald L. Gelpi, S.J.

PAULIST PRESS
New York / Paramus / Toronto

Library of Congress
Catalog Card Number: 75-44873

ISBN: 0-8091-1935-8

Published by Paulist Press
Editorial Office: 1865 Broadway, N.Y., N.Y. 10023
Business Office: 400 Sette Drive, Paramus, N.J. 07652

Printed and bound in the
United States of America

Contents

PART I: CHARISM   1

   I. The Experiential Approach   3

  II. The Mind of Jesus   27

 III. The Pauline Gifts   63

 IV. The Charismatic Experience   97

PART II: SACRAMENT   111

   V. Baptism in Water and the Holy Spirit   113

 VI. Marriage and Celibacy   157

VII. Apostolic Ministry   187

VIII. The Supper of Blessing   229

v

For Jerry McMahon, S.J.,
my brother and friend,
who no longer sees darkly in gifts and books
but knows even as he is known.
"My companion, my familiar friend,
we used to hold sweet converse together;
within God's house we walked in fellowship."

(Ps. 55)

Foreword

Charism and Sacrament is an essay in what Bernard Lonergan has called "foundational theology." But it attempts also to draw directly on categories evolved by American philosophers who have reflected on human religious experience. My hope in taking such an approach to charismatic prayer is to endow theological reflection on the charismatic renewal with a complexity and depth that have too often been lacking in the existing literature on the "movement."

The most basic question posed by the charismatic renewal is one of conversion to God. To understand the complexity of the conversion process one must come to some clarity about the meaning of experience and of religious experience. One must also reflect on those events and values that give specific shape to the Christian religious experience.

One of the most pressing areas of theological disagreement is sacramental theology. My hope is that by grounding a theology of gift and of sacrament in an understanding of the meaning of Christian conversion, we may begin to move from the experience of ecumenical prayer which the renewal has made possible to a serious discussion of those issues which continue to divide Christians who pray together charismatically. I also hope to provide a context in which traditional Catholics can begin to understand that their defense of sacramental piety is meaningless unless it also includes a defense of the charismatic dimensions of the Christian conversion experience.

I am extremely grateful to Robert Heyer for helping me to reduce a bulky manuscript to human and (hopefully) readable form. I also owe a tremendous debt of gratitude to Shiela Varnado and to Lois Thompson who bore the heat of the day in reducing the original manuscript to a readable typescript. Finally, I am indebted to all of those people in the charismatic renewal of the Church whose insights and experiences are reflected in this book: my students and friends in the charismatic tract of the Institute for Spirituality and Worship deserve special mention.

Jesuit School of Theology at Berkeley
Berkeley, California

PART I
CHARISM

I
The
Experiential
Approach

1. In 1971 I attended a conference for the Catholic charismatic renewal held at Loyola University in Los Angeles. I found myself sharing lunch with a Lutheran priest, a fairly conservative Catholic monsignor, and a classical Pentecostal minister. We agreed that only the power of the Holy Spirit could have brought us together as brothers in the Lord. And in the open and loving atmosphere created by the conference, we were able to share our personal experiences of God and our respective approaches to ministry and to worship.

The conversation drifted toward the sacraments, especially to the celebration of the Lord's supper. And we shared together our beliefs about the real presence of Christ in the eucharist. The classical Pentecostal minister observed that for him the Lord's supper was only a memorial. I agreed that it was indeed a memorial but suggested that there is a very great difference between recalling something like a dental appointment and recalling something in the power and anointing of the Holy Spirit. He agreed.

Our conversation went no further. But I left the table convinced that there was need for someone to attempt a book that explains the relationship between charismatic and sacramental worship. For as the Spirit continues to move powerfully in all the churches, He is beginning to heal the centuries of misunderstanding that have divided one Christian community from another. Sacramental theology has, of course, been one of the major cockpits of religious debate and mutual misunderstanding. And the antagonism that misunderstanding breeds has all too often stifled love, insight, and genuine religious and human growth. Bitterness has tended to transform all the Christian churches into bigoted sects rigidly entrenched in their respective theories of ritual worship.

The charismatic renewal of the churches is, however, beginning to provide a practical context in which Christians of different communions can worship together in the Lord. One would hope, then, that such shared worship might also free them to re-evaluate their beliefs concerning the ritual sacraments as well.

But if ecumenical dialogue on the sacraments is to advance, there would seem to be a need to find a new basis for discussing their meaning and purpose within Christian worship. Too often in the past Catholics have insisted that Christians of other communions accept a Catholic doctrinal stance as the only legitimate basis for discussion. But many Protestants do not relate at all to the ritual and dogmatic tradition of Catholics. Protestant piety tends more to be rooted in a devout understanding of Scripture than in dogma and ritual. Moreover, different Christian communions have assumed radically divergent positions concerning the meaning and purpose of sacramental worship. As a consequence, arguments about sacramental doctrine have usually generated more heat than light.

As I reflected upon my luncheon conversation at the Loyola conference, it occurred to me that an experiential approach to a discussion of the relationship between the gifts and the sacraments might be ecumenically fruitful. In that conversation, the reason why a conservative Catholic monsignor, a Lutheran priest, a classical Pentecostal minister, and I were able to make some small progress toward mutual understanding was that we were all initially willing to put aside our official doctrinal attitudes for an hour and to speak out of our personal experience of God in worship. What we discovered was that our experience of the Lord even in official ritual worship had much in common.

2. In these pages our theological approach to the relationship between charismatic and sacramental worship will, then, be experiential. But is it even possible to theorize about human experience? Take any cross-section of any human experience and it seems at first glance to be a buzzing, blooming confusion, a tangled miscellany of feelings, ideas, impulses, facts. To reduce experience

as a whole to anything like speculative clarity would seem at first glance to be a fool's venture.

One possible line of approach has been suggested by contemporary process theology. Process theory takes much of its inspiration from the writings of Alfred North Whitehead.[1] Whitehead has suggested that we think of ourselves not as having experiences but as being experiences. What I am is a developing experience. The kind of experience I am at any given moment is the fruit of my prior history, of my evaluative response to the facts in that history, and of the decisions I have taken in the light of my evaluative responses. The advantage of thinking in such terms is that "experience" ceases to be something "accidental" or "non-essential" to my makeup. It is the very stuff of which I am made.

If I am an experience rather than "have experiences," I may attempt to theorize about my personal development by sorting out the kinds of realities that shape me as an experience. I can certainly make the following minimal generalization about my experiential makeup. At any moment in my experiential development I may distinguish the realities I experience, my evaluative response to them, and the self that responds.

The first and most obvious realities I experience are the facts of my day-to-day existence: the food I eat, the clothes rubbing on my flesh, the light waves that strike my eye, the vibrations on my eardrum, my own bodily processes. Such facts endow experience with a certain toughness. They are forces that shape me, sometimes harshly. They resist direct volitional control. The food I eat is either nourishing or not, healthy or poisonous. If it is poisonous, no amount of mere wishing will change matters. If I am sick with cancer or influenza, merely wanting to be well will not effect my cure. I cannot wish away lights and sounds and smells and tastes and blows and caresses. Since I must conform initially to the factual elements in experience if I am to shape or change them, we will call the initial factual realm of experience "conformal feelings."

There are forces in the world that shape me as an experience. But within limits I also shape my world. I do so through decision and action. My words and deeds are also facts. I cannot unsay a harsh or a kindly word once it has been spoken. I cannot undo an angry or a loving deed once it has been done. But if my words and deeds are forces that gradually shape my environment, they also gradually shape me as a person, as a self. The kind of person I have become in the course of my growth is in large measure though not exclusively a function of my personal decisions. Reactive decision defines the subsequent realm of fact.

Moreover, if I *am* an experience (rather than one who has experiences) the facts that shape me as an experience are quite literally a part of me. Since they exist within experience, they exist quite literally *within me*! In a world of developing experiences, then, nothing exists (as philosophers once thought) "in itself but not in anything else." Things exist quite literally in one another to the extent that they shape one another. This is perhaps for many readers a new way of thinking about experience, and it deserves a bit of reflection.

Medieval theologians used to talk about the three persons of the Trinity as "mutually inexistent." The term "inexistent" does not mean "non-existent." It means "existing in" a reality other than oneself. Because from all eternity the Father generates the Son and because from all eternity both Son and Father spirate the Holy Spirit, the three divine persons are said quite literally to exist in one another. To say that persons "exist in one another" is to say that they are efficaciously interdependent and relationally distinct. They draw their life efficaciously from one another and yet are not identical with one another. An experiential approach to human development extends the same property of "inexistence" to all reality. One reality exists in another to the extent that it functions efficaciously in the other as an experience. To say so much is only to take quite literally the words of Jesus at the last supper: "On that day you will understand that I am in the Father and you in Me and I in you." It is to take quite literally the assurance of Paul: "Just as a human body, though it is made up of many parts, is a single unit because all these parts, though many, make one body, so it is with Christ."[2]

3. But if I reflect on myself as an experience, not only am I the facts that shape and mould me in my development, but I am also the way in which I respond to those facts. The most obvious way in which I react to facts is perceptually. My most vivid per-

ceptions are conscious experiences of sight, sound, touch, taste, smell. But such experiences in no way exhaust the realm of perception. Moreover, even the five senses vary considerably in vividness. Among human perceptions, sight is the most vivid; smells are among the vaguest. But we also experience vague perceptions of our own bodies: visceral and kinetic sensations, feelings of physical satisfaction and of pain. Our shifting moods also yield vague emotive perceptions of our bodily processes and of our surrounding environment. Fatigue leaves me edgy and irascible. A cloudy day leaves me depressed. A tastefully arranged room relaxes me. A prison threatens and oppresses me. Some perceptions may, moreover, be more or less conscious: sleepwalkers may react visually to sights of which they are unconscious. Automatic writers react perceptually without being conscious of what they are doing. Many moods and visceral perceptions elude consciousness.

What is descriptively common to all of these perceptual experiences is that they elude direct volitional control while presenting environmental forces to me for further evaluation and decision. But perceptual experiences themselves present facts evaluatively. Colors, sounds, tastes, smells are emotively charged. Moods, feelings of pleasure and pain are attitudes. But because they present my world to me initially for further evaluative response, perceptual feelings can legitimately be termed "dative," from the Latin verb "*do, dare*: I give, I present."

Of course, we do more than perceive things. We also adjust to them emotionally. Some of our adjustments are fairly automatic in character. A harsh word may evoke an immediate, unreflective blow. The sight of mutilation may cause me to vomit. We term such automatic emotive responses reflex. But not all emotional adjustment is so simple. It may come to visible expression in a broad variety of familiar activities: the reassurances of touch, of basic life rhythms, of sound, of speech; eating and drinking, smoking, gum-chewing, sleep, acts of self-discipline, laughing, dreaming, fantisizing, rationalization, talking things out, hyperactivity, aggressively seeking out the source of annoyances, slips of the tongue, minor accidents or mismanagements, sneezing, itching, coughing, scratching, pacing. When these emotional adjustments prove inadequate, more expensive coping devices are called into play, devices that range from bouts of "nervousness" to serious psychic illness and suicide. Although our emotional adjustments may accompany rational thought, they are themselves concrete processes, mediated either by activity or by the kind of imagistic thinking that occurs in dreams, whether conscious or unconscious. Our more complex emotional adjustments involve considerable conscious or unconscious fantisizing, and the images that accompany them assume a profoundly symbolic character for us, as, for example, do images in a dream. When emotional adjustments are symbolically mediated by images they cease to be reflex in character and become instinctive. The realm of instinct is, then, governed by free-floating fantasy and by free, imaginative association. We shall call emotive adjustments by the name "physical purposes." They are physical because they are tied to the concrete pole of evaluative response. They are purposes because they reorient experience evaluatively.

Physical purposes may be more or less conscious. Most dreams are in fact unconscious, although they can assume a conscious character. Emotional adjustments also lack the clarity of abstract, rational thought. We do not know fully why we react in a reflex or instinctive way to certain stimuli. Dream images are so rich in free associative connotations that it is often difficult to tell exactly what they mean. But through more abstract forms of reflection, one may clarify vague, concrete images. By reflection on a dream, for instance, I may come to an insight into its true meaning. By reflecting on a difficult poem, I may come to perceive the author's intent. Our abstract, theoretical interpretations of our vaguer emotive feelings may occur in a variety of explanatory contexts: our explanations may be ordinary, common-sense judgments; they may be either scholarly or strictly scientific. In any case, to enter the world of abstract thinking is to engage in some form of logical inference.

Our initial inferences about the things we experience are pretty spontaneous. They are often generated by an emotional response to some environmental fact. After a pleasant evening with friends, I may say: "That was a great party!" My statement is a kind of inference. It classifies a complex fact of my experience as a "great party." To make such a statement I must have a general idea of what parties are like and some set of criteria for evaluating their relative "greatness." And on the basis of these personal presuppositions, I classify the social gathering I have just experienced as "a great party." When I make such spontaneous, enthusiastic judgments, I often do not reflect too carefully on the reasons I have for classifying any given party as great. But if pressed to do so I could probably offer some abstract explanation of what the phrase means to me. Inferences like the one just described, which yield the initial classification of experiential data, are called "abductive." They are from a logical standpoint, the same thing as the formulation of an hypothesis. Because they give rise to concrete judgments about reality, inferences generate propositional insights. Hereafter we shall, therefore, refer to the initial formulation of an hypothesis as an abductive propositional feeling.

Many people live most of their "rational" lives at an abductive, hypothetical level. They go about making initial judgments about things, but never bother to ask whether those judgments are really accurate or adequate. Often we do not criticize our spontaneous abductions unless we are challenged. To my euphoric pronouncement: "That was a great party!" a friend may reply, "I think it was a lousy party." If we are to get beyond mere disagreement, we must begin to explain to one another what we mean by "great" or by "lousy." To justify the application of either adjective to the party in question, we must, then, both invoke some form of explanatory, deductive inference. I may, for example, explain that a great party is one in which the people are compatible, the conversations are lively, and everybody dances for most of the night. Since I believe the party in question was great, I predict deductively that a careful investigation will uncover facts that will justify my calling it "great." Such deductive inferences differ from abductive. While in abductive thinking, I conclude that if some kind of general principle holds true, then a concrete fact may be classified as an instance, or case, of that rule; in a deductive inference, I argue that certain predictable facts will be verified in a specific case because it is an instance of a general rule. In the case of the party in question, I predict, when pressed by my friend, that because great parties involve compatible people, lively conversation, and dancing and because the party in question was a great one, an investigation of what happened at the party will show that those who attended were in fact compatible, that they engaged in regular lively conversation, and that they danced the whole night through. In other words, because I believe a specific party to belong to the class of "great," I predict that certain facts will emerge upon investigation which justify such a classification. In the future, we shall term such an inference a "deductive propositional feeling." The example we considered is a fairly trivial, common-sense inference. But similar inferences occur in the realms of scientific and scholarly thinking.

But to justify my statement that the party was great, I must engage in more than deductive thinking. The verification or falsification of my deductive conclusions invokes a third kind of inference, namely, inductive inference. I may, for example, discover in investigating the personality profiles of those who attended the party that only 15% were emotionally compatible and that beneath all the politeness and surface gaity there was constant gossip and backbiting. I may discover that 75% of the people there found the conversation dull and trivial. I may discover that, while 25% did lots of dancing all night, I myself being one, the rest were wallflowers. If so, I must concede that according to my deductive criteria, the party was less than great. Inductive inference argues on the basis of fact to the applicability or inapplicability of a deductively clarified principle to a concrete case. In the future we will term such inferences "inductive propositional feelings."

As human experience grows evaluatively, it moves, then, through predictable stages. Initial evaluations are dative and perceptual. They give rise to emotive adjustments that are concrete and purposive. Emotive adjustments breed initial abductive beliefs. Reflection on spontaneous, abductive hypotheses yields their deductive clarification. And inductive inference yields the verification or falsification of deductively clarified beliefs. My dative perceptions, emotional adjustments, and inferences shape the quality of experience. They give experience its evaluative form. Hence, my evaluative responses to the environmental forces that shape me define an experiential realm of quality that is distinguishable from the experiential realm of fact.

My actions, however, may be the fruit of any or every phase of my personal evaluative adjustment. My deeds may express violent or erotic reflexes. They may express instinctive, symbolic fantasies. They may embody uncritical, spontaneous beliefs, untested deductive conclusions, or tested, verified beliefs. Clearly, then, my most adequate evaluative responses to the forces that shape me as an experience will be those which express inductively verified beliefs that yield the best available insight into my emotional motives for wanting to act in a specific way in the face of specific dative feelings.

My evaluative response to environmental forces within experience endows it with much of its temporal structure. The initial realm of fact defines the past as a concrete force within experience. Vague dative feelings, like feelings of pleasure and pain, present my immediate past to me for further evaluation. In so doing they ground an initial vague experience of my immediate past as present to me. Emotional adjustment yields a vague sense of a present shift in attitude. Sense perceptions and abductive propositional feelings yield a vivid sense of environmental forces present within experience. Deductive propositional feelings are predictive and therefore yield a vivid sense of the present as future. The inductive verification or falsification of a deductive prediction, like the performance of any consciously anticipated action, yields a vivid sense of the future as present. Finally, I experience the self that I am as a vague vectoral thrust toward an experienced future as future. On the basis of the preceding analysis, one may, then, schematize the dynamic structure of experience. See Diagram I.[3]

In such an approach to experience, the kind of person I am is the product of the facts that shape me as an experience and of my personal evaluative and decisive response to those facts. As I experience new things, I grow as a person: travel, study, a new job, change of citizenship mold me, make me different in some way. But the kind of difference environmental changes make is a function of the way I react to them perceptually, emotionally, inferentially, decisively. Moreover, my dynamic reaction to my world is itself a fact which shapes me and others as well.

The self that I am is, then, a growing, developing reality. And the kind of self I am is the product of my personal history. The dynamic tendencies that define me as a self, develop and decay, grow and decline in complexity. As a self, I exist in my own right but not in myself. For I am mutually inexistent with all those persons

DIAGRAM I
The Dynamics of Experience

The realm of QUALITY (EVALUATIVE FORM)

CONFORMAL FEELINGS	DATIVE FEELINGS	PHYSICAL PURPOSES	ABDUCTIVE PROPOSITIONAL FEELINGS	DEDUCTIVE PROPOSITIONAL FEELINGS	INDUCTIVE PROPOSITIONAL FEELINGS	DECISION
environmental impact: blows, caresses, collisions, radiation, etc. The initial realm of FACT. a sense of the past as actual	moods, pain pleasure, etc. vague sense of past as present	reflex reactions anger, joy, agitation, normal coping devices; vague sense of transition beyond past as present	initial hypotheses, classification of a fact as the case of a law. vivid sense of past as present	predictive clarification of an hypothesis. inference from case and law to verifiable facts. vivid sense of present as future	verification or falsification of predicted facts. inference from fact and case to law	reactive impact on environment. the subsequent realm of FACT

The Laws which ground the impact of environmental realities on the emerging self ←

The emerging self: the legal ground of evaluative and decisive response; a vague sense of the future as future. ↑

VECTORAL FEELINGS: the realm of LAW

and forces that shape me as an experience and that I shape in return. Moreover, the kind of self I have come to be comes to expression in the patterns of evaluation and decision that shape my life. At the same time, as a self I am also a dynamic thrust toward a relatively indeterminate future. Hence, as a self I am also ordered to growth and self-transcendence. For in every moment of experience I thrust forward beyond the self I have become to new possibilities of growth and self-actualization.

I am a human self. Human society is made up of selves like me: each with its own concrete history and character. But the environment that surrounds me is also filled with "selves" that are not human. For each reality in my world, every plant, thing, animal is a dynamic tendency to interact in a certain way with its surrounding environment. The poet Gerard Manley Hopkins had a remarkable sense of the uniqueness of each such "self" in the universe:

As kingfishers catch fire, dragonflies draw flame;
As tumbled over rim in roundy wells
Stones ring; like each tucked string tells, each hung bell's
Bow swung finds tongue to fling out broad its name;
Each mortal thing does one thing and the same:
Deals out that being indoors each one dwells;
Selves—goes itself; *myself* it speaks and spells;
Crying *What I do is me: for that I came.*

I say more: the just man justices;
Keeps grace: that keeps all his goings graces;
Acts in God's eye what in God's eye he is—
Christ—for Christ plays in ten thousand places,
Lovely in limbs, and lovely in eyes not his
To the Father through the features of men's faces.

4. But what relation does all of this talk of experience have to Christian faith and to openness to the Spirit? There is a hint in Hopkins's sonnet. The Spirit of Jesus is not an abstraction. He is a divine person, a divine self. He enters human experience as a life-force and a life-source. He is a salvific force alongside of spatio-temporal forces, shaping them, at times opposed to them. And like the purely natural forces in our environment, the Spirit can be experienced evaluatively in all of the ways we have just described.

We perceive the laws in nature by an inferential interpretation of their factual impact upon us. We perceive the Spirit of Jesus inferentially in the words and deeds of persons who believe in Christ and whose lives are open to the transforming presence of His Spirit. Such a statement may seem shocking to those unaccustomed to think of faith in experiential terms. But it is basic Christian doctrine. The first letter of John and his gospel are, for example, an extended theological reflection on what it means to perceive God enfleshed. For in a universe salvifically transformed through the Incarnation of God's Son, God's own life is made perceptually available within human experience: "Something which has existed since the beginning, that we have heard and we have seen with our own eyes; that we have watched and touched with our hands: the Word, who is life—this is our subject. That life was made visible: we saw it and we are giving our testimony, telling you of the eternal life which was with the Father and has been made visible to us."[4] For John, the divine life made visible in Jesus is a force that filled Him and came to expression in His teaching and miracles. That same salvific force, the Holy Spirit of God, dwells within His disciples and comes to perceptual visibility in their Spirit-filled words and deeds. Christians whose hearts are open to the Spirit and who share His gifts in common prayer know that His presence in men can indeed be perceived. What Christian has not seen human faces once filled with anguish and remorse transformed by the Spirit's healing power, filled with peace and joy in the Lord? What Christian has not seen lives reshaped by His gentle action? What Christian has not experienced His manifest anointing in the words and deeds that spring from His charismatic activity?

The presence of the Spirit can be perceived not only in others but in our own hearts. There His gentle touch is closer to a visceral perception than to the perceptions of the five senses. Sometimes the touches of the Spirit are only vaguely felt: they enter prayer in an undefined sense of peace and of the divine presence. At times His touch is clearer and breeds visions, insights, words, new understanding. Such impulses are as much a fact of experience as any other perceived environmental force; and like spatio-temporal facts they call out for correct inferential interpretation within faith.

But the Spirit of God not only touches us at a perceptual

level, He also summons us to repentance. He demands that we change our attitudes, come to terms with feelings of resentment, guilt, fear. He demands that anger-hardened hearts become hearts of flesh filled with Christlike love. Moreover, by His healing touch, the Spirit Himself changes our hearts and heals our disordered emotions. In other words, the action of the Spirit recreates our physical purposes and shapes them to His salvific purposes.

The Spirit also shapes our inferential processes. He leads us by grace to initial faith. And He teaches us to test the adequacy of our personal understanding of the good news by growing in a lived insight into its historical roots and practical consequences. Growth in religious understanding is mediated by deductive and inductive inference.

Finally, the Spirit leads us to do the deeds that witness to His saving presence within us. In other words, if every human self is a growing, developing experience, every stage in the growth of human experience is capable of transformation in the Spirit. By the same token, every human self who is open to the power and anointing of the Spirit becomes a different kind of self, a new creation, as every part of experience is penetrated by the Spirit's gentle presence. As we shall see, the preceding reflections have profound implications for understanding the gifts of the Spirit and how they function within human religious experience. But we would do well to postpone for the time being any consideration of the gifts as such and reflect first on the implications of the preceding analysis for an understanding of the dynamics of Christian conversion.

5. The integrally converted Christian is one who stands in complete openness to every impulse of the Spirit of God. But openness to the Spirit is not a purely passive state. The Spirit calls us constantly to respond in deed and in truth to His promptings and to the Word of God made flesh. For Christian religion is covenant religion; and it is the Spirit of God who seals the new covenant in our hearts. He does so by freeing us to consent to God and to one another in deeds transformed by grace.

But if the action of the Spirit touches every stage in the development of human experience, then conversion to God is a complex human process. Corresponding to the different stages in the growth of experience are four distinguishable kinds of graces present within conversion to God: environmental, emotive, inferential, and decisive.

An environmental grace is an event that is Spirit-led, Spirit-inspired. The words and miracles of Jesus were environmental graces. They were events that called out to others to acknowledge the presence of God and of His Spirit in the ministry of His Son. The words and deeds of all Spirit-led individuals and communities are also environmental graces. They are salvific facts to which I must respond with appropriate faith if I am to perceive the God whose saving presence they reveal. The direct action of the Spirit upon the human heart is also an environmental fact to which the one touched must respond appropriately. But an appropriate response to God engages me at an emotive, an inferential, and a decisive level. For religion is not, as Johnathan Edwards saw, a matter of the mind alone. It engages the heart as well. Conversion does not yield some detached scientific insight into objective divine truth. It is an abductive consent to God that is deeply felt and in its genesis shaped by strong emotional motives.

But religious beliefs, like other human beliefs, need to be understood. Inference, therefore, functions both in the initial formulation of the creedal content of any consent of faith and in the ongoing, critical re-formulation of one's personal religious creed. Faith, of course, lives at the level of decision. It is commitment to God rather than the inferential interpretation of any one creedal proposition. Creeds, however, help motivate the consent of faith.

Finally, faith without works is dead. Unless religious emotions and creedal insight give rise to acts of Christian love and service, their graced origin is suspect.

In a genuine religious conversion, therefore, one assumes personal responsibility for responding in an appropriate manner to every impulse of divine grace. Since we must respond to the efficacious impulses of grace at an emotive, inferential, and decisive level, authentic religious conversion also demands that we assume responsibility for our emotional, speculative, and practical growth as well. For disordered emotional attitudes, false and inadequate beliefs, and disordered patterns of activity can stand as an obstacle to adequate response to the Spirit's saving action and to the environmental graces that shape us.

Emotional obstacles blind us. The most obvious emotional obstacles to grace are anger, guilt, and fear. Resentment against God, His Church, against other racial or economic groups, against those who have hurt us harden and darken the human heart. Guilt keeps us from facing ourselves and acknowledging our need for God. Fear keeps us clinging to things that are not God. Guilt and fear together breed defensiveness, hypocrisy, self-deception.

False and inadequate beliefs also blind us to the action of the Spirit. False information breeds false expectations. And false expectations easily lead us to dismiss or ignore the saving action of God. The gospels are filled with stories of people who failed to acknowledge the event of grace present in Jesus because of false beliefs about the Messiah and His mission. The reason for such speculative blindness is not far to seek. We perceive facts (including events of grace) concretely but we grasp their meaning inferentially. Those who perceived Jesus' deeds with their eyes and heard His words with their ears had also to interpret the meaning of His words and deeds inferentially. Those who chose to do so without faith failed to see the divine reality confronting them in the Word made flesh. They saw without seeing. How often do we not sin against one another in a similar way? Because of some unacknowledged bias, we dismiss the Spirit-led words and deeds of others as mere human phenomena, whereas in fact they have the power to speak to us of God if we allow them.

If our disordered feelings and prejudices blind us, our disordered decisions and attachments bind us. We can understand all too well that God wants us to repent of some sinful attachment but be unwilling to consent to His grace because our hearts are sinfully or complacently wed to some person or thing, to some settled pattern of behavior. Money, job security, selfish lust, attachment to bourgeois comforts—such things can possess and imprison us until we are willing to relinquish them.

6. Within the conversion process, one may, then, speak not only of religious conversion but of affective, intellectual, and moral conversion as well. Affective conversion is the decision to assume personal responsibility for my emotional growth and development. It corresponds to the emotive stage in the growth of experience. Intellectual conversion is the decision to assume personal responsibility for my speculative growth and development. It corresponds

to the inferential stage in the growth of experience. Moral conversion is the decision to assume responsibility for the formation and consequences of my own decisions and for shaping them to what is truly valuable. It corresponds to decision in the growth of experience.

The presence of four distinguishable moments within the conversion process endows it with incredible complexity. Authentic religious conversion is a response to divine grace. It cannot be initiated or sustained by human effort alone. But human beings can achieve some measure of intellectual, moral, and affective conversion by dint of personal initiative and effort. The oppressive misery born of unacknowledged anger, fear, and guilt can eventually force me to face my need for professional psychiatric help. Exposure to natural and artistic beauty can convince me that I must henceforth cultivate a balanced esthetic sensitivity. Realization that many of my most cherished beliefs are only unexamined prejudices can make me decide to face and evaluate systematically my own personal presuppositions. Remorse at my own selfishness may cause me to resolve henceforth to make only responsible moral decisions by responding appropriately to every value that is present in experience.

What is common to these three decisions is the conscious assumption of personal responsibility for the development of some aspect of my own experience. Such decisions may be properly called a kind of conversion. For all conversion, religious conversion included, is the decision to turn from irresponsible to responsible behavior in some area of one's experiential development. As decisions, affective, intellectual, and moral conversion are dynamically interrelated by the laws of experiential growth. For emotive, intellectual, and practical habits of action are vitally linked within experience. One cannot develop true emotional balance while clinging to bigoted prejudices. One cannot subject the grounds of one's personal beliefs to critical examination without facing one's emotional biases and ethical commitments. One cannot truly reform one's vicious moral attitudes without facing the emotional kinks and rationalizations that motivate them.

Nevertheless, the decision to come to terms with one's emotional problems is not identical with the decision to fix one's speculative beliefs responsibly. Neither decision is identical with the decision to revise one's ethical commitments. Nor is conversion to God identical with affective, intellectual, or moral conversion. The fact that integral conversion is four-fold and involves four distinguishable kinds of interrelated decisions means that any given individual may enter the conversion process at any one of four levels. One may begin at the level of affectivity and move to moral, intellectual, and religious conversion. Or one may begin at an intellectual level and move on to religious, affective, and moral conversion. Or one may begin at a moral level and move on to intellectual, affective, and religious conversion. Or one may begin with religious conversion and then move on to affective, intellectual, and moral conversion. Any conversion at one level which is unaccompanied by conversion at other levels is to that extent inauthentic. And inauthenticity can eventually erode one's initial conversion commitment. Why is this so?

The morally converted individual is, as we have seen, one who has assumed responsibility for the proper formation and consequences of his or her personal decisions. Responsible decisions seek to shape choices by a true insight into all the values and laws operative in human experience. Implicit, however, in such a commitment is the willingness to do whatever is necessary to come to such valid moral insights. One obvious prerequisite for reaching valid moral insights is correct thinking on moral questions. Since correct thinking is deliberate, self-controlled activity, integral moral conversion demands that one assume personal responsibility for one's speculative beliefs as well. It presupposes, that is to say, intellectual conversion.

Similarly, the morally converted individual affirms an openness to accepting any valid insight into values that function normatively in personal decisions. The morally converted individual affirms at least implicitly, therefore, a dynamic openness to any authentic values (s)he has yet to feel, understand, and embrace. Among such values are, however, religious values. Implicit in moral conversion is, therefore, an openness to the ethical demands of religious conversion.

By the same token, the emotionally disordered or insensitive person is extremely prone to run roughshod over the feelings of others. As a consequence, such a person runs the risk of doing to others serious harm. If (s)he is ethically converted but esthetically unconverted, (s)he will tend to rationalize such insensitivity with the noblest kind of abstract moralizations. In other words, to be morally responsible in decisions that engage one emotively, one must come to terms with the effects one's unacknowledged feelings have on one's decisions. One must also be able to evaluate the effects which one's decisions have on one's attitudes and on the sensitivities of others. To do so demands affective conversion.

Logically, then, the morally converted individual who resists affective, religious and intellectual conversion inevitably introduces elements of inauthenticity into personal moral decisions. For as morally converted, (s)he affirms a commitment to act with moral responsibility in every decision (s)he makes; but in resisting esthetic, intellectual and religious conversion such a person affirms a willingness to act with moral irresponsibility in emotional, intellectual, and religious matters.

The person who has developed only to the stage of moral conversion may, of course, possess only an implicit openness to the further stages of conversion. (S)he may have yet to experience

DIAGRAM 2
The Dynamics of Conversion

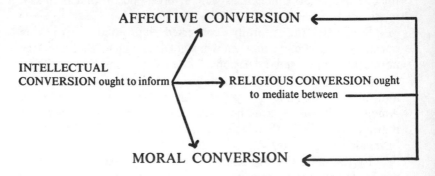

AFFECTIVE CONVERSION

INTELLECTUAL
CONVERSION ought to inform

RELIGIOUS CONVERSION ought
to mediate between

MORAL CONVERSION

consciously the liberation which these conversions bring. But when they occur, such an individual ought to experience them, on one hand, as adding a new dimension to moral conversion and, on the other, as dynamically convergent with it.

Intellectual conversion contains an implicit openness to affective, moral and religious conversion. Intellectual conversion is the assumption of personal responsibility for the consequences of one's beliefs. One's beliefs, however, have emotional, speculative, practical, and religious consequences. The intellectually converted individual who resists conversion at other levels is unable, then, to remain committed to complete intellectual honesty. For (s)he will resist facing speculative conclusions that contradict unexamined emotional, practical, or religious biases.

Moreover, conversion at any level involves a conscious, normative insight into oneself and into the emergent laws which ground personal human growth and development. Since, then, any such insight ought ideally to be expressive of genuine intellectual conversion, it follows that intellectual conversion ought to inform the conversion process at every level.

The affectively converted person who is religiously unconverted will remain insensitive to the full impact of some of the highest expressions of beauty, namely, religious art. If such a person is intellectually unconverted, (s)he will be prone to accept fallacious beliefs about his or her feelings uncritically. If such an individual is morally unconverted as well, his or her pursuit of beauty will be likely to degenerate into an effete estheticism.

The religiously converted individual is one who has assumed personal responsibility for his or her religious beliefs, attitudes, and decisions. Since authentic religious conversion is a response to God's salvific initiative, one cannot remain authentically converted at a religious level unless one is willing to meet God on His own salvific terms.

At the same time, the religious convert who resists intellectual conversion is soon transformed into the dogmatic fundamentalist. For the fundamentalist is one who arbitrarily closes off religious inquiry by adhering rigidly to a single abstract understanding of the meaning of divine revelation. One may do so because of uncritically accepted theoretical presuppositions, or because of an inordinate emotional attachment to some common sense or pseudo-scientific interpretation of religious experience. But whatever the cause, the fundamentalistic refusal to reflect on religious questions inevitably involves an implicit demand that God meet the believer on the believer's own intellectual terms. And such a demand, as we shall see, is incompatible with an authentic religious conversion.

Similarly, an individual may claim to be willing to accept the practical consequences of belief in God, while restricting personal moral choices exclusively to goods that yield immediate satisfaction irrespective of their consequences for oneself and others. Such an individual is implicitly absolutizing selfish needs and demanding that when those needs are involved, God meet one on one's own moral terms.

Finally, the religiously converted person who remains esthetically unconverted will find it difficult to distinguish the felt impulses of grace from personal neurotic tendencies.

Not every conscious human experience can be legitimately designated as religious. Experience takes on a conscious religious dimension when, in Paul Tillich's phrase, it is touched by "ultimate concern." Experience comes to be touched by ultimate concern when the religious question is raised. The religious question asks: what, if any, is the ultimate meaning and purpose of human life? Human experience takes on a more or less permanent religious character when the religious question is answered positively. To answer the religious question positively is to fix one's religious beliefs. The fixation of religious belief yields an insight into those realities and values which ought to concern me ultimately. Faith is the decision to consent to those values. To the extent that religious beliefs and the faith they motivate continue to shape the development of experience in a significant manner, to that extent will personal experience assume a permanent religious character. In other words, it is faith in realities that are affirmed as ultimately and absolutely meaningful which renders experience religious. For the Christian, the realities and values affirmed in faith are those revealed in Jesus and in the mission of the Holy Spirit. But not every religious conversion is Christian. One may be converted to Judaism, to Hinduism, to Buddhism. Christianity demands, of course, that beliefs in non-Christian religions which are false and inadequate be rejected and that the positive values in non-Christian religions be brought to salvific fulfillment in Jesus. But the fact remains that conversion to a non-Christian religion does endow the convert's experience with a religious character.

By leading one to affirm certain realities as ultimately and absolutely valuable, religious conversion creates the context within which ethical decisions can be made. Why is this so? A reality is affirmed as absolutely valuable when it is affirmed as worth striving toward under all circumstances. A reality is affirmed as ultimately valuable when it is affirmed as the goal of all one's moral striving. At the same time, a decision takes on a strictly ethical character when it is made in the light of those values which a person affirms as ultimately and absolutely valuable. Religious conversion, therefore, creates the evaluative context within which moral decisions in the strict sense can be made. Hence, religious conversion is linked by the dynamics of the conversion process to moral conversion.

At the same time, religious conversion has deep roots within human affectivity. Our most basic contact with God is emotive. The impulses of the Spirit are first vaguely felt and only subsequently understood with clarity and vividness. As a consequence, authentic religious conversion is never the result of controlled rational reflection. It has deep emotive roots that at the time of conversion remain largely buried and invisible. Disordered emotional attitudes stand, therefore, as an obstacle to religious conversion. Unresolved feelings of fear, anger, and guilt can prevent me from hearing the Spirit's call and from responding to it. Affective conversion, precisely because it involves a decision to come to terms with the obstacles to balanced emotional development is, then, in many cases a prelude to adult religious conversion. At the same time, religious conversion opens the heart to the healing power of the Spirit. In so doing, religious conversion provides the context within which effective emotional healing, often called the healing of memories, can occur. Clearly, then, religious conversion seeks to mediate between the affective and moral dimensions of human experience.

6. The preceding reflections allow us to put a Pentecostal theology of conversion into evaluative perspective, to acknowledge

what is valid in it, and to move beyond it to a more nuanced account of the conversion process. A traditional Pentecostal theology of conversion distinguishes conversion from baptism in the Holy Spirit. Some Pentecostals also distinguish baptism in the Spirit from the process of sanctification. Baptism in the Spirit is described as a "second blessing" over and above the grace of conversion. The meaning of such a theory becomes clearer when it is viewed in the light of the religious experience of the first Pentecostals. Prior to praying for baptism in the Holy Spirit, all were converted Christians. But they found their relationship with God so radically transformed by shared openness to tongues and to all the gifts that they felt justified in distinguishing the "second blessing" of Spirit-baptism from the experience of conversion to Christ. They also found that the growth in the Spirit which was the fruit of Spirit-baptism was a different kind of experience from Spirit-baptism itself and that it involved growth in holiness.[5]

But while one may concede that a Pentecostal account of conversion does interpret certain aspects of the experience of the first Protestant Pentecostals, there is reason to question its total adequacy as a theological theory. Here several key points should be noted. First of all, a theory of conversion is not the event of being converted. It is the attempt to formulate a language which allows one to speak of that event. To question the adequacy of a person's theory of conversion is not, therefore, to suggest that he or she is unconverted. It is only to suggest that there are ways of speaking about the event of conversion which take better account of its complexity. Second, to say that a theory is inadequate is not to say that it is devoid of all truth. A theory is inadequate when it is unable to give an account of every aspect of the event it is trying to describe. A traditional Pentecostal theory of conversion fails, for example, to differentiate between religious conversion, on the one hand, and affective, intellectual, and moral conversion on the other. For that reason alone it suffers from vagueness and inadequacy.

In addition, however, the language used in a Pentecostal theory of conversion could be misleading. The theory proposes a linear model of conversion. It suggests that growth in the Spirit proceeds in three distinct stages, like the segments of a line: first, conversion itself; then, Spirit-baptism; then, sanctification. The model seems to suggest, therefore, that the process of sanctification does not begin until after conversion and baptism in the Spirit. But everyone transformed by the Spirit is to that extent sanctified. And conversion itself is the work of the Spirit. It follows, therefore, that anyone who has experienced conversion enjoys some measure of sanctification. To separate the process of sanctification from conversion is, then, arbitrary and potentially misleading.

Similarly, the traditional Pentecostal model for religious growth distinguishes conversion from baptism in the Holy Spirit. There would, however, seem to be no solid scriptural basis for such a distinction. In the New Testament, conversion and baptism in the Spirit are two sides of the same coin. There is, then, solid reason for abandoning a classical Pentecostal model for conversion, not as false, but as inadequate to explain the complex dynamics of Christian religious experience. And we suggest as an alternative the model developed in this chapter. It is time, however, to begin to reflect on how the gifts of the Holy Spirit function within the conversion process.

Notes

1. For a helpful introduction to process thinking, see: Ewert H. Cousins, *Process Theology* (N.Y.: Newman Press, 1971).

2. Jn 14:20; 1 Co 12:12-13.

3. The working model for understanding the development of human experience here proposed is the conflation of a number of different themes in American philosophical thought. Though it has affinities with the thought of Jonathan Edwards, Charles Sanders Peirce, William James, John Dewey, George Santayana, and Alfred North Whitehead, it is not reducible to the thought of any one of these men. For an insight into some of the issues implied in the model see: Bernard Lonergan, S.J., *Method in Theology* (N.Y.: Herder and Herder, 1972) pp. 267-293; W.B. Gallie, *Peirce and Pragmatism* (Edinburg: Penguin, 1952); Murray G. Murphey, *The Development of Peirce's Philosophy* (Cambridge: Harvard, 1961); Vincent G. Potter, S.J., *Charles Peirce on Norms and Values* (Worcester:

University of Massachusetts, 1967); Victor Lowe, *Understanding White-head* (Baltimore: Johns Hopkins, 1966) Ivor Leclerc, *Whitehead's Metaphysics* (N.Y.: Macmillan, 1958); Francis E. Reilly, S.J., *Charles Peirce's Theory of Scientific Method* (N.Y.: Fordham, 1970); Roland Dellattre, *Beauty and Sensibility in the Thought of Jonathan Edwards* (New Haven: Yale, 1969).

4. 1 Jn 1:1.

5. Cf. Walter Hollenweger, *The Pentecostals: The Charismatic Movement in the Churches* (Minneapolis: Augsburg, 1972); Frederick Dale Brunner, *A Theology of the Holy Spirit* (London: Hodder and Stoughton, 1971); Kilian McDonnell, O.S.B., "The Ecumenical Significance of the Pentecostal Movement," *Worship*, XL (December, 1966) pp. 608-629; Herbert Schneider, S.J. "Heiligung und Geisttaufe: Herkunft und Geisttaufe: Herkunft und Ziele der Pfinstbewegung," *Stimmen der Zeit* (December, 1972) pp. 426-428; Simon Tugwell, O.P., "Reflections on the Pentecostal Doctrine of 'baptism in the Holy Spirit,'" *Heythrop Journal* (1972) pp. 402-414; James Dunn, *Baptism in the Holy Spirit* (Naperville: Allenson, 1970); John Hardon, S.J., *Protestant Churches of America* (N.Y.: Image, 1969) pp. 169-185.

II
The
Mind
of Jesus

1. Any discussion of the gifts of the Spirit and their place within an authentic Christian conversion should begin with a few terminological clarifications. There is a very real sense in which the entire salvific process is gift. The Incarnation is gift. The Spirit is gift. The tendency to designate certain movements of the Spirit as "gifts" derives, however, from the apostle Paul. Paul speaks of three distinguishable manifestations of the Spirit: gifts, or charisms *(charismata)*, works of power *(dynameis)*, and ministries *(diakoniai)*. Among the "gifts" listed by Paul are, however, fairly permanent and seemingly pedestrian, institutional functions, like the gifts of administration and of pastoral office. Moreover, in addition to specific charisms, Paul speaks of the Spirit of Jesus as giving the Christian community collective access to the mind of God and of Christ. This last Pauline suggestion is, as we shall see, pregnant with meaning.

Medieval discussion of the gifts of the Spirit employed different terminology from that of Paul. Medieval theologians distinguished the "gifts" *(dona)* of the Holy Spirit from His gratuitous graces *(gratiae gratis datae)*. The latter are the Pauline charisms: tongues, interpretation, prophecy, healing, miracles, discernment, almsgiving, pastoral office, etc. A grace gratuitously, or freely, given is, of course, a "gift." Hence, the designation of the Pauline gifts as "gratuitous graces" was in one respect only a verbal shift. But the medieval distinction between the *dona Spiritus Sancti* and the *gratiae gratis datae* had a deeper theological intent. The thirteenth chapter of the letter to the Corinthians argues that when any of the charisms is used without love it becomes trash. Medieval theologians reasoned that if this is so, then the charisms, or gratuitous graces, need not effect personal sanctification. Growth in sanctification is growth in faith, hope, and love. Such growth must be Spirit-led. The *dona Spiritus Sancti* are graces which mediate such sanctifying growth. Meditation on Is 11:1-2 led medieval theologians to equate these sanctifying gifts *(dona)* of the Spirit with the seven "spirits" mentioned in the Isaian text: wisdom, understanding, counsel, fortitude, knowledge, piety, and fear of the Lord. As sanctifying graces *(gratia gratum faciens)* these seven gifts had as their purpose to perfect the faith, hope, and love common to all Christians. The gratuitous graces, on the other hand, were described as seeking to effect, not growth in personal sanctification, but the building up of the Christian community. There is an imperfect insight coming to expression in these medieval distinctions. And we shall return to them in other contexts. We note them here, however, as an indication of the complexity of a traditional theology of "gift."

But there are further complexities still. The Protestant Pentecostal tradition distinguishes the "gifts" or charisms of the Spirit from "ministries." There is a tendency to equate the term "gift" with an occasional inspiration of the Spirit given for the edification of a specific community. The term "ministry" designates a more or less permanent call to service within the community. Contemporary Catholic theology, on the other hand, has taken a somewhat different tack. Catholic theologians tend, since Vatican II, to use the term "charism" in much the same way as Protestant Pentecostals use the term "ministry." By "gift" Catholic theologians tend to mean a more or less permanent call of the Spirit to serve the community in some way. But despite their verbal differences, both traditions acknowledge two types of pneumatic impulses: occasional graces and more or less permanent calls to the service of others in the name of Christ.

In the face of this vipers' tangle of terms, one is forced to attempt to clarify one's own terminology. To restrict the term "gift" to an occasional grace seems to me somewhat arbitrary as well as exegetically questionable. Hence, in the chapters which follow I will oppose the term "gift" or "charism" to the notion of an "occasional, or actual, grace," while acknowledging the reality of both phenomena. By the term "gift" or "charism" I mean "a more or less permanent, enabling call of the Spirit of Jesus." An enabling call is one that creates the freedom to respond. It makes one docile to the Spirit's promptings. With medieval theologians, I will also suggest that the call of the Spirit is twofold: it is a call to sanctification and it is a call to ecclesial and social service. These two charismatic impulses are dynamically interrelated, but they are not identical. In the present chapter, we shall concern ourselves with the Spirit's call to sanctification. In the chapter which follows, we will begin to reflect on His call to service.

2. What, then, does it mean to say that a Christian is called by the Spirit to holiness? The term "holy" ordinarily means "set apart by God for His own salvific ends." Jesus is then "the Holy One of God" in a privileged sense, the one set apart by God Himself to effect the final eschatological outpouring of the Spirit. For the believing Christian to be "set apart" or "sanctified" means to be assimilated to Jesus by the power of the Spirit. It means, in Paul's phrase, "to put on the mind of Jesus." For Jesus in His life and teaching stands in prophetic opposition to the principalities and powers of this world. His wisdom is not the wisdom of this world. To allow the Spirit to shape one's mind to the mind of Christ is, then, to allow God to set one apart from those who are ignorant of Jesus and closed to His Spirit. To be so set apart is to become holy: consecrated to God as Jesus was for the Father's own salvific purposes.

But what does it mean to "put on the mind of Jesus"? For the apostle Paul, it meant most obviously to enter into Jesus' *kenosis*, or salvific self-emptying, by serving God and one's brethren in Jesus' image. But what does it mean to enter into the *kenosis* of Jesus? And what are the distinguishing traits of Jesus' service? One would expect that the teachings of Jesus as they are preserved in the gospels would yield an important historical clue to His "mind." But Jesus left behind no systematic body of teaching comparable to the teachings of Plato or Aristotle. His words as they are preserved in Scripture are a collection of occasional sayings, some of them expanded or modified for catechetical purposes in the Christian community. Were it possible, however, to reduce the teachings of Jesus as they have come down to us to some kind of unified pattern, one would have an important clue to understanding how the first Christians, under the power of the Spirit, interpreted His "mind."[1]

One important hint of how the first Christians did in fact understand the "mind" of Jesus is to be found in the narratives of Jesus' desert temptations as they are preserved in the synoptic tradition. In all three synoptics, Jesus' desert sojourn is closely linked with His baptism.[2] And the accounts of His baptism give evidence of having been shaped by the early baptismal catechesis in the Christian community. Only the synoptic gospels mention Jesus' baptism by John, but all the gospels are careful to contrast baptism administered in Jesus' name with John's baptism of repentance. All the gospels insist that while John baptised with water, Jesus baptises with the Holy Spirit. For dramatic and polemic reasons, these basic truths of Christian faith are put on the lips of the Baptist himself. At the same time, the synoptics all portray the descent of the Spirit on Jesus at the Jordan at the time of His baptism as the inauguration of His visible revelation as messiah. The Spirit descends on Jesus in messianic plentitude to transform Him into the beginning of a new, pneumatic, charismatic Israel. And it is as the Spirit-filled beginning of the new Israel that Jesus descends into the desert. He does so to repeat in His own person the desert experience of God's people. In the desert Jesus meets Satan and confounds him. From the earliest days, Christian neophytes have been asked before receiving baptism to renounce Satan, his works, and his pomps. The symbolic caste of the baptismal and temptation narratives is unmistakable. It is entirely plausible, then, that the story of Jesus' desert confrontation with Satan was originally told to Christian catechumens as a way of explaining to them what it means to renounce Satan in the image of Jesus. It means to live not by bread alone but by every word that comes from the mouth of God. It means not to test God. It means to worship and serve the Father alone, and not the prince of this world.[3] There is, then, some basis in Scripture for suspecting that for the first Christians the three commitments made by Jesus in the desert as messiah and Spirit-filled founder of the new Israel provide a rough definition of the terms of the new covenant sealed in water and the Holy Spirit. If I scruple at such an interpretation of the Christian covenant I should ask myself whether, as a Christian, I consider myself covenanted to anything else. Am I as a Christian convenanted to live only by bread and not by every word from God's mouth? Am I committed to test God on every occasion? Am I committed to worship and serve the prince of this world rather than the God who is the Father of Jesus? Such questions are absurd. Moreover, when Jesus' teachings are read in the light of these three desert commitments they begin to take on a remarkable ethical consistency.

3. In the desert Jesus was first tempted to convert stones into bread. He refused because, as messianic Son of God and Spirit-baptiser of the new Israel, He had decided to live, not by bread alone but by every word that comes from the mouth of the Father. His temptation was not, then, a temptation to gluttony. It was a temptation to abandon the fast He had undertaken as an expression of His total abandonment to the Father in the fulfillment of the mission He had just received on the banks of the Jordan. If the baptised Christian ought, like Jesus, to live in total dependence on the Father, how ought such filial dependence to come to expression in the living of life?

In the Biblical accounts of the institution of the eucharist, Jesus speaks of His death as mediating a new covenant.[4] And it is clear from Acts 2 that the first Christians experienced the Holy Spirit as sealing the new covenant in their hearts. One of the defining characteristics of covenant religion is, however, that the measure of one's relation to God is the attitude one assumes towards one's fellow men. This principle is clear in the preaching of the prophets. It is repeatedly affirmed in the gospels and epistles of the New Testament.

One would expect, then, that the Christian convert's decision to depend in faith on the Father in the image of Jesus must in some way come to expression in the practical attitude which the convert assumes toward his or her neighbor. In Jesus' own teaching one clear test of a disciple's dependence on God rather than on bread or on the other temporal supports of life is personal willingness to share freely whatever one possesses with others.

Jesus' teaching concerning the need to share freely with others drew on the Old Testament archetype of the innocent poor man and its moralization in Wisdom literature. The innocent poor man is one who through his fidelity to God's law has every right to the material blessings promised to the obedient by the terms of the Sinai covenant; but he is a man who is unjustly deprived of them by the rich and powerful. Ironically, the latter possess the blessings God had promised, not as God's gift, but as a result of their sinful violation of God's law. The innocent poor man is, then, portrayed as unjustly deprived of all the ordinary physical supports of life. And because of his extremity, he is forced to depend upon God alone. The innocent poor man is an idealized literary archetype. And the reflections of the Old Testament sages eventually transformed it into a religious and moral ideal. The true believer in Hebrew wisdom is, then, one who avoids the accumulation of riches as an expression of a deeper desire to remain in an attitude of faithful dependence on God.[5]

Jesus' teaching as it is recorded in Scripture extended and developed these insights of the sages. Jesus rejected the notion that the possession of riches is in any sense a guarantee of God's blessing. "No one can be the slave of two masters: he will either hate the first and love the second, or treat the first with respect and the second with scorn. You cannot be the slave both of God and of money." He warned that wealth is tainted by human sinfulness and stands in need of redemption through use that expresses true faith in God.[6]

Jesus also extended the wisdom of the sages in three important directions. First, He taught that it is not enough to eschew riches: one must also share actively what one has with others. Second, one must share freely with everyone, irrespective of their merits. Third, one must do so as an expression of the fact that one is a true child of God living in the image of Jesus and in constant expectation of the coming reign of God. "You have learnt how it was said: *You must love your neighbor* and hate your enemy. But I say this to you: love your enemies and pray for those who persecute you; in this way you will be sons of your Father in heaven, for he causes his sun to rise on bad men as well as good, and his rain to fall on honest and dishonest men alike. . . . You must therefore be perfect as your heavenly Father is perfect."[7]

Jesus' demand that His disciples practice open and gratuitous sharing in the image of God may well have been an extension and embellishment of the teaching of the Baptist, who had held up the free sharing of possessions as one way of avoiding the coming retribution. In Jesus' preaching, however, gratuitous sharing has a more positive connotation. It is an expression of mutual reconciliation, of eschatological hope, and of childlike trust in God. Its purpose is the mediation of a community of atonement, a community of men and women reconciled to one another in mutual forgiveness, service, and love. "Yes, if you forgive others their failings, your heavenly Father will forgive you yours; but if you do not forgive others, your Father will not forgive your failings either." Hence, the mere heaping up of possessions is an abomination in the sight of God: one must labor, not to possess, but in order to have something to share with others, especially with those in need. "Sell your possessions and give alms. Get yourselves purses that do not wear out, treasure that will not fail you, in heaven where no thief can reach it and no moth destroy. For where your treasure is, there will your heart be also."[8]

The sharing Jesus demanded was profoundly personal. As a consequence, it gave rise to a startling ideal of hospitality: "When you give a lunch or a dinner, do not ask your friends, brothers, relations or rich neighbors, for fear they repay your courtesy by inviting you in return. No; when you have a party, invite the poor, the crippled, the lame, the blind; that they cannot pay you back means that you are fortunate, because repayment will be made to you when the virtuous rise again." Clearly, then, sharing in Jesus' image does not spare the most intimate of one's personal possessions. All must be at the disposal of the poor, the destitute, the outcasts of society.[9]

Jesus' summons to faith-sharing gives rise, therefore, to a certain kind of community ideal, that of a Christian "classless community." Such a community is neither the classless community envisioned by Marxist dialectic nor a democratic, bourgeois utopia. Instead, it is a community in which trust in God bears fruit in a personal willingness to use whatever one possesses in order to meet the needs of each individual in the community and in the human family. It is a community in which the desire to be reconciled in active sharing with one's brethren replaces any attempt to take economic advantage of another. "And so I tell you this: use money, tainted as it is, to win you friends, and thus make sure that when it fails you, they will welcome you into the tents of eternity."[10]

It should be clear that if I am willing to say yes to these ideals, I am giving a decisive orientation to my life, one that will demand a risk in faith of all that I possess as the pragmatic test of my determination to draw my life, not from bread, nor from any other physical support of life, but from the word and Spirit of God.

The gospel of John expresses the same insights in somewhat different categories. Outside the Samaritan village, Jesus refuses the food brought Him by the disciples because His meat and drink is to do the will of the one who sent Him. His words are clearly redolent of His first temptation as it is described in the synoptics. Moreover, in the first part of the bread-of-life discourse and in His last discourse, Jesus invites His disciples to feed in faith on Him just as He feeds upon the Father in trust. They must not seek after the bread which perishes but eat instead the bread which gives eternal life. That bread is the Word of God, Jesus, the eternal Logos who is the embodiment of God's saving word to human kind. The eucharistic section of the bread-of-life discourse places this teaching in an explicit sacramental context. One cannot eat the eucharistic body and drink the eucharistic blood of the Lord except as an expression of a faith-dependence which makes one live not by food and drink but by every word that comes from the mouth of God. Paul's reproaches to the Corinthian community over abuses in common worship bring together the same themes. One who celebrates the supper of the Lord but is unwilling to share of his or her possessions freely with any member of the community calls down the anger of God and transforms the eucharist from a saving act to an act of divine judgment.[11]

4. Jesus' second desert temptation was the temptation to test God. "Testing God" is the attempt to set the conditions God must meet before one is willing to trust Him. Jesus' rejection of His second temptation in the desert was then an expression of the unconditioned character of His trust in the Father. And it was a demand which He also made of those who followed Him.

Moreover, as one might expect in new covenant religion, the unconditioned character of my commitment to the Father finds expression in the unconditioned character of my commitment to others in the name of God. Such mutual commitment gives rise to specific kinds of activities in the community.

First and most obviously, it colors the quality of community sharing. One whose faith dependence on God comes to expression in free acts of sharing cannot, if he or she is unconditionally dependent on God in faith, place any conditions on the willingness to share with others. The scope of faith-sharing must, then, be unrestricted in principle. The true believer can exclude no one but must instead be willing to accept everyone without consideration of person or merits. Any cliquish attitudes or practices, any distinctions of class privilege must, then, be excluded from any authentic Christian community.

Since, moreover, the practical, gratuitous sharing of goods which is the sign of the authentic child of God mediates an atonement, it ought to be an expression of mutual reconciliation in love. For atonement means reconciliation. Sharing demands therefore a decision to be reconciled with others that is itself unconditioned, a mutual forgiveness that imitates the Father's own unconditioned forgiveness of men revealed in the love of His Son. Like God's forgiveness, it must be simply there before any offense is committed, while the offense is being committed, after it is done, even before there are any signs of repentence. It demands, therefore, that I love my enemies as unconditionally as my friends. "But I say this to you who are listening: Love your enemies, do good to those who hate you, bless those who curse you, pray for those who treat you badly. To the man who slaps you on one cheek, present the other cheek too; to the man who takes your cloak from you, do not refuse your tunic. Give to everyone who asks you, and do not ask for your property back from the man who robs you."[12]

As the apostle Paul realized, then, it is the unconditioned character of one's faith-dependence on the Father which finds expression in the peculiar character and quality of Christian love. For unconditioned love excludes boastfulness, conceit, rudeness and selfishness, as the causes of disunion rather than of reconciliation. It demands a commitment to others that is patient and kind, gentle, humble, self-effacing, and tolerant of any offense. Unconditioned love is opposed to every form of divisiveness. A forgiving love is not easily offended, it bears no grudges. It is ready to excuse for it is anxious to be reconciled. But Christian love is also realistic and truthful. It does not deny the reality of an offense; it forgives it in advance. But it refuses to base reconciliation on a lie or on deceitful pretense. Finally, it is a love rooted in one's unconditioned trust in the Father. Hence, it is always filled with hope and ready to endure whatever comes.[13]

5. The third temptation of Jesus was the temptation to found the Kingdom of God on the worship of the prince of this world rather than on the worship and service of the Father. Here four points are worth noting concerning His decision to reject that temptation. First His decision expressed His determination that the new Israel be a community of worship. "I tell you most solemnly if two of you on earth agree to ask anything at all, it will be granted to you by my Father in heaven. For where two or three meet in my name, I shall be there with them." Second, the pragmatic test of whether or not that community worships the true God rather than the forces of darkness is the means it employs in order to found the kingdom. "You know that among the pagans the rulers lord it over them, and their great men make their authority felt. This is not to happen among you. No; anyone who wants to be great among you must be your servant, and anyone who wants to be first among you must be your slave, just as the Son of Man came not to be served but to serve, and to give his life as a ransom for many." Third, to attempt to found the kingdom on political means alone or by the use of coercive violence is incompatible with authentic worship of the Father. "Mine is not a kingdom of this world; if my kingdom were of this world, my men would have fought to prevent my being surrendered to the Jews. But my kingdom is not of this kind." Fourth, the true kingdom of God must be rooted in a worship whose authenticity is measured by one's willingness to forgive one another in the image of Jesus. "So then, if you are bringing your offering to the altar and there remember that your brother has something against you, leave your offering there before the altar, go and be reconciled with your brother first, and then come back and present your offering."[14]

Once one has grasped the inner logic of the first two temptations, Jesus' recorded response to the third follows inevitably. For
if those who live as children of the Father must be inwardly free to
share material possessions with anyone, then membership in the
kingdom of God is incompatible with the pursuit of economic or
political power over others. And if the ideal of gratuitous sharing
necessarily involves a commitment of unrestricted, atoning love of
one's neighbor as an expression of one's radical dependence on
God, then the use of violence and coercion, whether military or
political, is simply inappropriate to found the kingdom.[15]

Such an ideal in no way precludes non-violent opposition to
oppressive economic and political structures. It may even demand
such opposition. To oppose such structures while eschewing violence means, however, that one must stand as Jesus stood, physically defenseless before the powers of darkness and of this world.
To demand that those powers abdicate their oppressive control
over others is to summon them to repentance in the name and with
the authority of Jesus himself.

6. It is, then, crucial to an understanding of Jesus' mission
and of the Christian call to sanctification that one see both as laying very specific moral obligations upon men. The Christian conscience stands polarized between two experiences: the concrete historical experience of human need, finitude, and sinfulness, on the
one hand, and, on the other, Jesus' vision of an ideal, Spirit-filled
community of "little ones" living in the image of God's anointed
Son and in hope of the coming reign of God. For the converted
Christian affirms that vision with ethical absoluteness and ultimacy.

Man's needs are physical, affective, cognitive, moral, and salvific. The ideal vision of a Spirit-filled community which emerges
from an integral Christian conversion is the historical revelation of
God's response to those needs; and it is a vision that is gradually
concretized in the pneumatic transformation of the believing community.

The saving word of God illumined by the Spirit establishes,
therefore, a normative communal context in which human and salvific needs must be met, if they are to be met with adequacy in the
sight of God. Simultaneously, the Word of God enunciates very

specific moral imperatives binding upon all who have heard God's call; and those imperatives enunciate the means demanded by God to fulfill man's salvific needs. To decide to follow Jesus is to decide to enter that community which is the historical expression and prolongation of His pneumatic anointing.

The recovery of the ethical imperatives of an authentic Christian conversion is, as we shall see, crucial to a sound understanding of the relation between the gifts and the sacraments. Moreover, it is in the believer's lived, practical response to the divine call revealed in Jesus under the guidance of the Spirit, that his or her faith commitment comes to visible, quasi-sacramental expression. For to use one's spatio-temporal environment as an expression of one's faith-dependence on the Father in acts of atoning love is to sacramentalize it, to transform it into a sign that both reveals and conceals the presence of God. To suffer in any way for justice's sake is to transform one's very suffering into a similar sign. The charismatic sacramentalization of the experienced environment from which we emerge as selves creates the possibility of perceiving the Spirit and His saving presence among us.

It should, however, be clear from the preceding reflections that in the teachings of Jesus as they are preserved in the gospels, one finds only the broad outlines of a basic ethical vision. The explicit teachings of Jesus preserved by first generation Christians sufficed as the foundation for its early common life and its early ethical development. But the Christian conscience has been forced to evolve historically in its very attempt to decide in the Spirit how concretely to live the ideals proclaimed by Jesus, in the variety of historical situations and contexts which came to confront it. The first such development in Christian ethics is to be found, of course, in the teachings of Paul.

The Christian's call to live, not by bread alone, but by every word that comes from the mouth of God comes to sophisticated theological expression in Paul's theology of faith. The faith of which Paul speaks in Romans is more than mere doctrinal assent. It is the willingness to trust in the Father's fidelity to His saving, justifying promises, made visible in Jesus and illumined by the Spirit of adoption. Precisely because Pauline faith is absolute trust in the saving power of God, that faith carries the believer beyond all human and this-worldly hope. "From the beginning till now the entire creation, as we know, has been groaning in one great act of giving birth; and not only creation, but all of us who possess the first-fruits of the Spirit, we too groan inwardly as we wait for our bodies to be set free. For we must be content to hope that we shall be saved—our salvation is not in sight, we should not have to be hoping for it if it were—but as I say, we must hope to be saved since we are not saved yet—it is something we must wait for with patience." In this context it is interesting to note that for Paul, humankind's tendency to turn from God in unbelief found its most basic expression in stinginess and cupidity.[16]

The Christian's refusal to test God comes to expression in Pauline teaching in the willingness to love others with a commitment that abolishes all human, economic, and social barriers. The true Christian must, then, live a life that reflects the belief that in Christ there is no longer Jew or Greek, slave or free, male or female. Moreover, for Paul, the true worship of God must come to expression not only in cultic acts, but in daily deeds of mutual service. Paul preaches therefore, the need for the free, gratuitous sharing of material goods with all in need, the subordination of the purpose of labor to the willingness to share freely with others, the importance of Christian hospitality as a practical expression of faith, the abolition of cliques and class distinctions in the act of sharing, the centrality of an unrestricted, atoning love in community living, the importance of entering into the *kenosis* of Jesus, the servant messiah.[17]

In all of these teachings, Paul simply proclaimed the basic moral message that would come to somewhat different expression in the gospels, but the immediate pastoral concern of his letters forced his thought beyond the general moral maxims enunciated by Jesus. For under the leading of the Spirit, he saw clearly that the ethical ideals of the new covenant reach into the most pedestrian aspects of human activity and make very special demands in the day-to-day living of the gospel. More specifically, Paul saw that one whose driving concern is to share one's personal possessions freely with anyone in need must repudiate acts of theft, usury, swindle, or any form of economic exploitation.[18]

Similarly, the Christian whose love imitates the unrestricted, atoning, forgiving love of Jesus will be ethically above slander, feuds, wrangling, jealousy, factionalism, revenge, dishonesty, quarrels, bad temper, envy, contentiousness. Even more, the true believer will be concerned to do nothing to scandalize the weaker members of the community. "We who are strong have a duty to put up with the qualms of the weak without thinking of ourselves. Each of us should think of his neighbors and help them to become stronger Christians. Christ did not think of himself. . . . And may he who helps us when we refuse to give up, help you all to be tolerant with each other, following the example of Christ Jesus, so that united in mind and voice you may give glory to the God and Father of our Lord Jesus Christ."[19]

The same atoning and forgiving love must, moreover, transform the Christian's use of sexuality. The Christian use of sex must, then, be more than the selfish satisfaction of bodily cravings. It must acknowledge the sacred character of the believer's body, consecrated to God as it is by His indwelling Spirit. "You know, surely, that your bodies are members making up the body of Christ; do you think that I can take parts of Christ's body and join them to the body of a prostitute: Never! As you know, a man who goes with a prostitute is one body with her, since *the two*, as it is said, *become one flesh*. But anyone who is joined to the Lord is one spirit with him."[20] Sexual activity informed by a Christ-like and atoning love excludes all irresponsible self-indulgence in sexual matters. Hence, it also excludes the works which self-indulgence inspires: fornication, promiscuity, gross indecency, sexual irresponsibility, adultery, sodomy, pederasty, foul talk, coarse or salacious language.[21]

In rejecting self-indulgence as incompatible with authentic Christian conversion, Paul was implicitly affirming that moral conversion is a necessary concomitant to authentic religious conversion. And on that basis, he rejected drunkenness and other orgiastic forms of self-indulgence.[22] Finally, in a Pauline ethic, dependence in faith on Jesus and the Father excludes idolatry, sorcery, and all forms of false worship.[23]

But Paul's ethical teaching went beyond the mere explicitation of the moral restrictions demanded by authentic Christian conversion. For he saw the converted Christian as instinctively drawn by the Spirit of Jesus to perform acts that are expressive of the divine indwelling. The converted Christian lives a life suffused by the praise of God for His saving love. Dependence on the Father in the Spirit teaches the believer to say "Abba" and draws the Christian to prayer on every possible occasion. There is joy in the Lord and the spontaneous concomitant of holy joy: the desire to praise God throughout the day for His forgiveness and His love. The converted Christian will be a person of devoted tenderness and sympathy, united in faith and love to the brethern, dedicated to serving the needs of others in the image of the servant Messiah. The believer's life will be marked by a Christ-like love, by a joy that is rooted in faith, by a peace that is grounded in a personal response to God, by patience, kindness, and goodness, by trustfulness, gentleness, and self-control. Sustained by the power of Jesus, the true disciple will live rooted in a faith that speaks to the heart of the full extent of God's saving love revealed in Christ. And (s)he will give glory to God in every word and deed.[24]

In other New Testament writers, one finds occasional moral exhortations which echo Paul's ethical doctrine. But none are as detailed as he in expressing the moral exigencies of a Christian faith commitment. The reason is not far to seek. The apostle of the Gentiles, who was concerned to exempt Gentile converts from circumcision and submission to all of the details of the Mosaic code, was equally concerned to show that the authentically converted Christian, who lives a life of faith sharing, unrestricted and atoning love, and mutual service in the image of Jesus, is one who acknowledges a personal obligation before God not only to observe the ethical substance of the Mosiac law, but to go far beyond the law's demands in a life of complete self-emptying in the image of a loving and crucified Lord.

7. The same evangelical and Pauline insights have, moreover, been implicit in much of the moral teaching of the official pastoral magisterium. In the practice of a gratuitous sharing which expresses one's salvific dependence on God, official Church teaching has made it clear that the word "alone" is crucial in Jesus' reply to His first desert temptation. The fact that one draws one's life from God does not mean that one ceases to possess, use, or alienate material goods, whether individually or in common.[25]

This doctrine clearly accords with biblical teaching. For apart from martyrdom, Jesus never demanded of His disciples the complete renunciation of all material, environmental supports to life. The renunciation of property which He asked of His close followers was a prelude to a life of communal sharing. It is mutual dependence in love which mediates one's sense of dependence on the Father, not a suicidal or quietistic renunciation of all material possessions.

It is no surprise, therefore, to find the official pastoral magisterium affirming unequivocally that economic destitution is an abomination in God's sight. For mere destitution is humanly degrading. It is a consequence of the misuse and exploitation of other persons, not of a loving faith-dependence on God. If the rich were concerned to share freely of their possessions with the poor, there would be no destitute people. The division of human society into "haves" and "have-nots" is, then, the visible social expression of the absence of authentic religious conversion.[26]

Not only, therefore, must the true Christian reject every temptation to transform the possession of riches into an end in itself, but active concern to share with others and to oppose prophetically those structures in society which are expressive of human greed and of social and political exploitation must imbue the believer with a willingness to "suffer persecution for justice's sake."[27]

It was sentiments such as these which motivated the great social encyclicals. While rejecting laissez-faire capitalism, the official pastoral magisterium has also repudiated any form of economic collectivism which would undermine a person's right to own and use material goods as an individual. At the same time, Church teachers have insisted that individuals are under serious obligation to use whatever possessions they have for the good of their fellow human beings.

Official pastoral teaching has also insisted on the importance and dignity of human labor. The conditions of labor must express a fundamental respect for the dignity of the laborer. Since, moreover, labor takes place at the expense of human vital energy, every laborer has the right to reap the fruits of personal labor. One has, therefore, the right to a living wage sufficient to support oneself and one's dependents.[28]

The official pastoral magisterium has also vindicated the basic rights of laborers to educational and cultural development. It demands the removal of economic inequity within nations and among the family of nations. It demands adequate aid to farmers in the marketing of their produce, social legislation to protect the erosion of family life, and the elimination of all forms of work which reduce the laborer to a mere tool of production.[29]

The unrestricted character of Christian love and trust in God comes to expression most obviously in the Church's universal missionary effort. But it is expressed too in a universal concern for the material needs of all culturally deprived people, including those of others nations. The official pastoral catechesis demands that Christians show active concern for the poor of other nations either through direct missionary activity or through financial support drawn even from the "substance" of one's possessions.[30]

Unrestricted commitment to others in the love of Christ also sets the believer in opposition to those forces in society which seek in any way to destroy or diminish human life, such as murder, genocide, abortion, euthanasia, suicide, mutilation, suffering in any form whether of soul or of body, arbitrary imprisonment and deportation, slavery, prostitution, subhuman living and working conditions. More positively it commits the Christian to active concern for the outcasts of society: for the aged, the migrant worker, the refugee, the abandoned or illegitimate child, the hungry, the poor.[31]

The Christian vision of a thoroughly converted, classless community in which each individual's personal needs are lovingly met in faith and mutual service has also set the collective conscience of the Christian community in opposition to any solution to social problems that trusts in economic or political means alone or which pits class against class in violence and hatred. The goal of Christian social action must be the abolition of class divisions through love, not their reinforcement through violence.[32]

We have been attempting an analysis of the basic ethical structure of Christian conversion as a prelude to a discussion of the seven gifts of sanctification. We have argued that to put on the mind of Jesus demands three distinguishable but interrelated decisions: 1) the decision to live, not by bread alone but by every word that comes from God's mouth; 2) the decision not to test God by placing conditions on one's trust in Him; 3) the decision to worship and serve the Father of Jesus rather than the prince of this world. We have suggested that these three commitments are dynamically interrelated. And we have explored some of their more obvious ethical consequences. In speaking of the demands made by Jesus' ethical teaching, however, it is important to remember that the call of Jesus to live as God's children in His image is irreducible to a mere philosophy of conduct. Central to an understanding of the Christian ethic is that it be a response to God's prior saving call. In all that touches the salvation of man, therefore, God holds the initiative. One must accept the values preached by Jesus, not simply as important moral insights, but as God's own word and as His summons to repentance. And as we shall see, one must ground any attempt to live them in prayerful docility to the Spirit. Consent to Jesus is, moreover, motivated by the beauty of His person and vision. At the same time, in consenting to the demands of the new covenant, the convert affirms them with ethical absoluteness and ultimacy, for they express the mind of God. Clearly then, Christian conversion mediates between the affective and ethical realms of human experience, and implicitly between affective and moral conversion as well.

It is time to address ourselves to a theology of the gifts of sanctification. But before we do, it will be useful to relate the preceding insights to an understanding of the Christian sense of sin. For that insight is crucial to understanding the relation between conversion to God and the "gifts of sanctification." The Christian comes to an authentic sense of sin, neither by meditating the decalogue or church law nor by reading the book of Genesis, but through a repentance-conversion to a religious vision of the world as it is revealed in Jesus.

8. Paul Ricoeur has correctly distinguished three stages in the development of religious consciousness of evil: defilement, sin, and guilt. Of the three, defilement is the most instinctive and least rational. It comes to symbolic, ritual expression in primitive taboos and purifications. What characterises the sense of defilement is its failure to distinguish clearly between deliberate sin and unconscious faults.[33] The sense of sin, by contrast, personalizes the expe-

rience of evil. It differentiates between mere ritual impurity and evil intent before God. The sense of sin is, therefore, closely bound to prophetic preaching: to a religious sense of divine displeasure at evil deliberately done and of divine pardon in the face of repentance. Guilt adds to sin the notion of degrees of personal malice.[34]

Ricoeur has suggested that it was the apostle Paul who brought the religious mind to its subtlest perception of guilt in his doctrine of the "servile will." The "servile will" is the product of the scrupulous conscience. It is a will determined to rid itself of all guilt in the practical observance of God's law. But in the process it is forced to confront its powerlessness to live a perfect moral life. As a result, the person of scrupulous conscience comes to acknowledge every effort to justify oneself before God as sin and guilt. (S)he is forced to confess that moral justification before God must be God's own work in the human heart. One is dead in one's sins until one accepts justification as God's free gift of life. The apostle Paul himself was forced to face the malice of his own servile will in the shattering realization that his zeal for the law had set him in opposition to His Lord and had led him to persecute the innocent servants of God.[35]

One may argue too that in Pauline theology the image of the servile will is paralleled by the image of the self-deluding mind. The self-deluding mind is one which in its very self-infatuated attempt to achieve wisdom independently of God blinds itself to the truth of divine revelation. The repudiation of such false wisdom is also implicit in Johannine denunciation of the children of darkness.[36]

If, moreover, every integral conversion has an affective dimension, then any adequate theory of religious repentance and conversion ought to include an account of the self-perverting heart, the heart which in its attempt to achieve emotional integrity independently of God reduces itself to emotional blindness and infantalism in moral and religious matters.

For the authentically converted Christian, then, there is only one way to put on the mind of Christ: it is to respond to the call which comes through the inner transformation of heart effected by the Spirit of Jesus. There is only one way to grow in that call: through the dependence of faith at every moment of one's religious growth. For, as Paul had seen most vividly, to attempt to put on the mind of God without being oneself taught by God is in effect to consent to the first temptation of Jesus. It is to refuse to live in an attitude of total trust and dependence upon the Father and the gift of His Spirit. Johannine theology of rebirth in the Spirit teaches the same doctrine. To be reborn in the image of Jesus one must, like the man born blind, acknowledge that without Jesus one lives in darkness. To be reborn in the image of Jesus one must, like Lazarus, acknowledge that without Jesus one is dead in one's sins. To acknowledge both is to repent and seek rebirth in water and the Spirit.

9. These reflections take on greater theological interest when they are set against the background of the analysis of religious conversion attempted in the preceding chapter. In an experiential approach to man, factual, environmental forces are immanent to the emergent self. As a consequence, an insight into the ethical demands of Christian conversion is double-faceted. It is, on the one hand, an insight into the religio-ethical ideals which give decisive salvific orientation to the self as it responds to the divine call to faith. And on the other hand, it is insight into those environmental factors which are factually immanent to the self but irreconcilable with the call of God revealed in Jesus and in the anointing of His Spirit.

As we have seen, however, each human self viewed as an emergent process defines itself in the course of its development to be a certain kind of self standing in a certain kind of relation to God and to the world. For in the course of its growth the self defines its dynamic and evaluative perspective on the universe. It decides which forces in its environment will nourish its life and which will not. For individuals react very differently to the same environmental stimuli. A ghetto may produce a saint or a pusher. As each self defines a perspective on its environment, it decides which elements in its past will continue to function positively in experience, which must be re-evaluated or excluded in the future.

It is possible, then, in the course of one's personal growth to define oneself into the kind of person who stands in radical or even complete opposition to the call of God revealed in Jesus. One may do so through a series of decisions which are opposed to that call at a religious, intellectual, moral, or affective level. Such decisions embody in some way a refusal to trust the God revealed in Jesus, a decision to live merely for the goods of this world, an attempt to place conditions on one's faith commitment, a choice to follow the way of violence rather than the way of service in atoning love, a refusal to bear witness against the sins and injustices of mankind.

If the analysis of conversion attempted in the preceding chapter is sound, the person who has come to stand in opposition to God will have difficulty in hearing the divine call proclaimed in Jesus, for the habits of thought, decision, and feeling which shape such an individual's conduct have either excluded the Spirit from the environment which nourishes the self or have devalued the things of God to the point of triviality.

Such a person cannot consent to God without a decisive reorientation of attitude. For, as we have seen, the past enters conscious experience as vague emotion. When, therefore, God takes the initiative and acts efficaciously to reorient a human self religiously, the convert may expect to experience initially a transformation of affectivity which yields a felt sense of God's presence and call. The consent of faith, if it follows, is the consent to admit into one's total environment the Spirit of God as a permanent, efficacious, healing, and transforming force. Hence, it is actions which proceed from an attitude of faith-dependence that are endowed with primordial sacramentality. For as co-action involving both God and man, they are simultaneously expressive of God's transforming presence in the believer and of the believer's response to that presence. Such actions are as a consequence lived signs of the new covenant.

Actions and sufferings which are expressive of an attitude of faith-dependence on God may, then, be described as imbued with a certain revelatory sacramentality, at least in the sense that they are environmentally immanent to the experience of others and must be interpreted inferentially as signs of the divine indwelling if they are to be adequately understood.

Graced actions and sufferings attain to full primordial sacramentality when they are not only imbued with revelatory sacramentality but are acknowledged by one who experiences them in another as expressions of the indwelling Spirit. For to grasp the full significance of Spirit-filled action and suffering, one must repent of interpretative, moral, and emotive habits which stand in opposition to authentic religious conversion. Hence, the full sacramentality of the Spirit-filled actions and sufferings of the believer can be grasped only by one who has personally decided to enter into an attitude of faith-dependence on God.

When the believer's faith-dependent actions and sufferings are environmentally immanent to the experiences of a nonbeliever and are accompanied by the healing and illuminating activity of the Spirit in the unbeliever's heart, they are, then, an invitation to the unbeliever to enter into a similar attitude of faith-dependence on God. Hence, to the extent that the believer's faith-dependence has been assimilated to Jesus' own filial dependence on the Father, the believer's actions and sufferings are a concrete revelation of Jesus himself and an historical prolongation of the Jesus-event.

10. We are now in a position to begin to evaluate a medieval theory of the gifts of sanctification. As we have already noted the "gifts of sanctification" derive their names and their number from the Isaian prophecy of the coming of a Spirit-filled Messiah. "A shoot springs from the stock of Jesse, a scion thrusts from his roots: on him the spirit of Yahweh rests, a spirit of wisdom and insight, a spirit of counsel and power, a spirit of knowledge and of the fear of Yahweh. (The fear of Yahweh is his breath.)"[37]

In a Thomistic account of the seven gifts of sanctification, they are distinguished both from the theological virtues of faith, hope, and love and from the moral virtues. The theological virtues are described as endowing human faculties with the power to act supernaturally; the "gifts" (dona), by contrast, endow the faculties with docility to the Spirit in their supernatural activity. This "docility" is described as endowing one's actions with a different kind of qualitative modality. It changes, not the object, but the quality of faith, hope, and love. A Thomistic theory of the gifts was, however, never universally held. A Scotist theology of faith denies, for example, any distinction between the gifts and the virtues.[38]

Thomists have attempted to distinguish each of the seven gifts by defining the genus and specific difference of wisdom, understanding, counsel, and the other gifts. How, they ask, does wisdom differ from understanding? How does understanding differ from knowledge? This attempt was, of course, a rough application of formal object analysis to the Isaian text. For in a classicist theology, "gift" is reduced to the Aristotelian category "habit," and habits are differentiated essentially by their formal objects.

Since, moreover, in a Thomistic hypothesis habits are essential modification of faculties, the traditional account of the seven gifts must logically attempt to relate them to the apparatus of human faculties, especially to the "spiritual" faculties of intellect and will. For in a world of static essences, these faculties, by their essentially immaterial character, ground man's basic contact with an essentially immaterial God. Since, moreover, in a substance theology, the gifts, by endowing human activity with docility to the Holy Spirit, also perfect the virtues, the gifts are defined in relation to the moral and theological virtues.

Traditional commentators on the "gifts of sanctification" are often deeply spiritual men; and their treatises often breathe with a sense of spiritual depth and wisdom. What they have written on the gifts is worth devotional study. Ordinarily there is no question of the truth of their ascetical insights, granted the kinds of questions they ask and the medieval problematic in which they have chosen to think. But if our reflections up to this point are fundamentally sound, there is serious question concerning the adequacy of their ascetical problematic.

In equating the seven "spirits" of the Isaiahan text with seven distinct, infused habits, a traditional theology of the gifts ignores the fact that the seventh of the "gifts" (fear of the Lord) was absent from the original Isaiahan prophecy and is in fact a scribal gloss explaining the meaning of the sixth "gift" (piety). The two "gifts," then, despite their essential differentiation in medieval thought, were not originally distinct at all. In the prophet's mind there were six, not seven "spirits."

Worse still, a traditional theology of the "seven gifts" assumes that one can adequately explain the meaning of the biblical text by projecting into it philosophical categories alien to the author's intent. Such a projection might be justifiable if truth were simply out there to be grasped, uniform and available for metaphysical insight. For in such a world, any mind addressing itself to the question of the "gifts," no matter what its age and circumstance, would supposedly be speaking in identical terms about the same reality. Unfortunately, however, the Isaiahan prophecy has little to do with medieval theological speculation on the gifts which it inspired. Isaiah did not intend to give a catalogue of supernatural habits capable of endowing moral theological virtues with the modality of docility. He intended to predict the coming of a Spirit-filled Messiah who would be a compendium of all the great charismatic leaders of the Old Testament.

Finally, a traditional theology of the seven gifts is built on epistomological and psychological sand. For it is inseparable from an untenable faculty psychology and from the equally untenable presuppositions of formal object analysis.

11. The reader may be tempted at this point to discard the traditional Catholic attempt to reflect on the "sanctifying gifts" as exegetically and theologically worthless. But a complete rejection of "gifts of sanctification" would be hasty and ill advised. There are valid insights struggling to imperfect expression in a theology of the "seven gifts." For the medieval application of the Pauline notion of charism to the experience of Spirit-led growth in faith, hope, and love is in the last analysis legitimate. Let us reflect on why this is so.

The religious experience corresponding to the Pauline use of the term "gift" is the experience of vocation, or call. What a medieval theology of the seven gifts grasped and grasped clearly is that beyond the initial call to faith, beyond the act of repentance it evokes, beyond the decision to enter into an attitude of faith dependence on God and to draw one's life from Him, beyond the permanent self-orientation that such a graced decision makes in one's life, there is a dynamic and efficacious lure of the Spirit of Christ in His presence to every believer to step beyond any present understanding of Jesus' mind in its application to the believer's own life, in order to reach a deeper lived experience and personal embodiment of God's word. The medieval attempt to reduce such an experience to the Aristotelian category of *"habitus"* also has its point, to the extent that it suggests both the enduring and constant character of the Spirit's call to sanctification and that call's capacity to be differentiated from the divine summons to faith, from repentance-conversion, from faith as a permanent attitude in the believer, from occasional actual graces, and from a specific service gift.

The medieval attempt to speak of these experiences in the categories of Aristotelian philosophy falters under the inability of a static, essentialistic world-view to provide an adequate account of faith as a genetic process. In an emergent experiential approach to faith, these deficiencies can be remedied. Medieval theologians held that because the gifts, the virtues, and created grace are supernatural, they are all "infused." Unfortunately, their theological language did not allow them to speak of the process of infusion in terms that have any discernible experiential correlate.[39]

These speculative inconveniences are considerably relieved, however, when one shifts from a medieval to an experiential, emergent problematic. In conscious adult experience, the "infusion" of created grace is the transformation of the self which results from a decisive response in faith to the saving impulses of the Spirit. The "infusion" of sanctifying grace and of the theological virtues is the decisive orientation given to the emergent self when, under the efficacious impulse of the Spirit, the believer accepts in principle the ethical consequences of living a life that is expressive of the threefold decision that Jesus made in His desert temptations. The "infusion" of the gifts is the cumulative, expansion of the convert's understanding of the consequences of that vision under the efficacious impulse of the Spirit in a charismatic community of faith. Hence, in an emergent problematic, the "infusion" of the "sanctifying" gifts is germinal in conversion but is ultimately accomplished in a process of evaluative and decisive growth in faith. In an emergent, experiential approach to human development, one must, then, distinguish the initial divine call to faith, the initial decision to believe, the permanent modification of the self consequent on the decision to believe, cumulative insight under the impulse of the Spirit into the consequences of one's decision to believe, and occasional actual graces. Let us begin to reflect on these insights in greater descriptive detail.

12. Thomistic theology correctly distinguished between the notions of "operative" and "co-operative" grace. The two terms describe distinguishable moments in the salvific transformation of experience. The term "operative grace" designates the moment of

divine initiative: the efficacious impact of God on human experience. "Co-operative grace" designates human response to the divine initiative. In an experiential problematic, the operative grace which leads to adult faith enters conscious experience as the felt impulse to believe. As an impulse to put on the mind of Jesus, that impulse is already sanctifying in its dynamic. Since the initial conceptual illumination of feeling remains an emotive impulse until the feeling is further clarified through inferential activity, the first stages of an adult conversion are apt to be emotionally charged. The same is true of any major religious reorientation of one's life after initial conversion. When authentic, these later experiences are a deepening and a clarification of one's initial turning to God.[40]

Less significant impulses of grace demanding less of an evaluative and attitudinal shift may occur at any time. Although they may be diminished in emotive tone by comparison with deeper experiences of conversion and repentance, these lesser impulses ought also, in an experiential approach to conversion, initially to be felt emotively and only subsequently understood.

In order for an operative grace to lead to conversion, however, it must pass from a vague emotive impulse to a relatively clear conceptual sense of God's call. In an experiential world-view the need for the ongoing, evaluative illumination of an operative grace is, moreover, one of the most fundamental grounds of human freedom under grace. That freedom has a twofold ground within experience. For the experienced open-endedness of one's personal conscious thrust toward self-transcendence combines with the highly abstractive character of evaluative, propositional feelings in order to prevent any single conceptual feeling from exhausting the possibilities for decision. Let us reflect a bit why this is true.

One of the constitutive traits of conscious activity is the presence within it of a negative judgment. I become explicitly conscious of something when I can differentiate it from something else. Minimal consciousness demands the ability to differentiate myself from the forces in my environment. To be conscious, an evaluative response must, then, be able to distinguish between what a potential object of decision is and what it is not. At the very least I must be able to distinguish between either choosing or not choosing the alternative facing me. The presence to consciousness of more than one potential for decision within a virtually unlimited horizon of self-development grounds the possibility of freedom in decision itself. For in such an evaluative context, no single potential can be exhaustive of value or desire. The more potentials that function in such an experience, the greater freedom and conscious indecisiveness prior to the act of decision. The ideal of Christian sharing may, for example, be embodied in an almost infinite number of ways. As I grow in an understanding of the different ways I can share the gifts of the Spirit, I am faced with the problem of choosing among the graced alternatives that confront me in faith.

The need for the ongoing evaluative illumination of God's efficacious impact on the self also grounds the possibility of illusion within religious experience. Such illusions are analogous to perceptual illusions, or even at times to hallucinatory experience. My religious beliefs may, for example, be colored by bigotry and selfishness. That same bigotry and selfishness can, on occasion distort my prayer, my prophetic utterances, my teaching. One finds, for instance, in charismatic groups individuals who feel moved to proclaim in God's name attitudes which reflect their own ability to relate positively to women or to the attempt to secure justice for women in human society. On occasion disordered attitudes may inspire visionary experiences.

In the experience of conversion, the emotive character of the early stages of the conversion process can, then, easily give rise to evaluative feelings which either imperfectly illumine or positively distort their causal source. This is particularly so when conversion occurs in the absence of sound teaching or in an environment which suggests false, fallacious, or inadequate interpretations of the efficacious movement of grace.

When authentic religious conversions occur outside of an explicitly Christian context, the possibilities of the evaluative distortion of the grace of conversion are multiplied, since the environmental, cultural forces which shape the self reflect even less the mind of Christ. Even within the Christian churches, decadent religious beliefs and attitudes, whatever their origin, can have a similar impact on the conversion process. I may, for example, turn to authoritarian, fundamentalistic forms of religion as a way of escaping the full consequences of authentic conversion to God.

Moreover, the total number of environmental forces operative in any given conversion experience is bewilderingly complex. And any abstract conceptual illumination of those forces conceals more than it reveals. There is, then, perennial wisdom in the old theological adage that I can never be absolutely sure I am in the state of grace. Such a judgment is either an abductive or an inductive inference; and every such inference is liable to revision, either because of some abductive or deductive oversight, or because of neglect and oversight within the process of verification.

When a conversion experience is authentically interpreted, it is a conscious confrontation in the Spirit with the person of Jesus as the historical revelation of the Father. It is a personal confrontation with His absolute commitment to me in love. And that confrontation brings with it a sense of the moral exigencies which a consent to the forgiveness of God revealed in Jesus must bring.

To interpret the Christian call to repentance as a summons to acknowledge my need to be forgiven by God is, then, false and misleading. Rather, it is a summons to acknowledge the fact that I have already been forgiven by God in Christ and that that irrevocable offer of divine forgiveness demands that I either open my heart to the healing power of the Spirit and submit to the moral exigencies of the new covenant or accept the damning consequences of my refusal. The true image of the repentant Christian is, then, the woman who was a sinner, bending at the feet of Jesus, and weeping with an amazement, sorrow, and joy at the realization that she had already been forgiven.[41]

But not every response to the divine summons to repentance is instantaneous, nor is it total. It is, moreover, in the experience of one's instinctive, personal repugnance to that divine summons that the Christian discovers a primordial experience of personal sinfulness. Paul Ricoeur is quite correct in insisting that the experience of sin is impossible outside of a theistic context. In a world without God, moral fault may be a blunder, it may even be deliberately wrong. But it is no sin. It is, as John Dewey realized, simply a mistake to be corrected as quickly and as completely as possible.[42]

Sin-consciousness implies God-consciousness. And for the Christian, God consciousness is consciousness of the lure of the Spirit to submit to Jesus as the personal revelation of the Father and as the revelation in his teaching and life of the Father's will for humankind.

In this context it is, moreover, important to insist that in an experiential approach to faith, sin-consciousness, even in its initial phases, can never be a purely subjective experience. For in an emergent universe, no experience can be purely subjective. Rather, sin-consciousness is simultaneously both environmental and evaluative. It is the awareness (initially emotive and vague perhaps) of all those forces in one's immanent, emergent environment which stand in opposition to the divine summons to repentance. This environmental dimension to sin-consciousness provides, as we shall see, important foundational grounding for the sense of "original sin."

It should, however, be clear from the preceding considerations that as a Christian, I do not derive my most basic sense of sin from a meditation on the decalogue. I derive it from a personal confrontation with Jesus' summons to repentance. The moral exigencies of Jesus' teaching go far beyond the demands of the decalogue, as Jesus himself was at pains to point out. Jesus demands not only the abstention from theft and covetousness, but the free sharing of all I have with others. He demands not simply the abstention from murder, but the unrestricted love of all men, including my enemies. He demands not only that I keep holy the Lord's day, but that my service of worship be an expression of my willingness to lay down my life daily for the brethren, even for those who hate me.[43]

If, moreover, as we have suggested, the major moral teachings of Jesus are an expression of His triple demand that I live, not by bread alone, but by every word that comes from the mouth of God, that I not test God, and that I worship and serve, not the Prince of this World, but only the Father, then I come to a basic sense of sinfulness in my awareness of those immanent forces in my environment which incline me to say "no" to each of these demands. Those forces would incline me to live a life of independent self-reliance, to set the conditions of my relationship to God, to disassociate my service of others from authentic worship of the Father, and to resort in my dealings with others to legal and coercive violence.

Among these five temptations, however, the most basic is the temptation to self-reliance. For religious self-reliance is implicit in every desire to set the conditions of one's relation with God, to disassociate service from worship, and to seek coercive power over others. For such desires presuppose self-reliance as their condition. Power, in a self-reliant world, is the key to personal success. The self-reliant person feels no need to depend in prayer upon God. Nor does such an individual sense the need to allow God to determine the conditions of their relationship.

But if the basic Christian sin is the sin of self-reliance, then true Christian repentance can only be, as Paul saw clearly in Romans, the decision to enter into an attitude of complete faith-dependence on God. For self-reliance in matters of salvation is the attempt to justify oneself in the eyes of God. Authentic Christian conversion is, then, repentance viewed positively, a turning to as well as a turning away. But there is only one turning. For one cannot turn from a proud self-reliance without simultaneously turning to faith-dependence upon God.

In a world of unconditioned faith-dependence, however, God must hold the initiative in all things. In such a world, the consent of faith can only be a response to the efficacious impulse of divine grace. And in the Christian dispensation that impulse can only be the work of the Spirit of Jesus drawing us to the Father through the Son.

If, then, these reflections are correct, to repent authentically as a Christian is to receive the Spirit of Jesus. But, if so, then any distinction between conversion and the reception of the Spirit is indefensible. By the same token, the most basic sign of openness to the Spirit is, not the gift of tongues or any of the service gifts, but a faith-dependence on the Lord whose sign is loving service of the brethren. We shall return to this last point in discussing sacramental baptism.

Once made, however, the decision to enter into an enduring attitude of unconditioned faith-dependence on God cannot be taken back without sin. It must function as the "leading principle" of all one's acts as a Christian. To the extent that it does not, one's life as a Christian is marred by an inauthenticity which could ultimately subvert one's initial faith commitment or reduce it to a formalistic sham. The term "leading principle" is logical in origin. C.S. Peirce uses it to denote a general rule which grounds a species of inference. It is applied analogously here to a generalized attitude which grounds a complex set of interrelated interpretative and decisive religious acts.[44]

13. To live by faith-dependence is to leave to God the initiative in every decision that touches salvation, either by following obediently what one has already been led under grace to acknowledge as His saving will or by seeking further enlightenment from him.

To experience God's constant leading as one grows through faith in an understanding of the mind of Jesus is to experience the "gifts of sanctification." Such an experience is legitimately termed charismatic, because it is the experience of an enabling and habitual call, a permanent lure of the Spirit of Jesus, who teaches and frees us from day to day to advance ever more deeply in understanding and living the mind of the Lord. Needless to say, such an experience presupposes the regular practice of shared and private prayer.

The initial call to faith is, then, God's operative grace summoning one to belief. The decision to believe is the initial act of faith, made under the efficacious impact of that call. The permanent modification of the self consequent on one's decision to live in abiding faith-dependence on God is aptly identified with what scholastic philosophy called "created grace" and the "infused supernatural virtues." The Spirit in His abiding, efficacious presence to the believer is aptly identified with "uncreated grace," the abiding salvific presence of the triune God to the believer. When that abiding presence comes to conscious conceptual clarity, it is felt as an abiding call to put on the mind of Jesus. Such a call is aptly designated as an experience of the "gifts of sanctification." For to put on the mind of Jesus is to grow in likeness to him. To grow in likeness to him is to be daily set apart by God from those who do not believe. And whatever is set apart by God for his own service and praise is holy, sanctified.

If the preceding analysis is correct then the experience of the gifts of sanctification grounds an ever expanding and cumulative horizon of understanding of God's salvific purposes. For putting on the mind of Christ is a genetic process composed of genetically interrelated evaluations and decisions that provide the concrete experiential ground for further religious growth and development. Hence, the evaluative form of any growing faith experience is charismatic; and theological fulminations against the experientially pervasive character of the charismatic dimension of Christian faith are as groundless as they have been, on occasion, tasteless. For nothing in the universe is static, including faith. One must either grow in an experientially integrated, cumulative understanding of God's call or in attitudes inimical or irrelevant to an authentic consent of faith. The fruit of the latter growth is religious disintegration and alienation from God as a life-source. At the same time, all authentic growth in faith is Spirit-led and the fruit of the charisms of sanctification.

The preceding analysis also allows one to distinguish between the experience of the gifts of sanctification and actual graces. For the gifts, as experienced, ground a permanent and cumulatively expanding horizon of understanding and decision within faith. Actual graces are, by contrast, experienced as occasional illuminations proportioned to the needs of a specific situation. They are the inspiration to avoid a specific temptation or to do some concrete Spirit-led act, impulses to apply achieved insights into the mind of Christ to some specific situation without that impulse adding any new insight into the mind of Christ itself.

Notes

1. Phil 2:1-11; 1 Co 2:6-16. The position assumed in this chapter is a distillation and precision of germinal insights developed in *Discerning the Spirit*. Although they were originally developed in the context of a theology of religious vows, it was clear from the beginning that they had implications beyond the religious life.

2. Dunn exaggerates somewhat the uniqueness of Jesus' Spirit-baptism; cf. James Dunn, *Baptism in the Holy Spirit* (Naperville, Ill.: A. R. Allenson, 1970) pp. 30-31. It is as a consequence of its hypostatic uniqueness that Jesus' human experience becomes normative both of who God is and what we are called to be.

3. Mt 3:13-4:17; Lk 4:1-21.

4. Mt 26:8; Mk 14:24; Lk 22:22.

5. Pr 19:1, 6:6-10, 10:4, 13:18, 17:5, 21:17, 22:1, 28:6, 30:9; Qo 4:13; Ex 22:21-25; Dt 23:15, 24:10-13; Ez 22:29-30; Mi 2:1-3; Jr 22:18-29; Am 8:7; Si 1:27; Ws 2:21-3:8; Is 11:1-4; Ps 72:12-13; Ze 3:11-13.

6. Mt 6:24, 13:22, 16:25-26, 19:6 ff; Lk 8:14, 12:15, 16:9-16.

7. Mt 5:43-48.

8. Mt 6:11, 31-33, 8:20, 19:16-30; Mk 13:38-40; Jn 12:6; Lk 3:10-14; 14:12-14.

9. Lk 12:37, 14:12-24; Mt 10:40; Mk 9:37; cf. Tt 1:7; 1 Tm 3:3-4; Jn 14:2-3.

10. Jm 1:9-10, 27, 2:2-4, 8-9, 13:5-6; Rm 12:13; 1 Th 5:14; Lk 16:9-12.

11. Jn 4:31, 6:25-63, 14:1; 1 Co 11:17-34.

12. Lk 6:27-35.

13. 1 Co 13.

14. Mk 1:22 ff., 2:1-12, 28, 4:41 ff.; Mt 5:20ff., 8:8 ff., 9:1-8, 17, 17:24-27, 18:19-20, 20:24-29, 23:11-12, 26:52-55; Jn 5:29-30; Lk 5:17-26.

15. Mk 10:43-45; Mt 16:21-26, 18:1-4, 20:25-28, 26:51-56; Lk 14:7-11, 17:7-9, 22:41-51; Jn 18:10-11.

16. Rm 1:16-17, 4:1-25, 8:1-27; Cf. Stanislaus Lyonnet and Leopold Sabourin, *Sin, Redemption, and Sacrifice* (Rome: Biblical Institute, 1970) pp. 50-51.

17. 1 Co 10:9, 13:1-13; 1 Tm 6:17; Rm 12:9-13; Phil 2:1-11.

18. 1 Co 5:9-13, 6:9-11; Col 3:5-9; Phil 2:1-11.

19. Rm 15:1-6.

20. Rm 14:1 ff.; 1 Co 6:9-11, 8: 1 ff.

21. Rm 12:14-21, 13:13-14, 14:1 ff.; 1 Co 3:16-17, 5:9-13, 6:9-20; Eph 4:29-31, 5:1-4, 29-32; Col 3:5-9.

22. Rm 13:13-14; 1 Co 5:9-13, 6:9-11; Gal 5:13-26.

23. Gal 4:8-11.

24. Eph 3:16-19, 5:4, 19-20, 6:1-8; Col 4:2-4; Phil 2:1-11; Gal 5:13-26; 1 Co 10:31.

25. DS 930-931.

26. *Gaudium et spes*, 31.

27. *Apostolicam actuositatem*, 4.

28. DS 3268, 3733-3737, 3946, 3960; *Gaudium et spes*, 68-71; *Populorum progressio*, 69.

29. DS 3733, 3735-3737, 3946, 3960; *Gaudium et spes*, 60, 66, 68; *Populorum progressio*, 61.

30. *Ad gentes*, 2; *Gaudium et spes*, 31, 69, 88.

31. *Gaudium et spes*, 27, 34-35, 60, 67; cf. DS 668, 1495, 2745, 3441.

32. *Gaudium et spes*, 4, 63, 69.

33. Paul Ricoeur, *The Symbolism of Evil*, translated by Emerson Buchanan (Boston: Beacon, 1967) pp. 25-46.

34. *Ibid.*, pp. 47-107.

35. *Ibid.*, pp. 118-157.

36. Cf. 1 Co 2:6-16.

37. Is 11:1-2.

38. Cf. *Summa Theologiae*, I-II, Q 68; John of St. Thomas, *The Gifts of the Holy Spirit*, translated by Dominique Hughes, O.P. (N.Y.: Sheed and Ward, 1951); M. M. Philipon, O.P., *Les Dons du Saint-Esprit* (Parish: Desclee de Brower, 1963); Adolphe Tanquerey, *The Spiritual Life*, translated by Herman Brandens (Westminster: Newman, 1930) pp. 119-120. In a classicist theology of gift, counsel is described as perfecting the virtue of prudence by making us judge promptly and rightly, by a kind of supernatural intuition, what must be done, especially in difficult cases. The proper object of counsel is the right ordering of particular acts. The gift of piety is described as perfecting the virtue of justice by begetting in our hearts a filial affection for God and a tender devotion toward those

persons and things consecrated to him, in order to make us fulfill our religious duties with a holy joy. It has as its proper object God as our master and loving Father, and created persons and things, to the extent that they are an expression of the divine reality. The gift of fortitude is described as perfecting the virtue of fortitude by imparting to the will an impulse and an energy which enable it to do great things joyfully and fearlessly despite all obstacles. It gives courage not only to act but to endure. The gift of fear of the Lord inclines us to filial respect for God, and it preserves us from excessive familiarity with Him. The gift of knowledge endows the mind with docility to the Spirit in the investigation of natural things insofar as knowledge of them leads to God. The gift of understanding is described as giving deep insight into revealed truths, without, however, giving a comprehension of the divine mysteries themselves. Finally, wisdom perfects the virtue of charity by enabling us to discern God and divine things in their ultimate principles and by giving us a relish for them.

39. Karl Rahner, S.J., "Some Implications of the Scholastic Concept of Uncreated Grace" *Theological Investigations*, translated by Cornelius Ernst (Baltimore: Helicon, 1961) I, pp. 319-346.

40. Bernard Lonergan, S.J., *Grace and Freedom*, edited by Patout Burns, S.J. (N.Y.: Herder and Herder, 1970).

41. Lk 7:36-51.

42. John Dewey, *A Common Faith* (New Haven: Yale, 1934).

43. Mt 5:17-48.

44. Peirce, *Collected Papers*, 2.465-467.

III
The
Pauline
Gifts

1. We have been attempting an experiential approach to the problem of Christian conversion. We have argued that the ethical commitment demanded by Christian conversion requires the assumption of an attitude of habitual faith-dependence on the Spirit in prayer. We have distinguished within the conversion process the operative grace which summons one to initial faith in Christ; the decision to assent in faith as a response to that grace; habitual, personal openness to the Spirit in putting on the mind of Jesus; and occasional, actual graces. We have identified what medieval theologians called the gifts of sanctification with the believer's habitual docility to the Spirit in putting on the mind of Jesus. And we have explored some of the ethical consequences of growth in the sanctifying gifts.

It is time, then, to turn our attention to the Pauline gifts of service. These gifts, it will be recalled were named "gratuitous graces" by medieval theologians. As such they were distinguished from sanctifying grace *(gratia gratum faciens)*; for, it was argued, they are ordered, not to the sanctification of the one who possesses them, but to the edification of the Christian community. As we have also seen, there is some basis for such a theory in 1 Co 13. But the theory becomes misleading if it causes one to suppose that there can be no connection within the dynamics of Christian conversion between the gifts of service and the process of personal sanctification. The connection becomes clearer, however, when one shifts from a medieval to an experiential problematic. For in an experiential approach to faith, one's primary concern is to establish genetic connections rather than to reify abstract essential differences. Those connections are not only individual and personal, but also social. For if the reflections of the preceding chapter are theologically sound, an integral Christian faith-commitment to God is impossible in anything but a communal setting. In new covenant religion, commitment to God demands an unrestricted love commitment to other persons, especially to one's covenant brethren. Hence, the growth demanded by the sanctifying gifts is communal as well as personal.

One cannot, however, grow in an active mutual service which expresses true faith-dependence on the Father through openness to the Spirit of Jesus without deciding to allow oneself to be led prayerfully by the Spirit to the precise form of community service to which the Father calls. The Spirit's call to a specific form of service—His charisms, or service gifts—ought, then, to be the normal outcome of growth in the gifts of sanctification. Far from being unrelated to the process of personal sanctification, a charism of service ought to be its specification and concrete personalization. One cannot, then, understand the gifts of service adequately by conceiving them as oriented exclusively to the service of others. For it is in serving others in the image of Jesus that one is sanctified.

At the same time, one cannot simply identify the charisms of sanctification with those of service. For while all are called to put on the mind of Jesus and all are called to some form of service in community, each individual is called to serve in a way that is personally appropriate.

It is this genetic distinction between the gifts of sanctification and of service which grounds the possibility of the latter's inauthentic exercise. For as Paul notes in I Co 13 and as experience teaches, it is possible to respond inauthentically to one's personal call to ecclesial service by separating that response from sanctifying growth in faith, trust, and love. But an inauthentic response does not negate the fact that one has been divinely called.

An experiential theory of the service gifts must, then, do three things. First, it must show in what sense each gift of service ought to be a particularization of God's call to holiness. Second, it must discriminate between the authentic and inauthentic exercise of the gifts of service. Third, it must relate this genetic analysis of the service gifts to the dynamics of experiential growth in general.

2. Paul the apostle gave us our first theological reflection on the gifts of service. His letters contain catalogues of the various gifts that were operative in the first Christian community. The lists overlap, but they are far from being uniform.

In the first letter to the Corinthians, Paul speaks of preaching with wisdom, preaching instruction, faith, healing, miracles, prophecy, discernment, tongues, and the interpretation of tongues. In the same letter he attempts what seems to be a hierarchical ordering of the gifts. In his hierarchical listing he speaks of apostles, prophets, teachers, miracles, healing, helpers, leaders, and tongues. Elsewhere in the same letter he speaks both of celibacy and marriage as gifts. Romans and Ephesians contain shorter lists of the gifts. Romans speaks of prophecy, administration, teaching, preaching, almsgiving, officials, and works of mercy. Ephesians lists apostles, prophets, evangelists, pastors, and teachers.[1]

Exegetes have not been able to reach a clear consensus concerning the precise meaning which each of these gifts had for Paul. Paul speaks of the service gifts as though they were familiar experiences in the communities he had founded. He therefore presupposed for the most part that extensive explanation of his meaning was unnecessary. He was no doubt correct. But his reticence leaves contemporary readers largely in the dark concerning his intent.[2]

It seems unlikely, therefore, that exegesis alone will ever supply us with a final theology of the gifts of service. In the absence of extensive evidence concerning a writer's intent, an exegete must conclude that the sacred author's meaning is vague. If the exegete is adept, (s)he will minimize the vagueness by indicating the possible senses a passage might have. (S)he may even indicate the sense (s)he judges to be most probable. But in the absence of decisive evidence, the exegete must rest content with textual vagueness.

Our own approach to the gifts is experiential, rather than purely exegetical. In an experiential approach to Christian conversion, the Pauline lists are, however, richly suggestive. For one discovers in them the hint of an overlapping spectrum of gifts corresponding to the emotive, the interpretive, and the decisive moments in the growth of human experience. Tongues is for example described by Paul in terms that suggest a vague, emotive response to God. As George Montague has noted: ". . . the gift of tongues as reported by Paul was essentially preconceptual without any connotation of foreign languages. It was a laudable type of personal prayer and entered into the community worship at Corinth and needed regulation, though not suppression."[3] Two other gifts mediate between the vague emotive impulse expressed in glossolalia and that impulse's conceptual clarification: the gifts of interpretation and of prophecy. Paul speaks of the gift of interpretation as reducing glossolalic utterance to intelligible human speech. And he assimilates interpreted glossolalic utterance to prophecy.

The various gifts of teaching and preaching of which Paul speaks prolong the conceptual illumination of the faith experience initiated in prophecy and interpretation. These word gifts would seem to be connected with the deductive and inductive moments within experience. There is, moreover, as we shall see, an intimate connection between the gifts of healing and miracles and the gifts of teaching. The gift of discernment mediates a certain kind of inductive judgment. It seeks to discriminate between authentic and inauthentic teachings, prophecies, and other charismatic impulses which appear in the community. Gifts like helping, almsgiving, works of mercy, administration are clearly associated with the decisive-reactive moment within experience. They are action gifts. They mediate the believer's reactive impact on his or her environment. But they too are in part dependent in their exercise upon sound teaching and upon discernment.

3. One can, then, correlate almost all of the different Pauline gifts with the different moments in the graced development of experience. There is, however, an important exception to the preceding insight: the gift of faith. Paul mentions this gift only once. But he does so in a context which suggests that he is speaking, not of the faith that is common to all believers, but of a special charism on a par with the gifts of teaching, prophecy, tongues, etc. Unfortunately, Paul never explained precisely what he meant by this gift. And his omission has led Christians to offer some fairly arbitrary explanations of it. One observes, for example, the occasional ten-

dency in charismatic circles to explain the gift of faith as an anticipatory certitude that a miracle or healing is about to be worked. Under such an hypothesis, an instance of the gift of faith would be Peter's apparent anticipatory certitude that the beggar at the Beautiful Gate would in fact be healed when Peter pulled him to his feet.[4]

There are problems, however, with such an interpretation of the charism of faith. The first is the absence of any positive evidence in the Pauline corpus to support it. A second difficulty is methodological. For the theory uses a Lukan pericope to explain a Pauline without establishing a connection between the two. A third difficulty lies in the restrictive character of such an interpretation. For it binds faith, as a special gift, to healing and to miracles. Such an interpretation smacks, however, of what Fr. Edward O'Connor has called "charismania."[5] It suggests the kind of excessive preoccupation with physical healing which sometimes mars both Catholic and Protestant charismatic piety.

We would like to propose here a different explanation of the gift of faith, one which is in better accord with an experiential approach to the gifts. We have explained the act of faith as a decision under the graced impulse of the Spirit to enter into an attitude of faith-dependence on the Father in the image of Jesus and under the anointing of the Spirit. We have suggested that in covenant religion such faith-dependence comes to expression in acts of worship, of gratuitous sharing, and of unrestricted and atoning service and love. We have equated the gifts of sanctification with docility to the Spirit in putting on the mind of Jesus, in growing in a cumulative insight into the lived consequences of one's basic faith commitment. All Christians, to the extent that their lives are authentic, believe in God and are in process of growing under grace in an understanding of what that belief demands of them. Both the commitment of faith which results from religious conversion and growth in the gifts of sanctification are, then, common to all believers authentically open to God.

In listing faith among the gifts of service, Paul seems to be suggesting that there can be a certain kind and quality of faith operative in individuals which lifts them out from the collectivity of believers and transforms them into outstanding examples of faith. Faith comes to visibility in their lives with a special vividness. Their service to the community lies in the example of faith they give and in their deeds of service, which are the practical expression of faith. At the same time, their practical service remains unchanneled into a specific charismatic ministry like administration, almsgiving, etc.

If this approach to the gift of faith is experientially sound, then there is clear genetic continuity between the gifts of sanctification and the gift of faith. For the gift of faith mediates an intensification and personalization of the insights and attitudes which are the fruit of growth in the gifts of sanctification. It is one thing to understand the mind of Jesus. It is another to trust Him concretely in the day to day living of one's life. One with the gift of faith will be moved to take concrete and personal risks that are expressive of authentic faith dependence on God; and such a person will do so in a manner that transforms his or her life into a visible and dramatic witness to faith.

It follows, therefore, that the gift of faith can come to expression in a broad variety of activities: in the habitual risk or renunciation of one's material possessions in order to share them with others who have nothing, in the habitual risk of one's life for the sake of others, in the habitual dedication to tasks that are humanly repugnant as an expression of one's desire to reach out in Jesus' name to those who are in greatest need. Since such risks can be undertaken out of unresolved guilt feelings or other emotional compulsions, an authentic gift of faith ought to be grounded in a carefully discerned sense of God's call. Since, moreover, a charism in the strict sense is an enabling call, not an occasional grace, one cannot speak of the gift of faith unless the risks taken are of a more or less permanent nature.

A final test of the presence and authenticity of the gift of faith will be the concrete character of one's faith expectancy. In undertaking the risks and renunciations to which one is summoned by God, one gifted with faith would be quick to acknowledge personal needs in prayer and would remain peacefully confident that God will provide for them. An authentic gift of faith will, then, bring a deepened belief in the power and concrete effacacy of petitionary prayer.

There are, then, five traits that characterize an authentic gift of faith: (1) experiential continuity with the attitudes and ideals which are the fruit of the gift of sanctification; (2) a practical visibility which endows the deeds which proceed from this gift with a public witness value; (3) the performance of such deeds in peace as a conscious and explicit response to God's prior call; (4) the enduring character of that call; (5) the intensification of one's conscious faith expectancy and reliance on petitionary prayer in the concrete living out of one's call.

Hence, one may legitimately describe the gift of faith as a "transmutation" of the experience mediated by the gifts of sanctification. The term "transmutation" is technical and needs explanation. A feeling, or experience, is transmuted: (1) when it develops in genetic continuity with a prior feeling; (2) when it includes novel, qualitatively distinguishable variables not operative in the prior experience; (3) when it integrates those novel variables into subsequent experience in such a way as to change its felt relational structure by reducing that structure to a mutually reinforcing unity. Graced experience too can be transmuted through the introduction of novel salvific variables into a faith experience. The gift of faith develops in continuity with the sanctifying gifts, and it enhances them by integrating into the call to sanctification the five traits listed above.

As the most basic genetic transmutation of the gifts of sanctification, the gift of faith ought to ground and interpenetrate all the other service gifts as well. Every other service gift ought to develop in continuity with it and with the gifts of sanctification. As a consequence, the other service gifts should incorporate within themselves the basic characteristics of the gift of faith. But this is not to say that the other gifts are identical with the gift of faith. Every transmuted experience has its own distinctive character. It is qualitatively distinguishable from feelings which precede and follow it. As transmutations of the gift of faith, the other charisms are, then, distinct from it in the sense that they are specific calls which lend a qualitatively distinct charismatic specification to an emergent faith experience. As a consequence, the other gifts are experienced as gifts in their own right. Moreover, while the gift of faith may be transmuted into other gifts, it need not be. There may, therefore, be individuals in the Christian community whose primary service consists in the fact that they are visible and outstanding embodiments of the kind of faith-dependence on the Father to which every child of God is called. Finally, if the preceding analysis of the gift of faith is sound, then a genetic, experiential, account of the service gifts must relate each gift both to the gifts of sanctification and to the gift of faith.

4. *Tongues*: Within recent years both Morton Kelsey and George Montague have made significant contributions to a theology of tongues. Montague notes correctly that the Pauline account of glossolalia is more primitive than the Lukan, and that with the exception of Acts 2. all of Luke's descriptions of glossolalia are compatible with Paul's account of the tongues experience. Montague also notes that there is no clear evidence in Paul that glossolalic utterance took the form either of a foreign language or of speech that is uttered in a trancelike state. For Paul, the gift is always subject to personal control. It can and should be used to edify the assembly.[6]

Paul describes glossolalic utterances as "pneumatic" speech rather than "noetic." It is a mysterious utterance expressive of the mysterious presence of the Spirit. It is a language of praise and thanksgiving. But it is devoid of clear conceptual content. The tongue-speaker does not understand what (s)he is saying unless (s)he possesses the gift of interpretation as well.[7] For Paul, glossolalic speech is a prayer to God. It edifies. It brings profit to the one who uses it. Moreover, Paul regarded tongues as bestowing a number of important positive benefits. It opens the tongue-speaker to God in prayer and produces personal edification. When accompanied by interpretation it has the same effect on the community as prophecy. Paul himself possessed the gift and found it important and beneficial enough to wish that all might have it. He encouraged all to seek the gift of tongues.[8]

The gift of tongues is controversial because it is surrounded by a host of misunderstandings. The causes of the confusion are multiple:

a. *Glossolaphobia*: Glossolaphobia may be described as the neurotic fear of tongues. The experience of tongues is linked with the vague, emotive pole of experience. Openness to tongues demands, therefore, conscious openness to feelings that often defy clear rational interpretation. Many individuals are perfectly at home with their pre-rational feelings. But there are hosts of others who are terrified by their own emotions. They have erected massive rational defenses against facing their own pre-conscious motivations. The tongues experience is apt to fill such individuals with terror. For it invites them to open their emotional monster closets. And that they are neurotically terrified of doing. Glossolaphobia is also a felt encounter with God. It is, then, also akin to theophobia: the terror of facing God out of fear of what that confrontation may demand.

b. *Philosophical and cultural attitudes:* Most western Christians are oblivious of the extent to which philosophical concepts have come to shape their religious attitudes. Much of Christian asceticism is colored by dualistic conceptions of man and the world derived, not from Scripture, but from Greco-Roman philosophy. Greco-Roman philosophy tended to divide the universe into matter and spirit. Platonism projected the same division into human nature itself. Plato taught that persons are essentially spiritual substances linked to another material substance called a body. This notion of human nature was condemned by the official pastoral magisterium at the council of Vienne. But occidental theologians continued to use the terms "matter" and "spirit" in speaking of human faculties and operations. The human intellect and will were described as purely "spiritual" faculties, devoid of organic basis, and ordered by their formal objects to God. God was also conceived as wholly immaterial.

The upshot of such thinking is that experiential access to God is located speculatively in the rational faculties of intellect and will. In such a view of human nature, emotions are non-cognitive and, being linked with the material part of human nature, are morally and ascetically suspect. They need to be carefully subjected to strict rational insight and volitional control. As a consequence, growth as a Christian can all too easily be misinterpreted as a Pelagian exercise in Stoicism rather than seen as openness and responsiveness to grace.

Contemporary psychology has tended to abandon such operational dualism in its account of human nature, and with good reason. The terms "matter" and "spirit" are simply not useful explanatory categories. The neat distinction between spiritual and material operations which fascinated ancient and medieval thinkers is all but impossible to verify experientially. There is, for example, evidence that rational activity is intimately linked to activity within the cerebral cortex. In the account of experience presented in the first chapter we have accordingly abandoned the terms "material" and "spiritual" altogether and replaced them with an account of the genetic transmutation of feeling. We regard emotions as cognitive, but vague. And in opposition of a dualistic approach to human nature, we locate initial salvific contact with God, not at the abstract, rational pole of experience but at its concrete, emotive pole. As a consequence, an experiential theology regards lack of affective conversion as one of the most serious obstacles to religious conversion.

A dualistic philosophy of human nature can, then, all too easily re-enforce the glossolaphobe's lack of affective conversion. For it provides such a person with a rich supply of pseudo-philosophical rationalizations for repressing and hiding from unsettling emotions. At a cultural level *machismo* and the social repression of feeling demanded by a male-dominated culture offer similar re-enforcement to the terror of the glossolaphobe.

c. *Fundamentalism:* But perhaps the greatest source of confusion over tongues is fundamentalistic teaching concerning the gift. One of the most common errors concerning tongues is that it is always the miraculous speaking of a foreign language. The confusion of xenoglossia with glossolalia rests exegetically on a fundamentalistic reading of Acts 2. This exegesis was popularized in the western church during the patristic era. It came to be widely held by western theologians. In point of fact the theory has no solid support either in Scripture or in fact. As Montague has observed, apart from Acts 2, there is no other passage in the entire New Testament in which glossolalic speech is described as xenoglossia. There is, moreover, strong exegetical evidence that in Acts 2 one is dealing with a midrashic interpretation of the meaning of the Spirit's visible manifestation in the community. A midrash is a theological reflection cast in imaginative form as a story.

In writing Acts 2, Luke seems to have drawn freely on a

number of ideas in the Jewish tradition. By the second century of
the Christian era, the Jewish feast of Pentecost had become a feast
of covenant renewal. And it is not impossible that the notion was
already abroad in the first century. By the dawn of the Christian
era, the rabbinic tradition had popularised the idea that all the nations of the earth were offered a share in the Sinai covenant. In the
writings of Philo, we find a description of the sealing of the covenant in *pneuma* (spirit) and in fire. And in the book of Genesis, the
tongues of men were confounded as a sign of their sinful rebellion
against God. Luke may well have interwoven all of these themes in
writing Acts 2. The appearance of tongues is described as one of
the first visible signs of the sealing of the new covenant in the
hearts of those called by God to become the New Israel. The first
Pentecost of the new covenant is, then, the re-assembly of the scat-
tered tribes of Israel from all the corners of the earth. Luke presents the event as a reversal of Babel, a new confounding of the
tongues of men from all nations, not as a sign of their sinfulness,
but as a sign of divine forgiveness and as a gift uniting them in the
praise of God.

Montague has correctly noted that there are several elements
in Luke's narrative which make no sense if the miracle of Pentecost had in fact consisted in xenoglossia. First, the apostles' glossolalic utterances startle the crowd and need explanation. Yet
Peter alone speaks to the crowds. Neither the explanation nor the
solitary witness of Peter would have been necessary, if each of the
apostles was already communicating to his auditors intelligibly in
some foreign language. Second, the bystanders' accusation of
drunkenness makes no sense as a response to a brilliant display of
linguistic competence. It is, however, understandable as an initial
reaction to glossolalia. Third, in replying to the charge of drunkenness Peter appeals to a prophecy of Joel which says nothing
whatever about speaking foreign languages. The text. however,
does refer to latter-day "prophecy," a term large enough to apply
meaningfully to glossolalic speech. Finally, there would have been
no need for a miracle to enable the apostles to communicate to the
Jerusalem crowds since those assembled for the feast would have
understood Greek, Aramaic, or Hebrew. There is, then, no unambiguous evidence in Scripture for the occurrence of xenoglossia

even on the day of Pentecost. And there is no evidence whatsoever for the glib theological theory that the apostles employed xenoglossia in the ordinary preaching of the gospel.[10]

Moreover, the contemporary existence of xenoglossia has yet to be documented scientifically. William Samarin has argued persuasively that the patterns of glossolalic utterances give no evidence of being languages with grammar, rules, and syntax. Glossolalic speech ordinarily consists of language-like sounds already familiar to the tongue speaker. And there is evidence that the glossolalist must to some degree learn the speech patterns in which (s)he prays.[11]

d. *Poor catechesis:* The terror of tongues which one finds not infrequently in institutional Christianity has all too often been re-enforced by poor popular catechesis concerning this gift. It has been argued popularly, for example, that the gift of tongues was exclusively a first-century phenomenon. The truth of the matter is, however, that glossolalia is available today to people who are open to the gift and seek it. It has been popularly taught that Paul the apostle in 1 Co 13:8 predicted the disappearance of tongues in the post-apostolic church. A careful reading of Paul's statement, however, reveals nothing of the sort. Paul predicted that the knowledge of God mediated by the gifts would one day be replaced by a face-to-face vision of God. Since we are all waiting still for the day of perfect vision to arrive, one can argue that the apostle would have been appalled at the the widespread absence of tongues and other gifts from contemporary Churches which call themselves Christian. It is also popularly believed that tongues was a gift necessary to the Church in its infancy but not in its maturity. Unfortunately, however, there is massive historical evidence indicating that the Christian community as a whole passed, not from infancy to maturity, but from initial fervor to widespread apathy and decadence. Since, moreover, the gift of tongues is readily available to large numbers of believers, apathy and decadence seem more plausible as an explanation for its disappearance than the spiritual maturation of the Christian community as a whole.

It is also erroneously taught and widely believed that the gift of tongues is an extraordinary gift. If the existence of xenoglossia could ever be documented, it could, of course, be characterised as

both statistically and theologically extraordinary. One could legitimately call it a miracle. But glossolalia is not statistically rare
among those open to the gift. There is evidence that about 80% of
contemporary charismatic Catholics lay claim to the gift. Nor is
glossolalia extraordinary in a theological sense. For it can be classified neither as one of the higher mystical graces nor as a miraculous preternatural utterance. Far from being a high mystical grace,
the gift of tongues is a beginner's gift. Paul places it last in his hierarchical listing of the charisms. One would, moreover, have to
search long to discover signs of higher mysticism among most contemporary charismatics, who nevertheless experience tongues as a
genuine grace.

A final misunderstanding concerning tongues is that it is the
only adequate criterion for baptism in the Holy Spirit. Luke in his
midrashic reflections on the Spirit's arrival in Acts 2 does mention
tongues as one of the signs of the Spirit's descent on those in the
upper room. But there is no mention of the gift being bestowed on
the three thousand who were baptised on that day. If Luke had
regarded tongues as the only decisive sign of the Spirit's coming, it
seems scarcely likely that he would have omitted such an important detail. There is no mention of tongues in the account of the
Spirit's descent on the Samaritans. There the Spirit's presence
seems to be associated more with healing and miracles than with
tongues. There is no mention of tongues in the baptism either of
the Ethopian eunuch or of Paul, although we know from Paul's
letters that he did at some point receive the gift.[12]

The appearance of tongues at the house of Cornelius has as its
clear purpose to link that event with the first Pentecost. It is what
exegetes have called "the Pentecost of the gentiles," a sign given
by God that gentile Christians ought to be admitted into the community without circumcision. But there is no indication that every
gentile received the gift of tongues. And there is decisive exegetical
evidence to the contrary.[13]

Paul's theology of the Spirit was formulated earlier than Acts
and gives us yet more primitive evidence of how the first Christians
understood baptism in the Holy Spirit. For Paul, one enters into a
salvific relationship with the Spirit by dying and rising with the
Lord in ritual baptism. He also makes it quite clear that the Spirit

dispenses His gifts of service by His own good pleasure and that not all receive the gift of tongues. We shall explore some of the implications of Pauline teaching on baptism in a later chapter. Our present concern is with tongues as an experience.[14]

As an experience, tongues can be characterised as one of the most basic of the Spirit's gifts. The Christian community whose worship is authentically expressive of an attitude of faith-dependence on God must acknowledge that prayer itself is a gift descending from the Father of lights. It is the Spirit of Jesus who ought to hold the initiative in prayer as in every aspect of the community's life. Hence, those who close themselves in principle to any of His gifts to that extent harden their hearts to the Spirit's call.

The gift of tongues is at one and the same time an experience and a sign of divine leading. It is a form of prayer which is clearly charismatic since not all receive the gift. At the same time, pastoral experience in charismatic prayer groups shows that when the experience of tongues is authentic, it brings with it a deepened sense of God's call to prayer and a deepened responsiveness to the Spirit within the prayer experience.

The experience of group prayer in tongues, and especially of group singing in tongues, transforms the personal experience of tongues into a shared communal experience. Such a prayer experience not only serves as a vivid, concrete reminder of the charismatic character of Christian prayer, but it also reminds the worshipping Christian community that its prayer is only the prolongation in space-time of the pneumatic impulse that transformed the apostles on the first Pentecost from a community of timid faith to one of public praise.

Shared openness to the gift of tongues would, then, seem to be demanded of every authentically converted Christian community: not in the sense that one must expect everyone in the community to possess the gift, but in the sense that genuine value is given to the gift in the teaching and lived piety of the community. The authentically converted Christian should acknowledge that this gift is one of the means God commonly uses to build up a people of praise. And the authentically converted Christian community will make place for the exercise of the gift in its common worship.

But tongues is also a transmutation of the gift of faith. Yielding to tongues demands that one step out in faith and abandon one's attempt to control rationalistically one's growth in prayer. It demands instead a willingness to follow in worship the felt promptings of the Spirit. We have suggested that growth in the gift of faith can be measured by the following criteria: (1) experiential continuity with the gifts of sanctification; (2) the visible transformation of one's life through deeds of faith; (3) a carefully discerned sense of God's call; (4) the enduring character of that call; (5) the intensification of concrete faith expectancy. All of these elements are present in the experience of tongues. The authentic tongue-speaker is one who prays visibly in the Spirit. (S)he is one who has said "yes" to a particular way of responding to the pneumatic call to worship issued to all Christians in the gifts of sanctification. The authentic tongue-speaker is one whose prayer is marked by an abiding docility to the leadings of the Spirit. And to the extent that one's response to the call subjects one to ridicule and to slanderous charges like emotional imbalance and even insanity, the tongue speaker is one who is willing to step out in faith to bear witness to the good things which the Lord has done.

Finally, when the gift of tongues is situated within the spectrum of feelings that shape experience, its emotive character serves as a vivid and concrete reminder that the impulses of the Spirit are in God's ordinary providence initially vague emotive impulses and only subsequently understood. For the impulse to pray in tongues is preconceptual. But it is an experience of the power of God which demands conceptual explanation.

If, however, these reflections are sound, one can anticipate the experiential consequences of an inauthentic exclusion of the gift of tongues from personal and communal worship. Where such an exclusion is rooted in a lack of conversion, it will mediate a diminished sense of the charismatic character of Christian prayer. It will, therefore, tend to be accompanied by different varieties of do-it-yourself worship. Even authentic acts of worship are in part the activity of man. Quietism in all its forms must, then, be excluded from Christian prayer. But so must self-reliant, Pelagian rationalism. Inauthentic worship tends to express, to a greater or lesser degree, not faith-dependence on the graced and charismatic initiative of the Spirit, but personal self-reliance and oppressive human control. It will be imbued with a desire to teach oneself to meditate rather than to seek that teaching from the Spirit of Jesus. Inauthentic shared worship will be dominated by the desire to subject every aspect of worship to strict rational and legal restrictions. Or it will be more concerned to "create humanly meaningful liturgies," than to open people in their hearts to the power and anointing of the Holy Spirit, who alone can teach them to pray.

Where the absence of tongues is, then, expressive of a significant lack of conversion at an affective, intellectual, and religious level, one can also anticipate that personal and communal faith-dependence on God will be undermined and that worship will assume an increasingly formalistic of pseudo-humanistic character. Moreover, the overall approach to worship in such cases will reflect the absence of that felt passivity which characterises an authentic Christian prayer experience.

Finally, if prayer in tongues were to be located within the spectrum of feelings described in the first chapter, it would have to be classified as primarily dative in character. It yields a vague emotive sense of the presence of the Spirit in prayer. For prayer in tongues is devoid of that clear, inferential understanding which characterises propositional feelings. Nor is it primarily an experience of emotional adjustment, whether reflex or instinctive. Prayer in tongues can, however, and often does give rise to feelings of joy and praise of God. When such feelings grow they assume a physically purposive character, which is often expressed in individual or group singing in tongues.

5. *Interpretation:* Paul in his letters speaks of two distinguishable manifestations of tongues: praying in tongues and messages in tongues requiring interpretation. He speaks too of the gift of interpretation.[15]

Since, as we have seen, the experience of glossolalia is ordinarily to be distinguished from the experience of xenoglossia, the ordinary gift of interpretation should not be confused with the gift of "miraculous translation." By it Paul seems to have meant the reduction of garbled, oracular speech to syntactical clarity much as the priests did with the oracles of Delphi. The Delphic prophetess often spoke nonsense syllables; and it was the job of the priests to "interpret" the meaning of those utterances to those who sought the prophetess's advice.

Here several points should be noted. First, when one is prompted to speak a message in tongues, one is speaking as Paul notes, not only to God but to a concrete community. The impulse to speak a message in tongues transmutes the more common experience of prayer in tongues. And this transmutation links it to the gift of interpretation. Second, the impulse to speak a message in tongues stands in continuity with the experience of praying and singing in tongues. The "message" spoken is glossolalic in character. Third, the impulse to speak a message in tongues is characterised by an internal paradox, which Paul is careful to note. For when one feels moved by the Spirit to speak a "message" in tongues, the message is delivered in a pseudo-language devoid of conceptual meaning. Fourth, the interpreter of tongues is one who is subsequently moved by the Spirit to make sense out of this paradox. The interpreter is one who senses in prayer that the message in tongues is a sign from the Lord that He has a word to speak to the community. And (s)he feels moved to speak that word in the Lord's name. Hence, to interpret a message in tongues does not ordinarily consist in translating literally from one language to another. Ordinarily, what is interpreted is not the pseudo words of the tongue-speaker but the paradoxical impulse of the Spirit who has moved the glossolalist to speak to the community in an unintelligible manner.

To one of rationalistic bent, such a process may seem initially unintelligible. But tongues and their interpretation are linked with the emotive pole of experience. And emotions follow the laws of free association, not the laws of inference and of logic. The "rationale" behind messages in tongues and their interpretation becomes clearer, however, when one reflects on their dynamic relationship within prayer. The message in tongues has the same experiential results as praying and singing in tongues. It is a sign of the Spirit's presence and a concrete reminder of the first Pentecost. The fact, however, that a message is spoken in tongues also serves as a signal to the community to prepare itself for some word the Lord wishes it to hear. Prayer for an interpretation of the tongue further disposes the community in an attitude of openness to God. When the word of the Lord is finally spoken by the interpreter it is spoken to a group which has been explicitly moved by the glossolalic message to prepare for and receive that word.

The reason why Paul equates the practical impact of an interpreted message in tongues with that of prophecy is, then, clear. In both instances, a word of the Lord is spoken to a specific community as an expression of a concrete impulse from the Spirit to speak. We may, then, postpone any consideration of the genetic continuity which exists between the interpretation of glossolalic messages and the gifts of sanctification and of faith, until we reflect upon the gift of prophecy itself. For the same principles apply to both experiences.

Here it suffices to note that if interpretation of glossolalic messages is the equivalent of prophecy in its consequences, it is unlike prophecy in being an interpretative process that is distinct in its causal source from the pneumatic impulse it seeks to interpret. No prophecy is, as we shall see, logically infallible. But the dissociation of the impulse to speak from the impulse to interpret increases even further the degree of fallibility in the interpretative process. For the interpreter is attempting to make sense out of an impulse of the Spirit manifested in someone else, a hazardous process at best even when one is dealing with conceptual language. An interpretation of the Spirit's movement would in principle be less liable to error, if it were the interpretation of an impulse which the interpreter has personally experienced. Such a self-interpreting impulse is prophecy.

6. *Prophecy:* a prophecy is a felt impulse from God which elicits an interpretative response from the prophet that convinces the prophet that (s)he is called to speak a message to a specific community in the name of God. Even this preliminary description should make it obvious that prophecy is an experience of considerable complexity. For prophecy, like every human experience, must emerge from a total environment and be an interpretative, evaluative response to factual variables present in that environment. Prophecy can, then, no more be conceived as a purely subjective experience than can any other human experience. The prophet's environment is immanent to the prophetic experience; the prophecy, an evaluative interpretation of that environment.

The evaluative elements in prophetic utterance can be assimilated logically to abduction. They are an initial, instinctive conceptualization of a felt impulse from God. Abductive thinking transmutes physical purposes into inference. It emerges from an emotive matrix and is heavily charged with vague and inchoate feeling. Abductive thinking gives initial propositional formulation to instinctive beliefs, hunches, gut feelings, imaginative leaps.

The emotive, abductive character of prophetic speech colors spontaneously its literary expression. Prophecy need not, as Gerhard von Rad has correctly insisted, be ecstatic. The prophet need not undergo trance-like or visionary experiences, although some have. The emotion expressed in prophecy need not be violent. But prophecy is, as von Rad also notes, "impassioned dialogue."[16] It is an emotive impulse of grace bursting into initial conceptual clarity by being named and brought to conscious symbolic expression. As an experience prophecy brings together physical purposes and abductive inference. Complex physical purposes breed vague, symbolic images. Their presence in prophecy accounts for the poetic character of prophetic discourse. The abductive elements in prophecy endow it with doctrinal content.

Prophetic discourse has an affinity for poetic, imagistic thinking for two obvious reasons.[17] First, it is a word that is itself deeply felt. Second, it is a word that seeks to engage its auditors totally—affectively, intellectually, decisively—in order to orient them totally to God. To demand a re-orientation of the self is to demand a change in attitude. Hence, the prophetic word addresses itself to the physical purposes that motivate a community's life and social structures. These two observations deserve further reflection.

It is a distortion of Biblical thought to imagine the prophet as a detached news reporter carrying to society the latest factual bulletin from God. In Scripture the word of God is a force that comes to the prophet. It is a power that takes hold of, possesses the prophet until the prophet becomes a personal incarnation of that word. In an experiential approach to the gifts, one does not have prophetic experiences, one is a prophetic experience. And experience is irreducibly symbolic in structure. The facts in experience are symbolically expressive of the laws in which they are grounded. Evaluative responses are interpretative symbols that reflect the kind of self one has come to be. The prophet in responding to the divine summons to speak becomes an expressive symbol of God's word to all who hear.

But there is more. The prophets of the Old Testament were intensely political people. They were deeply involved in the burning social and religious issues of their day. They confronted kings and rulers fearlessly. They denounced economic and political exploitation. They demanded repentance in high places. They passed judgment in God's name on the policy decisions of priests, rulers, and politicos. The words they spoke to others expressed the values they embodied through active involvement in social and political conflict. All that they were spoke of God. To this Scripture testifies, and Scripture cannot be gainsaid.

When the prophecy ordinarily practiced in charismatic groups is contrasted with the Biblical norm, it pales somewhat by comparison. The charismatic renewal has done a great service by renewing popular belief in the perennial character of the prophetic gift. Charismatic prophecy is, however, highly ritualized. It tends to occur within the context of a prayer meeting and to follow predictable patterns of diction. There can be no doubt that the Spirit touches communities through such words. But they do not exhaust the prophetic gift. The great Biblical prophets were not far removed from street preachers and political reformers. Contemporary, charismatic prophecy has yet to address itself in a significant way to the social and political issues of our day. This failure should be of concern to leaders of charismatic groups. Moreover, those involved in the charismatic renewal need to become attuned to the prophetic voices in our society which speak outside of prayer groups and who eschew King James English. For God also speaks through such as these.

The fact that authentic prophecy is totally engaging links it experientially to the gifts of sanctification. The authentic prophet must have put on the mind of Jesus. (S)he is one who has meditated the word of the Lord spoken to Israel and brought to fulfillment in the mission of God's Son. And (s)he is one who speaks out of the plentitude of an intimate, Spirit-inspired understanding of that Word. By the same token, authentic prophecy is a transmutation of the gift of faith. For it lifts the prophet from out of the rest of humanity and sets the prophet in public opposition to those forces in human society which are anti-God and anti-Christ. One cannot follow such a call without growing in those attitudes which are the fruit of the gift of faith.

But a prophet's response to the divine call is also a human response. As human it is fallible in its source, in its formulation, and, on occasion, in its consequences. The prophetic word is fallible in its source because no human prophet is the definitive embodiment of God's word to men. Only Jesus is the very Word of God made flesh. Jesus alone, therefore, is the historical measure of the truth or adequacy of prophetic utterances. The prophetic word is also fallible in its source because the prophet remains in part, despite God's grace and call, a sinful human being. Not every prophet need have experienced an integral, fourfold conversion. And even the integrally converted prophet may retain pockets of inauthenticity capable of obscuring or distorting the true and full meaning of the divine prophetic impulse.

The prophetic word is fallible in its formulation because it is, in its logical structure, abductive. And no abductive inference can lay claim to absolute logical certitude. It needs clarification and testing. The prophetic word is also fallible in its formulation because it is in part abstractive. It seeks to differentiate and express conceptually and imagistically the divine impulse to speak to a concrete community in its concrete religious situation. But the prophet is capable of mistaking disordered, neurotic, and even sinful impulses for the voice of God. The false prophet is, as history shows, even capable of standing in opposition to the true word of God.

The prophetic word can also be fallible in its consequences because it is a vague word. The affinity of the prophetic utterance for imagistic language has all the advantages that attend richly imaginative speech. It is concrete and affectively engaging. But prophetic language also suffers from the limitations of imagistic speech. It is often difficult to tell precisely what a prophet means. A prophetic word becomes fallible in its consequences when it occasions false and divisive interpretations of the divine intent which is attempting to come to expression in the prophet's speech.

If, then, the prophetic impulse is self-interpreting, its fallibility prevents it from ever being self-evaluating. To evaluate the truth of prophetic oracles one must appeal to interpretative criteria that go beyond the prophetic experience. One must, that is to say, engage the gift of teaching in its different manifestations.

But before proceeding to a reflection on the gift of teaching, it will perhaps be useful to contrast the theory of prophecy here presented with a Thomistic theory of prophecy.[18] For the latter has bred many misunderstandings about this gift and its proper use. A Thomistic theology of prophecy correctly insists upon the graced origin of every prophetic impulse. But it arbitrarily restricts the "formal object" of prophecy to truths that can be grasped through preternatural or miraculous enlightenment. Prophetic knowledge is thus reduced to clairvoyance or ESP, to knowledge of mysteries that transcend the natural powers of the intellect, and to knowledge of free future events. Theological theories about prophecy must be tested against the norm of Scripture. When so tested, however, there is scarcely a Biblical prophecy which actually deals with the kinds of objects to which Thomism seeks to restrict the prophetic word. The theory here proposed acknowledges the graced origin of the prophetic impulse, but does not restrict in principle the potential objects of prophetic discourse. Moreover, a Thomistic theory of prophecy seeks to ground prophetic insights in infallible access to the immutable mind of God. Our theory makes no such claims and acknowledges the prophet's fallibility in interpreting the felt impulses of grace. Finally, Thomism assimilates prophecy to the intellectual contemplation of eternal truth. Our theory presupposes no metaphysics of the divine mind and links prophecy more with the felt, emotive pole of human experience than with the intellect.[19]

7. *Teaching.* Paul the apostle speaks cryptically of a variety of teaching gifts. In 1 Co 12:28-30, he speaks of "teachers." In Rm 12:6-8, he mentions "teaching" and "preaching." In Ephesians there is mention of "evangelists" and of "pastors and teachers."

"Preaching with wisdom" is sometimes popularly translated as "a word of wisdom"; and "preaching instruction," as "a word of knowledge." There is a tendency in charismatic circles to correlate these Pauline terms somewhat narrowly with very specific types of religious experience. The "word of wisdom" is sometimes explained as a word from the Spirit that touches another directly and deeply. The "word of knowledge" is explained as a special word of revelation: one may, for example, receive a word that a healing has been granted to a given individual. There can be no doubt that such experiences occur in charismatic communities. But there are more gifts of the Spirit than those Paul enumerated. And it is highly questionable that Paul was referring to such experiences when he spoke of the "word of wisdom" and the "word of knowledge."

Paul seems, rather, to have envisaged two pastoral exercises of teaching: the evangelization of unbelievers through the proclamation of the good news and the on-going pastoral instruction of believers by resident teachers. The Biblical evangelist is the herald of good tidings from God. (S)he brings to others the divine word of pardon, forgiveness, and reconciliation.[20] In the New Testament, evangelists are portrayed as prolonging in space and time the evangelical preaching of Jesus Himself, who began His public ministry by summoning His hearers to repentence and to an acceptance of membership in the community of those who look forward to the coming reign of God.[21] The evangelist's summons is, therefore, a summons to faith-dependence on the Father in the image of Jesus through sharing and mutual love.[22] It is a summons to openness to the Spirit and to His gifts of sanctification.

For Paul, moreover, true wisdom is the summit of religious knowledge. It is an insight that comes only through faith in Jesus Christ, who is divine Wisdom personified. For Paul, therefore, the "word of wisdom" may well have meant merely the kerygmatic proclamation of the good news about Jesus, who is the power of God, the wisdom of God.

Such a kerygmatic proclamation of the gospel is akin to prophecy in that it is a summons to repentance. It also resembles the oracular tone of prophecy in that it is the proclamation of God's word. But it differs from prophecy in its concern not only to proclaim but to explain, to clarify. Under this hypothesis, examples of early kerygmatic preaching, or of "teaching with wisdom," would be Peter's Pentecost sermon and his sermon at the Beautiful Gate.

"Teaching instruction" ordinarily presupposes at least an initial repentance-conversion in one's auditors. It is concerned less with initial proclamation and more with the transmission and authentic interpretation of the meaning of the good news that has already come to be believed. It is more explanatory than kerygmatic in tone. A word of wisdom may, however, also be addressed to a believing community. Such a word seeks to deepen a community's initial conversion by summoning it to repent of inauthenticities that mar its relationship to God and to one another in Christ.[23]

Both forms of teaching have a cumulative impact upon the Christian community. For both produce a corpus of preaching and instruction which is in turn in need of further interpretation if it is to be correctly understood by succeeding generations of believers. In speaking of "pastors and teachers," Paul may be hinting that "teaching instruction" came to be one of the chief responsibilities of the resident leaders of the community.

Christians in charismatic communities relate instinctively and positively to the kerygmatic word of proclamation. The mere phrase "Jesus is Lord" is enough to evoke an enthusiastic "amen" from any typical prayer community. But the charismatic renewal is a grass-roots religious revival. And it shows all the strengths and limitations of popular religion. Charismatic Christians have been criticised for being fundamentalistic. That they are more fundamentalistic than the average Sunday worshipper or ordained pastoral leader remains to be demonstrated. But one does discover from time to time a certain impatience in charismatic communities and in local parishes with technical theological instruction. There are charismatic Christians just as there are Sunday-go-to-meeting believers who want only simple answers to any question they raise about God, religion, and the Church. Unfortunately, however, not all the questions people raise are simple. And simplistic answers to complex questions are misleading. Fundamentalism is the search for the ready answer to complex religious problems. It is rooted in fear and in lack of intellectual conversion. It needs to be combatted by the gifts of teaching with wisdom and of teaching instruction.

The proclamation and personal witness now available in charismatic communities needs, then, to be supplemented with a call to intellectual conversion and with competent, systematic instruction at almost every level of theological inquiry. The same instruction is also badly needed in every local parish. To be more specific, there is need for sound teaching in all of the following areas: (1) the history of the Bible: who wrote it, how it came to be written, and why; (2) exegesis: the meaning of Scripture and of the more important creedal statements of the Christian community; (3) church history: especially the history of the reformation and of the ecumenical movement; (4) dialectics: instruction on those issues which continue to divide different Christian communions; (5) foundational theology: instruction concerning the meaning of conversion to Christ and its socio-ethical consequences; (6) Christian doctrine: meditation on Christian teaching in the light of a sound understanding of Christian conversion; (7) systematic theology: the reduction of sound Christian doctrine to a unified vision of faith. Too much charismatic teaching is the sterile repetition of old Protestant Pentecostal canards.

There is also need to incorporate the valid insights of liberation theology into the instruction given in charismatic communities and in local parishes. To hunger and thirst after justice is the mark of a true Christian. Liberation theology has insisted correctly that integral Christian conversion demands that those who profess Christ face and attempt to solve the political and economic injustices that plague human society. Moreover, theologians of liberation have something to learn from charismatic piety, with its vibrant, expectant faith in a just and living God.[24]

Finally, charismatic communities need to be warned against theological incest. Too much teaching in the renewal is inbred. The teaching gifts of the Spirit are not restricted to those who participate in charismatic prayer groups. Balanced growth in faith demands openness to all the gifts present throughout the Church universal.

The authentic charismatic teacher, like the prophet, proclaims God's word to other persons. But the gift of teaching transmutes the gift of prophecy and is therefore distinct from it. The propositional element in prophecy is primarily abductive. The gift of teaching, however, extends the inferential moment present in prophetic experience beyond the stage of abduction. The charismatic teacher does more than proclaim in oracular fashion the word (s)he has received from the Lord. The teacher seeks in addition to interpret not only the historical origin but also the theoretical and practical consequences of divine revelation and to render them plain to others. Teaching, therefore, demands both a contextual and a deductive clarification of the word proclaimed and its inductive verification in the data of revelation. As a consequence, the gift of teaching in both of its forms mediates the charismatic transformation of the inferential phase of experience. Authentic teaching ought, then, to be grounded in intellectual as well as religious conversion.

As a transmutation of the gift of prophecy, teaching shares some traits in common with the prophetic impulse. Like the prophet, the Christian teacher is called not only to speak about God's word but to be that word to others. The "word of the Lord" must then come to the teacher as it comes to the prophet. It must interpenetrate the teacher's life and transform it into a human embodiment of the word (s)he speaks.

As a transmutation of the prophetic, authentic teaching is also situational. It can never be a mere academic exercise. It is the attempt to interpret the message of salvation to a concrete community in terms that will lead it to repentance and to a deeper charismatic openness to the Spirit. When, therefore, Christian teaching loses its prophetic character it becomes shot through with inauthenticity. It degenerates into cerebral academic exercises.

The gift of teaching has either a Christological or a pneumatic focus. Christological teaching proclaims Jesus as the normative historical and environmental revelation of who God is and what we are called to be. Pneumatic teaching seeks to illumine the process by which the believing community is historically and charismatically transformed into the image of Jesus. The study of pneumatology also encompasses, therefore, the study of the Church in its graced, charismatic, and sacramental transformation by the dynamic indwelling of the Spirit. And it encompasses the whole of that process: its historical preparation, its present implementation, and its final consummation.

The charismatic basis of Christian teaching also affects its mode of exercise. An authentic gift of teaching is a transmutation of the gifts of sanctification. To the extent that the charismatic teacher is limited in insight into the mind of Jesus to that extent will his or her teaching be vulnerable to falsehood, inadequacy, and inauthenticity. One cannot become the word proclaimed without putting on the mind of Christ. Moreover, the authentic Christian teacher must undertake to instruct the community, not as the result of a choice reached with self-reliant human prudence, but as an act of public, personal witness in docility to God's call. And the Spirit-led teacher must minister to others in an attitude of habitual faith-dependence on the Lord. The gift of teaching is, then, also a transmutation of the gift of faith.

8. *Healing.* Healing and sickness are correlative terms. To define one is implicitly to define the other. Moreover, the way we think about both is very much a function of the way we think about ourselves. Illnesses have been traditionally classified as physical, psychic, and psychosomatic. There is basis in experience for the distinction, but it can be interpreted in terms that are too rigidly dualistic. That is to say, the term "physical" can be understood to mean "material, bodily" ailments; the term "psychic," illnesses which touch a person's "spiritual soul." But an experiential approach to human illness rejects too rigid a distinction between the physical and the psychic. Experience certainly has a physical and an evaluative pole. But they are dynamically interrelated within the emergent self. The physical pole of experience is shaped in part by evaluative decisions: facts are presented within experience as vague emotions and as more or less vivid perceptual judgments. Sickness too is a fact, and as a fact it changes, not just bodies but feelings, persons, selves. And attitudinal adjustment affects physical processes. Evaluative decisions shape experience and can breed bodily dysfunctions. When viewed as an experiential process, all illness is psychosomatic, although the chief causes may be located either in the physical or in the evaluative pole of experience. Hence, too rigid a distinction between the healing of bodies and the healing of attitudes is ill advised. It is whole persons, not bodies alone or souls alone which need healing.

Moreover, an experiential approach to personal development also affirms the principle of mutual inexistence. We shape our world as our world shapes us. There is, then, also an intimate connection between personal and environmental disorder. Physical or psychic disorder in any individual introduces disorder into the lives (s)he touches. Sinful decisions breed sinful situations and oppressive, sinful institutional structures. And those situations and structures shape other persons as experiences. The healing of individual persons cannot, then, be dissociated from the healing of society. We shall return to this point in discussing "original sin."

Healing can be the result of human insight and initiative. But the healing which is born of faith takes three basic forms. The first is conversion itself. The unconverted individual is diminished as a person by a disordered relationship with God and with other persons. The re-ordering of social and religious attitudes effected by faith heals the human heart in its deepest center. The second form of faith-healing is the transformation of mere suffering into grace. Without faith, psychic and physical suffering is devoid of ultimate meaning. But the believer who suffers with Christ in faith transforms mere suffering into deepened trust in God and openness to His life-giving Spirit. For faith tested in the crucible of pain is purified by the refusal to test God, even in the midst of personal suffering. Finally, the healing born of faith can even effect the removal of suffering and its causes. When such faith-healings are striking and defy rational explanation, they are termed "miracles."

The gift of healing is a transmutation of the gift of teaching. For the proclamation of the word creates the context of faith in which divine healing and even miracles occur. When a word ministry is blessed not merely with conversion and with the transformation of suffering into grace but is also confirmed by the complete removal of physical and psychic illness, it is transmuted by its consequences into the gift of healing. When such a ministry is regularly accompanied by healings that are striking and inexplicable, it becomes the gift of miracles. As a transmutation of the gift of teaching, the gifts of healing and of miracles are also transmutations of the gifts of sanctification and of faith. Of the two, the gift of miracles is both statistically and theologically extraordinary.

God wills our salvation; and salvation brings healing. No Christian should ever doubt God's will to heal. But those who pray for healing must also allow God to be God and to heal in the way He chooses. He may not choose to remove suffering but to transform it instead into an occasion for deeper conversion and growth in faith. To affirm that God always responds to the prayer of faith with the removal of suffering is theologically and factually false. The authentic Christian healer, like the authentic teacher, will not, then, be concerned with demonstrating his or her charismatic power. (S)he will be concerned to proclaim the Lordship of Jesus in expectant faith. And (s)he will leave the healing to God. The authentic healer is not concerned superstitiously with the human mechanics of healing: with saying the "right words" or performing the "right gestures" to insure God's healing action. Nor will (s)he attempt to dictate to God in advance the form that healing must take. The authentic healer will rest content with a deepened conversion or with the transformation of suffering into grace, if that is the Lord's saving will. At the same time, (s)he will not attempt to contain God's healing power by discouraging others from believing in the divine power to heal efficaciously and even miraculously. Finally, in praying with others for healing, (s)he will be concerned that they be properly disposed and properly instructed, so that in approaching the divine healer they may truly seek Him in selfless love, rather than covet His healing gifts. And in every healing granted, the authentic healer will be careful to give all glory to God.[25]

9. *Discernment.* The gift of discernment seeks to authenticate impulses which claim to be Spirit-inspired and Spirit-led by evaluating their genesis and consequences against religious, ethical, and psychological criteria. Here several points should be noted.

First, the gift of discernment is an attempt to evaluate religious impulses within a context of faith. The true discerner seeks to be led by the Spirit in prayer to a sound judgment concerning His presence and activity in others. Hence, while discernment invokes not only religious but also psychological and moral criteria, it does so in a context of prayerful faith-dependence on God. As a public service to the community exercised in prayerful dependence on the Spirit, discernment transmutes the gift of faith.

Second, the authentic exercise of discernment presupposes that the discerner has advanced significantly in understanding the mind of Jesus. For any impulse which violates Jesus' mind cannot be the work of His Spirit. The authentic exercise of discernment ought, then, to transmute the gifts of sanctification as well.

Third, the exercise of discernment employs many evaluative criteria derived from the Spirit-led teaching of other members of the community. Authentic discernment is never off the top of one's head or rooted in personal feeling alone. It is factually, doctrinally, ethically, and psychologically informed. But in applying the fruits of sound teaching to the evaluation of specific impulses within the community of faith, discernment transmutes the gift of teaching into a gift of concrete, practical wisdom. As a consequence, the gift of discernment breeds its own kind of practical insight into the working of the Spirit. The discerning heart understands the normal patterns of graced human growth in both individuals and communities at an affective, evaluative, and moral level. The wisdom born of discernment is embodied in books like *The Spiritual Exercises* of Ignatius Loyola, *The Interior Castle* of Teresa of Avila, *The Ascent of Mount Carmel* of John of the Cross, and Jonathan Edwards's *Treatise Concerning Religious Affections*.

Fourth, the gift of discernment mediates the formation of a Spirit-led judgment concerning the authenticity of impulses which claim to be from God. In its logical structure, therefore, the judgment of discernment is an inductive inference. By verifying or falsifying certain predictable psychological, doctrinal, and ethical attitudes in actions and impulses which claim to be from God, the discerner concludes that the law or dynamic tendency which grounds them is or is not the Spirit of Jesus.[26]

10. *The action gifts*. The gift of discernment transmutes theoretical insight into the promptings of the Spirit into sound pastoral judgments. The action gifts, like helping, almsgiving, works of mercy, administration, transmute sound pastoral judgments into deeds. In speaking of the action gifts, Paul takes refuge in a certain amount of vagueness. "Helping" is, for example, vague enough in its scope to include almost any activity not explicitly named by one of the other gifts. Gifts like administration, official responsibility, works of mercy, and almsgiving are more specific in their focus. But even they are subject to a variety of interpretations. What is common to the action gifts is that they seek to facilitate shared activity in the community. The gift of almsgiving or of works of mercy, for example, very likely encompassed not only

personal deeds of charity but the supervision of charitable works undertaken by the community as a whole. A contemporary list of the action gifts might then also include gifts of community organization and of community mobilization for shared social and political action.

Charismatic communities are founded in a shared prayer experience. And experience testifies that shared charismatic prayer breeds shared practical concern for one another. But charity exercised exclusively within a prayer community is inbred. The mobilization of prayer communities to rectify social, economic, and political injustice is the task of those who are called to serve through action. The evocation of such gifts through instruction and prayerful openness to the Spirit is one of the most pressing pastoral needs of most parishes and charismatic communities. It is all too easy to sit around waiting for God to reveal to us something He has already made perfectly clear. And it is quite clear that the committed Christian has a serious responsibility to minister to the oppressed. Concern with the poor, with the rights of oppressed minorities, with the social, political, and economic rights of women is not a religious extracurricular. It lies at the heart of Christian service.[27]

That community service which flows from the action gifts ought to be a transmutation of the gifts of sanctification and of faith should by this point be sufficiently clear. For to be authentic, community action must express the mind of Christ; and as a personal call, each action gift endows the more generic personal witness of faith with a specific purpose and direction.

In closing this discussion of the Pauline gifts, we note that the preceding discussion has failed to take account of three gifts mentioned by Paul: marriage, apostleship, and celibacy. These gifts cannot, however, be treated adequately until we have reflected on the Christian sacraments of community initiation.

Notes

1. 1 Co 12:8-10, 28-31; Rm 12:6-8; Eph 4:9.

2. Arnold Bittlinger, *Gifts and Graces*, translated by Herbert Klassen

(London: Hodder and Stoughton, 1967); *Charisma und Amt* (Stuttgart: Calwer Verlag, 1967); "Gnadengaben im Neuen Testament" in *Kirche und Charisma* (Marburg an der Sahn: Oekumenischer Verlag, 1966); Josephine Massingberd Ford, *Ministeries and Fruits of the Holy Spirit* (Notre Dame: Catholic Action Service, 1973); Gotthold Hassenhüttle, *Charisma: Ordnungsprinzip der Kirche* (Freiburg: Herder, 1969); Gabriel Murphy, *Charisms and Church Renewal* (Rome: Catholic Book Agency, 1965); Karl Rahner, *The Dynamic Element in the Church* (N.Y.: Herder and Herder, 1964); Hans Küng, *The Church*, translated by Ray and Rosaleen Ockenden (N.Y.: Sheed and Ward, 1967) pp. 151-203.

3. George Montague, "Baptism in the Spirit and Speaking in Tongues: A Biblical Appraisal," *Theology Digest*, XXI (Winter, 1973) p. 363. See also: Michael P. Hamilton, *The Charismatic Movement* (Grand Rapids: Eerdmans, 1975).

4. Act 3:6-7.

5. Edward O'Connor, *The Pentecostal Movement in the Catholic Church* (Notre Dame: Ave Maria, 1971) pp. 225-228; Vincent M. Walsh, *A Key to the Charismatic Renewal in the Catholic Church* (St. Meinrad: Abbey, 1974).

6. Cf. Montague, *op. cit.*; Morton Kelsey, *Tongue Speaking: An Experiment in Spiritual Experience* (N.Y.: Doubleday, 1968); 1 Co 14:26-28, 32, 34.

7. Montague, *op. cit.*, pp. 349-351; 1 Co 14:2, 5, 18.

8. Montague, *op. cit.*, pp. 351-355, 1 Co 14:5.

9. Montague, *op. cit.*, pp. 352-353.

10. *Ibid.*; see also: George Montague, *The Spirit and His Gifts* (N.Y.: Paulist, 1974).

11. William Samarin, *Tongues of Men and Angels* (N.Y.: Macmillan, 1970) pp. 62-72, 226-236.

12. Act 2:41, 8:4-40.

13. Act 10:44-11:18; 1 Co 12:30.

14. Rm 6:1-8:39; 1 Co 12:12-30.

15. 1 Co 14:1-33, 12:30. Cf. Montague, *The Spirit and His Gifts*, pp. 30-50.

16. Gerhard von Rad, *Old Testament Theology*, translated by D.M.G. Stalke (2 vols.; Edinburgh: Oliver and Boyd, 1965) II, pp. 8-10, 130. See also: Oscar Cullmann, *Christ and Time*, translated by V. Filson (Philadelphia: Westminster, 1964) pp. 94-106.

17. von Rad, *op. cit.*, II, pp. 90-97.

18. *Summa Theologiae*, II-II, QQ. 71-72, aa. 1 & 2.

19. Cf. John L. McKenzie, "The Social Character of Inspiration," *Catholic Biblical Quarterly*, XXIV (January, 1962) p. 121; "The Word of God in the Old Testament," *Theological Studies*, XXI (June, 1960) pp. 183-206; Karl Rahner, "Visions and Prophecies" in *Inquiries* (N.Y.: Herder and Herder, 1964) pp. 8-190; K.L. Crenshaw, *Prophetic Conflict* (Berlin: Topellmann, 1973).

20. Is 40:1-9, Mk 2:10, 17, 21 ff.

21. Mk 1:15; Lk 4:43.

22. Mt 5:3; Mk 10:17-23, 11:28; Lk 9:48, 10:21.

23. I Co 2:6; Col 1:9. This account of these gifts differs significantly from that popular in Protestant Pentecostal circles. Cf. Douglas and Gloria Wead and Elaine Cleeton, *The Word of Knowledge* (Ellendale, N.D.: Action Evangelism, 1973).

24. Paulo Freire, *Pedagogy of the Oppressed* (N.Y.: Herder and Herder, 1972); also see, Gustavo Gutierrez, *A Theology of Liberation*, translated by Sr. Caridad Inda and John Eagleson (N.Y.: Maryknoll, 1973).

25. Cf. Donald Gelpi, S.J., "The Ministry of Healing" in *Pentecostal Piety* (N.Y.: Paulist, 1972), pp. 3-58; George A. Buttrick, *God, Pain, and Evil*, (N.Y.: Abingdon, 1966); Dan H. Gross, *The Case for Spiritual Healing*, (N.Y.: Nelson and Sons, 1958); Morton T. Kelsey, *Healing and Christianity*, (N.Y.: Harper and Row, 1973); Francis McNutt, O.P. *Healing*, (Notre Dame: Ave Maria, 1974); Dennis Linn and Matthew Linn, *Healing of Memories* (N.Y.: Paulist, 1974); Francois-H. Lepragneur, O.P., "The Place of a Sick Person in a Christian Anthropolicy," *Theology Digest*, XVI (Summer, 1968) pp. 137-141; Frances Meredith, "Suffering and the Will of God," *Mount Carmel* (Winter, 1972) pp. 156-162; Karl Rahner, S.J., "The Saving Force and Healing Power of Faith," *Theological Investigations*, (Baltimore: Helicon, 1966) V, pp. 460-467; Maura Ramsbottom, "The Ministry of Healing," *The Way*, Supplement #17 (Autumn, 1972) pp. 28-39; Robert W. Gleason, S.J., "Miracles in Contemporary Theology," *Thought*, XXXVIII (March, 1962) pp. 12-34;

Réné LaTourelle, S.J., "Vatican II et les signes de la revelation," *Gregorianum*, XLIX (1968) pp. 225-252; "Miracle et revelation," *Gregorianum*, XLIII (1962), pp. 492-509; Louis Monden, S.J., *Signs and Wonders* (N.Y.: Desclee, 1966) Anton Friedrichson, *The Problem of Miracle in Primitive Christianity*, translated by Roy Harrisville and John Hansen (Minneapolis: Augsburg, 1972).

26. David T. Asselin, "Christian Maturity in Spiritual Discernment" *Review for Religious*, XXVII (1968) pp. 581-595; Michael Buckley, S.J., "The Structure of the Rules for Discernment of Spirits," *The Way*, Supplement #20, vol. 2, pp. 19-37; Francois Charmot, "Discernment des esprits et direction" *Christus*, II (1965) pp. 9-38; Don Falkenberg, "The Holy Spirit in the Counseling Process", *Pastoral Psychology* XV (November, 1964) pp. 31-41; Jonathan Edwards, *A Treatise Concerning Religious Affections* edited by John E. Smith (New Haven: Yale, 1959); Jacques Guillet, *et al.*, *Discernment of Spirits* (Collegeville: Liturgical Press, 1970); Raymond Hostie, *The Discernment of Vocation* (N.Y.: Sheed and Ward, 1963); Karl Rahner, S.J., *The Dynamic Element in the Church*, (N.Y.: Herder and Herder, 1964); William Spohn, S.J., "Charismatic Communal Discernment of God's Will," *The Way*, Supplement #20, vol. 2, pp. 38-54; John H. Wright, S.J., "Discernment of Spirits in the New Testament," *Communio* (Summer, 1974) pp. 115-127.

27. We shall return to a consideration of the action gifts in discussing the sacrament of orders. Cf. George Croft, S.J., "Leadership, Authority, and Community," *Spode House Review* (December, 1972) pp. 8-15; Charles-André Bernard, S.J., "Experience spirituelle et vie apostolique en Saint Paul" *Gregorianum*, XLIX (1968) pp. 38-57; Sr. Ellen Gielty, S.M.P., "The Tradition of Leadership in the Christian Church, *Spode House Review* (December, 1972) pp. 5-8.

IV
The
Charismatic
Experience

1. Every writer knows that vagueness has its uses. In writing *Pentecostalism: A Theological Viewpoint*, I repeatedly used the term "charismatic experience" but deliberately avoided defining it. For its explanation would have demanded a host of technical considerations that lay beyond the scope of that book. The reflections of the past three chapters have, however, brought us to the point where we can attempt the needed clarification.

Experience is the harmonization of conformal, evaluative, and vectoral feelings. A charismatic experience is a faith experience whose evaluative form and concrete satisfactions are shaped by habitual and prayerful docility to the call of the Spirit of Jesus. One need not, then, attend charismatic prayer meetings in order to be genuinely charismatic, although, as we shall see, shared charismatic prayer lies at the heart of authentic Christian piety. For coveted graces wither; shared graces grow and develop. Still, any Christian who is growing in a prayerful insight into the mind of Jesus or in the sense of a personal call to serve others in Jesus' name embodies a "charismatic experience."

The charismatic character of a growing faith experience is effected initially by docility to the Spirit in putting on the mind of Jesus. But it is intensified and enhanced through the reception of one or more of the Pauline gifts. For the service gifts personalize and concretize one's public ecclesial witness to Jesus. (N.B., the term "service gifts" refers to all of the Pauline gifts, not just to the action gifts)

Moreover, each of the Pauline gifts speaks directly to one or other moment in the factual and evaluative transformation of shared human experience. As we saw in the first chapter, the transmutation of experience gives rise to a variety of genetically linked feelings: conformal feelings; dative feelings; physical purposes; abductive, deductive, and inductive propositional feelings; and decisions. The gift of tongues is primarily dative in character. It is a vague, emotive response to the impulse of the Spirit. The abductive illumination of a message in tongues is effected by the gift of interpretation. Prophecy synthesizes the charismatic elements which are separately present in an interpreted message in tongues: it is a self-interpreting impulse of the Spirit. Because prophecy enunciates a demand for emotive and attitudinal adjustment to forces in one's environment, it is ordinarily an abductive propositional feeling integrated with a conscious physical purpose. When the inferential moment in prophecy expands to include deductive and inductive inference, the prophetic impulse is transmuted into the gift of teaching. Discernment transmutes teaching into sound pastoral judgment; and that judgment is an inductive propositional feeling. Finally, the action gifts address themselves to decision, to the graced transformation of one's environment. This parallel between the Pauline gifts and the transmutation of human experience suggests five important consequences.

First, since the Pauline gifts correspond to different moments in the process of experiential growth, the charisms of service manifest the same genetic dependence upon one another as is present in the different phases of experience itself. That is to say, authentic interpretation and authentic prophecy must be open in their genesis and ecclesial exercise to the kind of charismatic impulse expressed in tongues. Authentic teaching, to the kind of charismatic impulse expressed in prophecy. Authentic discernment and authentic healing, to the kind of impulse expressed in teaching. And authentic charismatic action, to discernment. When this genetic order is violated, the gifts tend to inauthenticity in their exercise.

Second, one can respond authentically to a service gift only if it is in its exercise a transmutation of the gifts of sanctification and of faith. For one truly called to a ministry like tongues, prophecy, teaching, healing, miracles, discernment, or practical service may in fact choose to exercise that ministry in a way that does not express the mind of Jesus. Or one may do so out of other motives than a personal response to God's call. When one responds inauthentically to a personal gift that response does not alter the fact that one has been called to a specific from of service. But the inauthentic exercise of a service gift does, as Paul warns, render the service done worthless in so far as it touches one's personal salvation. And inauthentic charismatic service is also apt to have a negative impact on the shared faith-consciousness of the community in which it occurs. For as a response to God it is informed, not by the mind of Jesus and by charismatic faith, but by human limitation and sinfulness. One of the chief tasks of community discerners will, then, be to judge whether the exercise of a service gift is rooted in an integral fourfold conversion and is a transmutation of the gifts of sanctification and of faith.

Third, a theory of the transmutation of gifts lends confirmation and clarification to the Pauline principle that the authentic exercise of any service gift demands charismatic openness to all the gifts operative in the community. For it reveals the inability of any gift to function authentically in isolation from the others. The tongue-speaker as tongue-speaker is incompetent to interpret and explain his or her own religious experience. The prophet as prophet is incompetent to understand the full significance of his or her words. The teacher as teacher is incompetent to evaluate the impact of his or her teaching on the community. The discerner as discerner is incompetent to derive all the criteria (s)he needs to reach a correct judgment. Those with action gifts are incompetent as such to discern the best course of action to take in order to build up the community. All need authentic teaching and discernment in order to grow in the authentic exercise of any gift. None are excused from responding in faith to the authentic prophetic impulses in the community or to the authentic exercise of leadership.

Needless to say, one individual may be endowed with more than one service gift. But even one so gifted must recognize the presence of the same gifts in others and must be willing to be open in faith to the voice of the Spirit who speaks and acts in the community as a whole. Discerners must, therefore, evaluate the inauthenticity of any gift in its exercise by its possessor's degree of charismatic docility to the tested gifts operative in the Church universal. The absence of such charismatic docility renders the exercise of any gift potentially heretical.

Fourth, the preceding analysis reveals the chief purpose of the Pauline gifts to be the heightening of shared faith-consciousness.[1] To understand the meaning of such a statement, we must reflect on three interrelated questions. What is consciousness? When does consciousness become shared consciousness? When does consciousness become faith-consciousness?

Human consciousness has both a personal and a social dimension. Moreover, as Alfred North Whitehead has observed, all consciousness, including faith-consciousness flickers. It waxes and wanes, grows and declines in intensity and complexity. Consciousness is not a "thing" to which I can point. But it is an aspect of the evaluative form of an experience, of the way in which any given self experiences its world. The teenybopper and the music theoretician experience the Beethoven Ninth differently because the latter approaches the symphony with a differentiated awareness of its structure, history, and purpose which the teenybopper has never acquired.

Human consciousness grows through both analytic differentiation and synthetic insight. To one who has never studied botany all plants and trees look more or less the same. There is a vague sense of difference but no clear conception of what those differences are. As one learns the difference between families and species of plant life, one begins to perceive each shrub and tree with a new awareness. The act of differentiation which grounds consciousness in general is the differentiation of the self from its environment. When I sink into sleep, I revert to a subconscious form of experience. A clear sense of the things around me fades. And when it disappears, I lose consciousness altogether.

But personal consciousness is also heightened through synthetic insight. Synthetic insight is the grasp of relationship. It presupposes (1) that I have already differentiated factual elements in experience which stand in some kind of relationship with one another but (2) that I have yet to grasp that relationship inferentially. In other words, initially analytic discrimination heightens consciousness of facts, while synthetic insight discriminates those facts from the law(s) grounding them and articulates the specific character of those laws. Of course, once a law is recognized as such, it may be discriminated from other laws in yet other consciousness-heightening acts. Any conscious act includes, therefore, an act of discrimination.

Shared consciousness is a more complex experience than personal consciousness. Shared consciousness is a community's awareness of itself as a community. Human communities achieve shared consciousness when certain conditions are fulfilled.

a. Shared consciousness is shared experience. The actual sharing of experience is, then, the first condition for the possibility of a conscious community. In smaller communities like families and friendships, much of the sharing is immediate: it is the result of the mutual and immediate impact of the members of the community upon one another. But in large communities with a history, such immediate sharing is impossible. Such communities can, however, come to a conscious sense of shared experience if each member of the community projects back into history to a common originating event which is interpreted as that event which founds the community as such.

b. A large historical community must, however, also come to a consensus concerning the meaning of that originating event. For if different members of the community affirm contradictory evaluations of that event, they do not experience it as the same event. Hence, lack of community consensus about the significance of the community's founding event diminishes shared consciousness among its members. Consensus, on the other hand, endows a community with a present corporate sense of identity. For the interpretative re-appropriation of those historical forces which have shaped the community renders them experientially present to its members.

c. Shared consciousness is, however, further intensified when it gives rise to a corporate sense of purpose. A community will, then, grow in a common sense of identity if it is able to derive from reflection on its history a consensus among its members about the kind of community it ought to become.

d. Shared consciousness is, however, further intensified when shared ideals are translated into corporate action. For corporate action lends novel complexity to experience and is the laboratory for discriminating the experiential applicability and adequacy of projected ideals.

e. The level of shared awareness in any group will also be a function of its ability to integrate into a synthetic vision of its common origin and purpose the greatest diversity of personal contributions from its members to the shared life of the community. The contribution of individual members must, then, be orchestrated in such a way that they are mutually re-enforcing. Individual activity done at cross purposes or for divergent and unrelated ends diminishes community consciousness.

f. The communal orchestration of personal gifts is possible only if each member of the community stands committed to every other. Full membership in any human community is, therefore, impossible unless the individual who seeks membership personally desires it. It is also impossible unless the community accepts the neophyte. If, moreover, any member of a community betrays the community, readmission into the community is possible only if the community is willing to accept in loyal and atoning love the negative consequence of its having been betrayed. Mutual commitment in an atoning love is then an indispensable condition for the possibility of community consciousness.

g. The practical orchestration of individual gifts is possible only if there are a variety of leaders within the community who know how to evoke the best from the individual members of the community and to facilitate the integration of their gifts into the life of the community as a whole.

h. Finally, community consciousness is a function of the personal conversion of its members. Conversion heightens personal self-awareness. The absence of conversion at any level tends to introduce confusion and diminished self-awareness into shared communal life.

Clearly, then, the dynamics of shared consciousness are the dynamics of personal consciousness writ large. For community consciousness is heightened through the introduction of novel factual variables into the life of a developing group, through the evaluative discrimination of those facts and through their integration into the interpretative consensus which shapes a community's sense of historical identity and common purpose. But since communities are made of many individuals, growth of community consciousness presupposes in addition a mutual commitment among its members strong enough to survive the vicissitudes of physical and evaluative growth.

Personal consciousness and community consciousness are transmuted into faith-consciousness when consciousness heightening activity is undertaken at either a personal or communal level in response to an impulse of divine grace. The gifts of the Spirit mediate such activity within the Christian community. Growth in the sanctifying gifts and in the gift of faith intensifies the self-awareness mediated by religious conversion. The integration of glossolalic prayer into the shared worship of the Christian community serves as a vivid and concrete reminder of the community's common historical origin, for tongues recreates that salvific, pneumatic event which in Acts is described as having founded the Church as such. Prophecy and interpreted messages in tongues yield a vivid sense of the Spirit's presence to the community as a guiding power. Teaching heightens a community's awareness of its origins and destiny. It also mediates the creedal consensus which grounds shared faith-consciousness. Healing and miracles lend divine sanction to authentic teaching. Discernment lends discriminating clarity to a community's understanding of which impulses among its members need to be approached in faith. The action gifts, orchestrated by gifts of leadership translate the believing community's sense of its historical origins and destiny into shared communal activity.

If, then, communal self-awareness is mediated in a faith community by the active presence of the charismatic gifts, the disappearance of any gift from the community can be expected to diminish proportionally shared faith-consciousness. Where the gifts of sanctification and of faith are absent, the life of the community is a counterwitness to the faith it professes nominally. Where glossolalia is absent from a Christian faith community, one may expect to find a diminished sense of the community's pneumatic, Pentecostal origins. Such diminished awareness could take a variety of forms. Among them might be: a diminished sense of the place of the Spirit in the redemptive process; a diminished sense of the importance of yielding to the felt impulse of the Spirit together with the rationalism, moralism, legalism, and formalism that such inauthenticity breeds; a diminished sense of the basically charismatic character of Christian prayer; and a diminished sense of the importance which feeling plays in Christian faith and worship.

Where prophecy is absent from a community one may expect

DIAGRAM 3: THE DYNAMICS OF CHARISMATIC EXPERIENCE

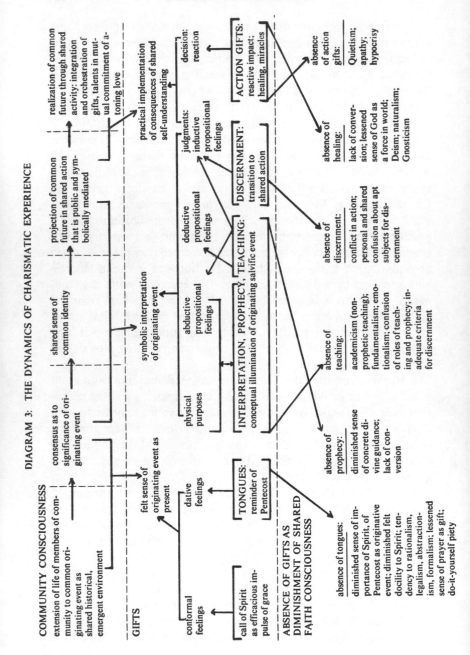

to discover a diminished sense of being collectively guided by the Lord in the living out of one's shared faith commitment. One may also anticipate a tendency to confuse authentic prophecy with other merely human phenomena. One may, for example, anticipate the tendency to designate any human protest as prophetic, whether or not it is authentically expressive of the mind of Christ or of a personal response to God's call.

Where the gift of teaching is absent from a community, two divergent inauthentic tendencies can be expected to arise. Since authentic teaching is a transmutation of the prophetic impulse, inauthentic teaching will be apt to degenerate into a effete academicism devoid of any summons to repentance. This form of inauthenticity has tended to plague the teaching ministry of the institutional churches. Since, however, authentic teaching also prolongs the abstract, conceptual moment present in the prophetic impulse, where sound teaching is absent, there may also develop a tendency to give exaggerated importance to the felt emotive dimensions of experience. In such a community one may expect to encounter the excesses of emotionalism as well as a tendency to substitute the gift of prophecy or personal witness for that of teaching. Such problems have in fact tended to plague charismatic communities of fundamentalistic bent.

Where healing and miracles are absent from a community, one may expect to find a diminished sense of the efficacious presence of God to that community. The members of such a community will be prone to adopt either a Deistic or a Gnostic stance toward God. For both of these religious creeds exclude God from the world as an efficacious salvific presence. The secularization of the institutional churches can in fact be attributed in part to the diminished presence of these gifts: and the presence of secularizing tendencies in the community can normally be expected to pose an obstacle to the appearance of these gifts.

Where authentic discernment is absent from a community, shared communal activity will tend to express impulses that proceed from other sources than the Spirit of Jesus. Such a community will manifest an inadequate understanding of what decisions are apt subjects for discernment and of what criteria ought to function in Spirit-led group decision making. Charismatic prayer communities who lack discerning leadership frequently experience just such problems.

Finally, where action gifts are absent from a community, one may expect community self-consciousness to be vague and theoretical, without any awareness of the practical moral demands of authentic faith commitment. Both charismatic communities and the institutional churches have suffered from this symptom of inauthenticity.

If these suggestions are sound, only a worshipping community which is active and authentically open to all of the Pauline service gifts can come to adequate self-awareness as a faith community. A community cannot, however, grow in self-awareness as a faith community without growing in the gifts of sanctification. The relationship between the gifts of sanctification and of service is, then, even more complex than we have already indicated. On the one hand, the authentic personal exercise of a service gift demands that it be the transmutation of the gifts of sanctification and of faith. On the other hand, personal growth in the sanctifying gifts is mediated by openness in faith to the all of the gifts of the Spirit present within the Church universal. Moreover, shared openness to all of the service gifts of the Spirit gives rise to charismatic activity which transforms personal growth in the sanctifying gifts into shared faith consciousness. The faith experience which is the fruit of such a process can indeed be called a "charismatic experience."

Fifth, precisely because they mediate the heightening of faith-consciousness, the gifts of the Spirit are integral to the primordial sacramentality of the Church. Let us reflect on why this is so. In the following chapter, we shall begin to explore the meaning of ritual sacramental worship. But the notion of "primordial sacramentality" is broader than the seven ritual sacraments.[2] The notion implies: (1) that the idea of sacramentality cannot be restricted exclusively to ritual sacraments; (2) that any event is imbued with a degree of sacramentality which simultaneously reveals and conceals the saving presence of God; (3) that the Incarnation is just such an event and is indeed the normative sacramental event against which lesser sacramental revelations of God should be measured; (4) that the Church participates through Pentecost in the normative sacramentality of the Incarnation inasmuch as it is an event of grace which consciously prolongs the experienced consequences of the Incarnation; (5) that only when the seven ritual sacraments are seen as the conscious explicitation of the primordial sacramentality of the Church can they be adequately understood as sacraments.

Every graced transmutation of experience is, then, endowed with some degree of primordial sacramentality. Experience is irreducibly symbolic in its structure. It is the dynamic interrelation of three basic kinds of variables: qualities, facts, laws. A symbol is, however, any reality that mediates the grasp of intelligibility. Facts are clues to the laws in which they are grounded: every fact is, then, an expressive symbol of the law which explains it. Evaluations are clues to the kind of self one has become in the course of personal development. The fact that certain things anger me or that I approach life with a common-sense, a philosophical, or a scientific bias is explicable in terms of my biological and educational development. Moreover, our emotive and inferential responses to facts are more or less vague, more or less adequate attempts to interpret their meaning. If, then, the facts which impinge on me are expressive symbols of the laws in which they are grounded, my evaluative responses to them are interpretative symbols which both reveal the character of my personality and which seek to interpret the forces which shape me as a person. Experience may, then, be divided into expressive and interpretative symbols. And apart from experience there is nothing.

A word or deed performed in faith is an event which reveals the power and anointing of the Spirit in the one who performs it. Such an environmental symbol of grace is endowed with expressive sacramentality. Any adequate evaluative response to such an event must be informed by faith in God and in His saving acts within history. Faith endows experience with interpretative sacramentality. Experience takes on integral primordial sacramentality when expressive and interpretative sacramentality fuse within the same experience, when an event of grace is perceived in faith to be such and evokes the proper graced response.

It should, however, be clear from the preceding analysis that the charisms of sanctification and of service are integral to the Church's primordial sacramentality precisely because they mediate the conscious transformation of the Christian community in faith. For the Christian community cannot grow in faith unless it does so in response to the Spirit's abiding call. And the Spirit's abiding call is a charism, or gift. There is, of course, a sense in which any act performed in response to an actual grace is visibly expressive of the salvific presence of the Spirit. But such a presence is occasional. The permanent commitment to God in faith, hope, and love and the gifts, by their very habitual character, give an abiding and dynamic orientation to the self which comes to repeated expression in words and deeds of faith. They are, then, more clearly expressive of the presence of the Spirit than occasional graces. By mediating the visible transformation of experience, the gifts transform human activity into expressive symbols of grace and endow them with primordial sacramentality.

Similarly, every response in faith to an event of grace is, as we have seen, suffused with interpretative sacramentality. To so respond is to grow in faith. But one cannot grow in faith without docility to the gifts. Hence, the gifts of the Spirit also endow experience with interpretative sacramentality. In a community of faith both forms of sacramentality are operative. Hence, it is by sharing the gifts of the Spirit in faith, that the Christian community creates the revelatory sacramental context from which sacramental worship derives its meaning.

By the same token, however, where the gifts are inoperative in a given faith community, the primordial sacramentality of that community will be correspondingly diminished. Such a community will tend not to experience itself or to be experienced by others as an event of grace. And its sacramental worship will tend to be infected either by an empty ritualism or by the self-conscious and self-reliant pursuit of "humanly meaningful" liturgical experiences.

Finally, we note in closing this chapter that our reflections on the Pauline gifts cast light on the distinction made at the second Vatican Council between the "extraordinary" and "ordinary" gifts of the Spirit. Moreover, the council warned against seeking the "extraordinary gifts" without proper counsel and direction.[3] The only gifts which one might legitimately designate as "extraordinary" are xenoglossia and miracles. The tendency of theologians in the past to regard tongues as extraordinary was the fruit of misunderstanding concerning the character and availability of this gift. Similarly, the tendency to characterise prophecy as "extraordinary" was rooted in the mistaken medieval notion that the prophetic word is always preternatural or miraculous in character.

In his perceptive study of mystical psychology, Joseph Maréchal has suggested, quite correctly, that the extraordinary graces of higher contemplation exist in genetic continuity with the more ordinary manifestations of Christian prayer.[4] Our analysis of the service gifts suggests that a similar judgment applies to them. If so, it is false and misleading to characterise this or that gift as "essentially extraordinary." In a post-resurrectional, Spirit-led Church, every gift ought to be regarded as ordinary unless it is accompanied by some inexplicable or miraculous phenomenon. The ordinary experience of tongues, prophecy, and healing is not, however, inexplicable or miraculous. Every service gift from glossolalia to administration is, then, capable of both ordinary and extraordinary manifestations. And it is against the intemperate desire of the latter that the bishops at Vatican II warned. The problem is not, of course, that there is anything wrong with extraordinary manifestations of the Spirit but that the desire for such gifts can be all too easily marred by pride and disordered self love. Aspiration after the extraordinary should, then, be carefully scrutinised. Unfortunately, however, there is too much false teaching abroad in the churches concerning the "extraordinary" character of perfectly ordinary gifts. The mere statistical rarity of a gift is no proof that it is "extraordinary." For when Christians open their hearts to the working of the Spirit, gifts which may have been statistically rare among them suddenly begin to appear in abundance. The truth of the matter is that too many Christians prefer to measure God's generosity by their own fear, apathy, and tepidity.

Notes

1. This analysis of the conditions for the possibility of a conscious community is heavily indebted to a perceptive article by Francis Oppenheim, S.J., "A Roycean Road to Community," *Proceedings of the Jesuit Philosophical Association* (April, 1969) pp. 20-61.

2. Cf. Eduard Schillebeeckx, O.P., *Christ, the Sacrament of the Encounter with God* (N.Y.: Paulist, 1968); Karl Rahner, S.J., *The Church and the Sacraments* (New York: Herder, 1963); William Van Roo, S.J., "Reflections on Karl Rahner's 'Kirche und Sakremente,' " *Gregorianum*, XLIV (1962) pp. 465-500; Juan Alfaro, S.J., "Cristo Sacramento de Dios Padre: La Iglesia Sacramento de Cristo Glorificado," *Gregorianum*, XLVIII (1967) pp. 5-27; G. Martelet, S.J., "De la sacramentalité propre à l'église ou d'un sens de l'église inseparable du sens du Christ," *Nouvelle Revue Théologique*, CV (January, 1973) pp. 25-42; Herbert Musurillo, S.J. "Sacramental Symbolism and the Mysterion of the Early Church," *Worship*, XXXIX (April, 1965) pp. 265-274; Matthew J. O'Connell, S.J., "New Perspectives in Sacramental Theology," *Worship*, XXXIX (April, 1965) pp. 195-206.

3. *Lumen gentium*, 12.

4. Joseph Maréchal, S.J. *Studies in the Psychology of the Mystics*, translated by Algar Trorold (N.Y.: Magi, 1964) pp. 154 ff.

PART II
SACRAMENT

V
Baptism
in Water and
the Holy Spirit

1. We are attempting to understand the relation between the gifts of the Spirit and the sacraments by grounding both in a sound understanding of the dynamics of Christian conversion. We have seen that the consent of Christian faith is the decision to enter a religious community that is bound together by the free and gratuitous sharing of the gifts of God and of His Spirit, by mutual service in an atoning, Christ-like love, and by prayerful expectation of God's saving action. We have also seen that the initial consent of faith is inauthentic unless it includes personal openness to whatever gift of service the Spirit may choose to give. Moreover, personal growth in faith and in holiness is mediated by responsiveness to all of the gifts of the Spirit operative in the believing community— from tongues to the action gifts. We have seen too that admission into a pre-existing community is never a unilateral act. It demands of a candidate a willingness to share in the community's life as its member, and it demands the community's willingness to accept the candidate. A community acts by authorizing one of its members to act in its name. The act by which new members are accepted into the Christian community is, of course, the sacrament of baptism.

A Christian ritual sacrament has the following experienced characteristics: (1) *It is a public act of covenant worship.* It is public because it proclaims the word of God to a believing community assembled in worship. It is an act of worship because it is born of faith in God's saving action and challenges those who participate to deeper openness to the call of the Spirit. It is an act of covenant worship because it measures commitment to God by commit-

113

ment to the community of faith which proceeds from the covenant of grace sealed in the death and glorification of Jesus and in the mission of the Holy Spirit. (2) *It engages the faith of the Church universal.* The word of God proclaimed in sacramental worship is the faith that is binding on all Christians. Hence, while sacramental worship demands a personal profession of faith, it also demands that that personal profession embody consent to the word of salvation proclaimed by Jesus and transmitted from generation to generation in the Christian community by the power of the Spirit. Consent to that word is consent to the historical community in which it is proclaimed. And that community is the Church universal. (3) *It challenges the sacramental worshipper prophetically in the name of Jesus either to seal or to renew the Christian covenant by openness in faith to the Spirit.* The Christian covenant is sealed in official public consent to the historical act of grace embodied in the death and glorification of Jesus and in the sending of the Spirit. Since covenant consent binds one to God in a community of faith, the initial sealing of the Christian covenant culminates for the adult in baptism. The covenant may be renewed either in private acts of devotion or in public acts of worship. But sacramental covenant renewals are by definition public, in the sense defined above. The sacramental renewal of one's baptismal covenant may occur in a variety of life situations. (4) *It is the act not simply of a private individual but of the Christian community as a whole, which confronts the sacramental worshipper in faith through the ministry of one who has been authorized to speak in the community's name.* Sacramental worship is the ritualization of the shared faith-consciousness of the Christian community. As a consequence, the authorized minister of the sacrament confronts the sacramental worshipper not only in the name of the Father, Son, and Spirit but also in the name of the community of all Christian believers.

The preceding descriptive definition of a sacrament is more complex than the familiar Catholic definition: "a sacrament is an outward sign instituted by Christ to give grace." But it also has the advantage of avoiding some of the vagueness and inadequacy latent in the traditional Catholic formula. The phrase "outward sign" can, for example, be misleading. What is outside of me is by definition not a part of me. It does not affect or engage me personally. A sacrament, however, demands a personal commitment of faith that engages one totally. Moreover, as an event it is immanent to a worshipper's experience and shapes it efficaciously. As we shall see, there is a sense in which Jesus may be said to have instituted the ritual sacraments. But the Catholic theological justification of such a belief has in the past been marred by legalism and by historical naiveté. Too often, Catholic theologians attempted to portray Jesus as carefully defining the legal, canonical essence of seven distinct ritual acts and as establishing them by "divine law." Their proofs, however, were exegetically naive, and ignorant, by and large, of the historical development of sacramental worship. Finally, Catholic attempts to explain how the sacraments "give grace" have in the past been too often couched in language that seemed to transform grace into a "thing" and its conferral into an automatic, almost mechanical process. There are, to be sure, legitimate insights struggling to expression in the traditional Catholic definition of a sacrament and in its different scholastic explanations. But when a formula gives evidence of inadequacy and when its traditional explanations breed misunderstanding and confusion, it is better to replace them by more comprehensive theories that are truer to experience.

2. To relate any ritual sacrament to a theology of conversion, one must explore the faith commitment to which it challenges the sacramental worshipper. The Christian neophyte has been traditionally asked: (1) to renounce Satan, (2) to believe in the Father, Son, and Holy Spirit, and (3) to believe that by baptism the sin of Adam in which all humans participate is taken away. These three commitments are different in character. The first implies the renunciation of realities and values that are opposed to Jesus. The third is the "belief that" a certain proposition is true. The second is "belief in" a tri-personal God: it demands, therefore, that one enter into a certain kind of relationship with God, one dictated by the historical mission of the Son and of the Holy Spirit. What, then, is the meaning of such a commitment?

To understand the meaning of a sacramental ritual, one must reflect on the evaluative elements that structure it, for those elements give shape to the kind of commitment it demands. Among the interpretative structures present in the Christian baptismal commitment there are two figures that are clearly mythic in origin: Satan and Adam. The suggestion that Satan and Adam are mythic figures is sure to raise some theological hackles, but anyone who has survived the analysis of the preceding chapters is likely to respond to such a suggestion at least with a certain initial openness. The problem with the suggestion is that the term "myth" is surrounded by a host of misunderstandings. There is, then, need before we proceed to reflect briefly on the dynamics of mythic thinking and the way it functions in human experience.

The first thing to be observed is that myths are a way of interpreting reality.[1] Myth defines a general frame of reference like science, mathematics, scholarship, and common sense. When confronted with a problem the scholar or scientist concocts a theory, and the mathematician writes a formula. But the mythmaker tells a story. Mythic thinking about the forces which shape experience is, then, concrete and imagistic, though images occur outside of mythic tales. Moreover, as in the case of poetry or prophecy, mythic patterns of thought are deeply rooted in the physical purposes which shape human experience.

Conscious dreams teach us that different laws govern the association of images than the laws of logic. As we adjust emotionally to reality, dream images blend and fade in fantastic associative patterns. A concrete image like an old chair, a familiar tree, one's childhood home, is linked by free association with a host of other images and feelings. The images present in myths are no different. The figure of Adam and Eve in the garden of Paradise, the serpent-tempter, the tree of knowledge of good and evil—all these images speak directly to religious emotions and evoke a host of imaginative associations from us all.

The fact that myths are stories constructed through the free use of the imagination rather than by strict logic makes it difficult to explain the meaning of mythic thinking with abstract clarity and precision. The meaning of a myth is symbolically vague, and a vague affirmation is one to which the principle of contradiction cannot be applied. Myths tantalize human reason, they call out for explanation. But their theoretical clarification is the work of the scholar, not of the mythmaker. The mythmaker is content to let the images which shape a mythic tale stand in both their naked ambiguity and richness of connotation.

The scholarly study of myths has revealed distinguishable stages in the development of mythic patterns of thought. The study of comparative religion reveals, for example, that certain mythic images tend to be associated with predictable regularity in male-dominated cultures. The sky and the lights of heaven tend on the whole to be personfied as masculine forces; the earth, the moon, the sea, as feminine. Some myths are closely tied to the processes of personal human development. The myth of Osiris, for example, recounts his castration and dismemberment, the reassembly of his body, and his return to life transformed.[2] The plot is improbable but the myth gives evidence of speaking to different stages in the socio-psychological development of personal consciousness. As myths are popularized they are transformed into art. The plot and narrative structure become more complex, more self-conscious, more realistic. Eventually, myth becomes epic; and ritual, drama. Of special theoretical significance are, however, myths about the origin and end of all things. Such myths are the matrix of abstract speculation. For they are generalizations cast in story form. A myth about the first human being is a story that seeks to reveal something about the meaning of every human experience. Myths about the end of the world seek through narrative to comment on the destiny of all creation.

3. The figure of Satan is mythic in origin. He first appears in the book of Job, which is not a historical book but a poetic parable. The figure of Satan has, however, had an interesting intellectual history. In popular catechesis, Satan is normally described as a fallen angel. But most accounts of his angelic powers are a fusion of biblical and medieval patterns of thought.

The roots of Christian angelology are in the Old Testament. As the Hebrews conquered the Promised Land they were forced to come to terms theologically with the rival deities whom their adversaries worshipped. Their enemies adored a variety of natural and cosmic forces which they had personalized in myth and ritual. Convinced that only Yahweh is God, the writers of the Old Testament were loathe to acknowledge the divinity of these nature gods. At the same time they were loathe to dismiss them altogether as unreal. They chose a middle path. Convinced that Yahweh had created all things, they symbolized the subjection of the "gods" of their adversaries to the Lord's dominion by reducing them to the status of courtiers in the palace of Yahweh. In time, the Hebrews came to imagine the heavens themselves as the court of God and the stars as His courtiers assembled to do Him homage.

Moreover, since the gods of their enemies were also national deities, angelic beings were conceived as the personification of the state that did them homage. Their inclusion as courtiers in the retinue of Yahweh was, then, also an affirmation of the Lord's power over all the nations. In the New Testament, these angelic guardians of the state became the "principalities and powers of this world."

As Hebrew thought developed, it began to insist more and more upon the transcendence and otherness of Yahweh. And this insight came to mythic expression in the transformation of the divine courtiers into messengers sent by God to bring His word to His people or to accomplish some concrete task of salvific significance.[3]

Medieval theologians embellished these mythic images in Scripture with ideas that were frankly derived from Greek philosophy. They found in Aristotle that the stars and the planets were propelled by unmoved movers, purely spiritual beings who were by nature subsistent intellects, wholly free from the limitations of matter. They concluded that the stellar retinue of the Lord described in the Scripture and the unmoved movers of Aristotle must be the same beings. They accordingly attributed to the angels of Scripture the natural, intellectual, and volitional characteristics of the Aristotlian unmoved movers.

In medieval angelology, Satan is an Aristotilized biblical angel gone bad. He is a rebel against God and the leader of the demonic powers who fight against the Lord and obsess and possess men. The image of Satan which emerges from medieval reflection has been admirably summarized by Walter Farrell. Satan is pure spirit, ageless because immaterial, immune to injury, pain, sickness, and death. He is not restricted in his activity by the limits of time and space. He has the perfect knowledge of a disembodied intellect. And he has fallen from grace by a single sin committed before the creation of the world.[4] The grounds for such a belief are, however, as scientifically solid as Aristotelian astronomy and metaphysics. Moreover, the renunciation of Satan was demanded of the Christian long before the Aristotlization of biblical angels. It is, then, to a more primitive tradition, rather than to medieval theologians, that we must turn to unlock the meaning of the baptismal formulas.

4. In a perceptive analysis of Pauline demonology, G. B. Caird has thrown considerable light on the place occupied by the figure of Satan in early Christian belief.

When Satan first appears in Ze 3:1-5 and in the book of Job, he is the "Accuser." He functions in the Lord's court as an angelic prosecuting attorney zealously committed to testing the sincerity of all those who pretend to live upright lives in the sight of God. As a mythic figure he is, therefore, linked imaginatively with the law. And the misery he brings upon Job expresses the popular tendency of the Hebrew mind to interpret suffering and disaster as accusations of sinfulness on the part of God for transgressions of His law.

In Job Satan is not yet "the devil," he is one of the "sons of Elohim" obediently subservient to the will of the Lord. But already in Job Satan possesses a somewhat sinister character. He is the author of accusatory suffering. He brings sickness and utter misery to Job, destroys Job's family and possessions, and in the process successfully convicts Job of sinful pride.[5]

Caird has suggested that Satan's function as angelic prosecuting attorney provides part of the theological background necessary for understanding a Pauline theology of the Mosaic law. The law is a revelation of God's will for men; but because the law is powerless to save men, it confronts them as a divine accusation. As a result, its functions in Pauline theology and those of the angelic district attorney tend to fuse. Paul speaks of the law as the great accuser; like the Satan of Job, it tempts human beings and convicts them.[6]

Caird has also noted that there is a strain of New Testament theology which dates Satan's fall differently from medieval angelology. There are passages in the New Testament which suggest that the fall of Satan actually occurred contemporaneously with the ministry of Jesus. Jesus by His ministry breaks the power of the Accuser because there is no place in the New Israel for the law and its condemnation.[7]

Satan, for his part is transformed by his very function as angelic prosecutor into a demonic force. For as the Accuser, he sets himself in opposition to Jesus and His mission. In the process he becomes the adversary, i.e., the devil. Through the ministry of Jesus, Satan thus becomes the mythic personification of all those forces that stand in opposition to the divine plan of salvation made visible in Christ. For the first Christians, Satan came to stand, therefore, for the rigors of the law, its power to convict, coerce, and condemn. As a consequence, he was transformed into the leader of the principalities and powers of this world, which follow the path of violence and the sword. The purpose of Jesus' mission is, by contrast, neither the conviction and condemnation sought by the Accuser nor conquest by violence, but the revelation of the Father's saving mercy.[8]

These reflections cast further light on the meaning of the temptations of Jesus as they are recorded in Matthew and Luke and link them more closely to early baptismal catechesis. Jesus' anointing on the banks of the Jordan began His revelation as the Spirit-filled messiah predicted by Isaiah, the one sent to inaugurate the new spiritual Israel. The new Pentecostal Israel would, as a result, draw its life, not from the law, but from the participation of each believer in Jesus' own Spirit-baptism. For Jesus is sent to baptise men, not with water alone, but "with the Holy Spirit and fire." It is this belief which comes to expression in the creedal formulas of baptism. At the same time, Jesus' pneumatic anointing, by transforming Him visibly into the beginning of the new Israel, sets Him in irreconcilable opposition to the Accuser. Matthew and Luke accordingly embellished the cryptic account of Jesus' desert temptations recorded in Mark by introducing the figure of Satan into the dramatic narrative.

Moreover, we have some reason to believe, on the basis of the logia of Jesus preserved in Scripture, that it was because the figure of Satan functioned interpretively in Jesus's own catechesis of His disciples that it was preserved in the catechesis of the post-resurrectional Church. Jesus is portrayed in the New Testament as interpreting disease, demon-possession, and the evil and weakness of men as signs of their sinful state, and therefore of their subjection in bondage to the Accuser. Moreover, when the disciples began to participate efficaciously in Jesus' own ministry of healing, He interpreted it as a sign that the power of Satan had been broken and that the Accuser had been cast out from the presence of the Father. Jesus' rebuke to Peter suggests that He regarded any person or force as "Satan" which tempted Him to deviate from His messianic commitments.[9]

The accounts of the temptations of Jesus reflect the same kind of catechesis. Jesus confronts the Accuser in the desert as the one who tests Jesus by seeking to undermine His trust in the Father. The Accuser is the one who would have Jesus himself become a "Satan" by testing the Father's fidelity, just as Satan himself tests Jesus' own fidelity to the Father. The Accuser is the one who would seek to build the Kingdom of God, not on authentic worship and atoning love, but on trust in the principalities and powers of this world: upon law, politics, coercive violence.

A similar catechesis is reflected in the renunciation of Satan demanded by the baptismal ritual. To renounce Satan is to repudiate all that is opposed to trust in God as a merciful Father and to openness to the Spirit who transforms the community of the faithful into the Church, the new Israel. For by the power of the Spirit the personal participation of each believer in the atonement of Jesus, rather than the law and its accusations, is the rule of life in common. To renounce Satan as a Christian neophyte is, therefore, to pledge oneself to stand open to the Spirit in putting on the mind of Jesus in the sense explained in chapter II.

5. But in baptism the believer is also asked to affirm that by this bath of regeneration (s)he ceases to be a child of Adam and is reborn instead as a child of God in the image of Jesus. Clearly, the images of pneumatic rebirth and adoptive divine childhood are intimately linked in the baptismal commitment to the mythic figure of Adam. A clarification of these images is, therefore, also linked to a clarification of the way in which the figure of Adam functions interpretively in the baptismal commitment.

Paul Ricoeur's analysis of the Adamic myth offers some helpful and suggestive approaches to this complex question. Ricoeur has suggested that the Adamic myth is not a myth of the fall of the human race but a myth of human deviation. In this he is quite correct. The image of man's fall is more proper to Gnosticism and Neoplatonism than it is to Sacred Scripture. The image of a "fall" presupposes a dualistic division of the cosmos into a higher, eternal realm of spirit and a lower, temporal realm of matter. In such a cosmos, the fall of humankind from grace is the lapse from a purely spiritual existence into one tainted by contact with matter and the body. In Gnosticism, man's fall is the effect of personal guilt. In Neoplatonism it is the result of metaphysical necessity.[10]

As an eschatological myth rather than a myth of "fall," the Adamic myth differs from other mythic accounts of the origin of evil in its stance toward human history. In the Gnostic and Neoplatonic traditions, for example, the soul's salvation consists in its deliverance from matter, time, and history by its restoration to an eternal, spiritual mode of existence.

Mircea Eliade has argued that every religion as it grapples with the problem of evil is forced to face the terror of time, the fact that life slips away and all things end in death. And he has also suggested that a comparison between the Judeo-Christian tradition and other traditions reveals that the former is distinguished from the latter by its unique stance toward time and the historical process. For Judeo-Christian soteriology insists that man is not saved by an escape from history but by immersion in it. It therefore opposes a soteriology of flight from this world by a soteriology of transforming commitment to this world.[11]

Because it is eschatological in character, the Adamic myth is a special kind of myth. It is similar to other myths in that it speaks in archetypal imagery and casts its religious statements in narrative form. It also resembles other myths of human origins in that it signals its universal significance by constructing a story about the origin of all human beings. But it differs from most other myths by being an attempt to make a religious statement about the salvific significance of the historical process itself.

Adam enters the story as mankind personified. As the narrative unfolds he becomes the sole author of sin and of the moral and religious ambiguity that plagues the human condition. But the author of the Adamic myth stands in clear opposition to the tragic

Greek vision of a god who is a *kakos daimon,* a malignant power in need of repentance. Unlike the Greek deities, Yahweh is subject to no fatal power beyond Himself. A good God, He has created a good world. It is the human race, not God, who is in need of repentance for sin. As the sole author of sin, Adam is also the sole author of religious hypocrisy. His deviation from God's will transforms nature into a hostile force, labor into an oppressive burden, childbearing into sorrow, and the human experience of death into a meaningless return to dust.

Adam is conquered by the serpent. The serpent as it appears in the original myth is not explicitly demonic in character. It is, as Ricoeur has suggested, a chthonic animal borrowed from other mythic traditions and introduced into the narrative for symbolic purposes. As a symbol, rather than an abstract, conceptual sign, the serpent resists clear definition. But his presence in the narrative is expressive of the fact that, while man is the author of sin, he is led to deviate from the command of God by forces outside of himself. The figure of the serpent is, therefore, a vague religious symbol for those cosmic powers within us, among us, outside us which lead us to stand in opposition to God and to his saving plan.[12]

6. In baptism, the Christian is asked to consent, not to Adam, but to the Father in heaven who has revealed Himself in the mission of His Son and of His Spirit. From its earliest days, however, the Christian community recognized Jesus' mission as the penumatic messiah to be the reversal of Adam's sin. Hence, in consenting to Jesus as the new Adam, the Christian neophyte decides to accept Jesus as the author of the "Adamic reversal." What, then, are the implications of such a decision?

The old Adam was chthonic in origin, sprung from the earth and progenitor of men in their unredeemed, earth-bound existence. Jesus, as the new Adam, comes "from heaven." He is divine and pneumatic rather than chthonic in origin. The divinity of His origin comes to full historical expression in His resurrection, which in turn completes the process of visible pneumatic transformation inaugurated on the banks of the Jordan and mediates the final eschatological outpouring of the Spirit. Moreover, the enduring visible sign that Jesus is risen is His power to transform sinful men, even in our day, through the mission of the Spirit who recreates them in

Jesus' own image. As the ritual inauguration of vital pneumatic transformation, baptism is, then, a species of rebirth. Since, moreover, the Christian neophyte consents to pneumatic assimilation to Jesus as Son, baptismal consent is participation in Jesus' sonship. It is becoming a child of God by God's free call and gift. Hence, the sonship of the believer is adoptive, not "natural" as Jesus' was. It is experienced as free gift rather than as a human birthright. The old Adam was the author of salvific ambiguity. The new Adam dispels that ambiguity by being the final and definitive revelation of God's salvific intent and the embodiment of what person is called by God to become.

An analysis of the baptismal commitment reveals, therefore, that baptismal consent terminates at the Adamic and Satanic myths only insofar as they illumine and are illumined by Jesus, His ministry, glorification, and mediation of the Spirit. Both the Adamic and Satanic myths illumine Jesus' mission and its consequences by supplying a cerain number of archetypical mythic symbols for interpreting their meaning. Jesus' mission illumines the Adamic and Satanic myths by revealing Jesus himself, not any mythic construct, to be the definitive revelation of those salvific truths which come to inchoate expression in the first chapters of Genesis and in other related biblical myths. The Christian neophyte is not asked, therefore, to believe in Adam or Satan as historical realities; but (s)he is asked to believe in Jesus as the unique historical author of the Adamic reversal and as regal victor over the serpent/Satan. In other words, the mythic formality under which baptismal consent is made belongs to the personal evaluative form of the baptismal experience rather than to the physical data.

As the new Adam, Jesus counters the hypocrisy of the old with His summons to repentance. He reverses the disobedience of the old by His trust in the Father.

He also reverses the consequences of the old Adam's sinfulness: He overcomes the hostility of nature by mediating the redemption of our environment through the free sharing in faith of the environmental supports of life. He redeems labor from the oppressive consequences of sin by endowing it with a new purpose: to share in faith and love rather than to possess in self-reliance. He redeems human sexuality from the oppression of sin by transforming the use of sex into an expression of redemptive, atoning love.

By his sin the old Adam had transformed death into a meaningless return to dust; the new Adam conquers death by revealing it to be total transformation in the Spirit for those who believe.

The old Adam was conquered by the serpent as the symbol of cosmic evil: of the chaos within man, in his social relations, and in his world. The new Adam triumphs over the serpent by endowing cosmic evil with redemptive significance. He does this by subsuming suffering itself into God in order to transform it into a source of divine life.

In addition, however, the new pneumatic Adam triumphs over the chaos in the human heart by the gifts of the Spirit. He effects the healing of human social relations through the charismatic activity of his Spirit. And He effects the redemptive transformation of the world by freeing those who believe in Him to love this world and one another with the same unconditioned commitment as the new Adam himself. And in so doing, the new Adam sets the race of pneumatic children of God in redemptive opposition to Satan and to the principalities and powers of this world.

Finally, by freeing those who believe in Him from the bondage of the law, Jesus frees them from the dominion of Satan, the serpent/Accuser. And this liberation is the spiritual exodus/covenant experience dimly foreshadowed by the original exodus.

7. The Christian neophyte is asked to believe that by baptism original sin is taken away. The meaning of this creedal proposition has however been hotly disputed by theologians. The notion of "original sin" is of post-biblical origin. The phrase as such never occurs in Scripture. It was the creation of sacramental theologians of the fourth century in their attempt to respond to the Pelagian crisis. Since the Pelagian controversy focused attention on the nature of sin and its relation to baptism, the anti-Pelagians were forced to reflect upon the speculative implications of the mythic, imagistic, and creedal categories which function within a Christian baptismal commitment.

As a conception evolved by speculative theologians, the phrase "original sin" is closer to a conceptual sign than to an imaginative or mythic symbol. Hence, it is capable of quasi-definition, although it is too complex a notion to be defined by genus and species alone. But "original sin" and "personal sin" do divide the genus of "sin." Moreover, as "sin," "original sin" is also opposed speculatively to the notions of "nature" and "grace." The terms "personal sin," "nature," and "grace" are here understood, not as fixed metaphysical essences, but as dimensions of the evaluative, personal form of a developing experience, i.e., of the way in which an emerging self responds to the forces that shape it. One may, then, respond to the forces which shape experience graciously, naturally, sinfully. What distinguishes a natural from a graced response is faith. A natural response is sensitive to the values which characterise spatio-temporal reality, but it is untouched by an awareness of God or by the need to depend upon Him in faith. Personal sin, by contrast, presupposes some measure of God-consciousness but assumes a stance that is opposed to what one understands to be God's demands.[13]

As a speculative concept, "original sin" can, therefore, be descriptively defined both negatively and positively. It may be defined positively as everything in human experience apart from one's sinful, natural, and graced personal responses which is proper to a human self as such, when (s)he is understood as one who is redemptively called to transcend mere human life by living in faith as a child of God in the image of Jesus. It can be defined negatively as anything in human experience apart from one's sinful, natural, and graced personal responses which is in need of redemptive transformation by the Spirit. But what is there in experience apart from my sinful, natural, and graced responses? What but the situation to which I respond? But "original sin" designates the human situation only under a specific aspect, namely, its distortion by the sinful acts of other human beings.

As a situational concept "original sin" may, then, be described in the following concrete terms: It means that human beings with no faith dependence on God face death as devoid of salvific meaning. They experience life as charged with moral and religious ambiguity. They find themselves prone to a self-reliant rejection of God's word. They are apt to deal hypocritically with one another and with God. They are inwardly divided, confused and vacillating in the face of feelings they cannot understand or evaluate properly. They are victims to the servility of their own wills, prone to the self-righteous attempt to save themselves rather than to accept salvation as God's free gift through faith. They live in a world that fails to reflect the ethical vision of Jesus. It is a world where human actions and institutions do not express the desire to share freely the good things of life as the sign of one's trust in God. It is a world in which human acts and institutions attempt to define the conditions which God must meet before humans will enter into relationship with Him. It is a world in which humans trust in law as a salvific force, seek power rather than atoning love, prefer punishment to forgiveness, and hypocritical worship to the worship of Christian service. It is a world in which the actions and institutions of men express their stinginess, their desire for class privilege, their mutual exploitation, and their sexual perversions.

As an abstract, speculative idea, therefore, "original sin" is a "situational" concept in that it designates a broad range of variables which function efficaciously within any experienced human situation. When the variables in human experience which it designates are grasped in mythic terms, they can be legitimately interpreted as those dynamic, environmental forces in one's situation (not one's sinful, natural, or graced personal responses) which give efficacious definition to a human person as a "child of Adam": that is, as one who has yet to decide to live as the child of God in the image of Jesus. When these situational variables are grasped in non-mythic, imagistic terms they can be understood as those dynamic, environmental forces in one's situation (not one's sinful, natural, or graced personal responses) from which the children of God have been freed. When they are grasped in ethical terms, they can be understood as those dynamic, environmental forces in one's situation (not one's sinful, natural, or graced personal responses) which are not expressive of the "law of Christ." When they are grasped in creedal terms, they are all of those dynamic, environmental forces in one's situation (not one's sinful, natural, or graced responses) which undermine faith in Jesus as the revelation of the Father through the power of the Spirit.

As a situational concept, the notion of "original sin" has implications for a theology of conversion. For it designates variables that function efficaciously in the environment of each emerging self. The environmental forces designated as "original sin" shape each self, are immanent to it, and cry out for correct evaluation in faith. Indeed, the disorder in the environmental forces designated by "original sin" desperately needs prophetic confrontation and redemptive, re-evaluative transformation. They are those forces from which the Christian convert must turn evaluatively in repentance and which (s)he must seek to change in the name of Christ. But as environmental factors they are immanently constitutive of the convert's developing experience prior to personal repentance. Clearly, then, a theology of conversion lends support to Tridentine teaching that original sin is not acquired by imitation of bad example but functions positively in human experience prior to personal sin.

At the same time, it should be clear that "original sin" cannot be adequately grasped in all of its complexity under the category of "situation" alone. Nor can it be adequately understood as the sum total of all sinful acts, as Piet Schoonenberg suggests.[14] For "original sin" does not include my own personal sin. The experienced consequences of the collective sinfulness of mankind is, of course, part of the situational reality which the notion of "original sin" seeks to interpret. But those consequences can be grasped formally and explicitly as an aspect of "original sin" only when they are seen to stand in redemptive opposition to Jesus as the unique salvific author of what we have called the "Adamic reversal." In other words, "original sin" is a notion that can be grasped interpretatively only from within Christian conversion. It is the sum total of those unredeemed elements in my situation (as opposed to my sinful, natural, or graced personal responses) from which I am freed through a conversion that culminates in sacramental baptism.

If the preceding analysis is sound, then all of the following theological frames of reference are inadequate to interpret the meaning of "original sin." First, any theological interpretation of the meaning of "original sin" will be inadequate which rests on an exegesis of Genesis and Romans alone. It is methodologically inadequate because it prescinds from the post-biblical, speculative context from which the notion of "original sin" arose and from the philosophical, doctrinal, systematic, and pastoral problems which teaching on "original sin" has raised. Second, equally inadequate will be any approach to "original sin" which prescinds from the redemptive mission of Christ and from the sacrament of Christian baptism, for one is led to the notion of original sin by an analysis of the interpretative elements which function within the baptismal commitment of the believer. Third, no speculative approach to original sin will be adequate which seeks to grasp its meaning in philosophical, psychological, or anthropological categories alone. Such abstractionism has marred many of the contemporary attempts to explain the meaning of "original sin." Finally, any approach to "original sin" will be inadequate which is marred by the absence of intellectual conversion. Such an approach will fail both to differentiate the speculative frames of reference which have functioned in the interpretation of a Christian baptismal commitment and to evaluate how they have so functioned.

Intellectual conversion provides, moreover, the key to unraveling the theological problems posed by the encyclical *Humani generis*. The encyclical lent some degree of official sanction to the idea of biological monogenism: the notion that the human race descends physically from Adam.[15] This official "defense" of monogenism was not, however, the assumption of a definitive position. It was diagnostic and cautionary. The encyclical predicated continued official espousal of monogenism upon the inability of theologians to advance beyond the theological understanding of original sin prevalent at the time the encyclical was written. In focusing attention on the inadequacies of existing theological thought, the encyclical pointed the way prophetically to a resolution of the very questions it raised. For it forced theologians to acknowledge that the reason why they had attempted to defend biological monogenism on exegetical grounds was their failure to distinguish adequately between a mythic and a scientific frame of reference. At the basis of that failure was the naive objectivism of the medieval classicist mind. The theological shift from a classicist optic to the greater critical sophistication demanded by intellectual conversion mediated the speculative rehabilitation of mythic patterns of thought. And that rehabilitation enabled theologians to identify certain "traditional" problems surrounding original sin as nonquestions. For they were forced to recognise that it is as illegitimate to draw scientific conclusions from mythic presuppositions as it is to dismiss mythic insights on scientific presuppositions.

Sensitivity to the eschatological character of the Adamic myth also casts light on the pope's unwillingness to dismiss it as unhistorical. The Adamic myth is precisely a mythic rendering of the salvific meaning of the historical process itself. But while the myth is an interpretation of the religious significance of human history, it remains in its interpretive structure a myth, not a scientific or scholarly hypothesis. The biological descent of all men from Adam described in Scripture is, therefore, a mythic image, not a scientific or scholarly theory. As a narrative element in the Adamic myth, the image of biological descent affirms the salvific solidarity of all men within a unified history of salvation.

But while that real solidarity is affirmed in mythic categories in Genesis, it is factually revealed, not in Genesis, but in Jesus and in the sending of the Spirit. Human salvific solidarity is historically grounded, therefore, not in the scientific verifiability of biological descent from a single couple but in the salvific solidarity of all men effected by the death and glorification of Jesus and by the Pentecostal sending of the Spirit.

We are now in a position to understand what it means to say that ritual baptism "takes away original sin." "Original sin" is a situational, Christocentric concept. It designates those forces in one's experienced environment (as opposed to one's natural, sinful, or graced evaluative response to them) which have yet to be transformed by the Spirit of Jesus. Baptism "takes away original sin" by radically modifying one's salvific situation. A situation is modified factually through decision. A battle is changed through the charge of new troops. A society is changed through the passage of a law. A salvific situation is modified by some novel fact of redemptive significance. Formal acceptance into a Christian community is such a fact. It embodies the joint decision of a neophyte and of the believing community (s)he joins. Its effect is to make one's relationship to God henceforth a function of one's relationship to the other members of that community.

As we saw in the last chapter, the Christian community can be adequately understood only in dynamic, charismatic terms. It is a community called by God to put on the mind of Jesus by the active sharing of the blessings of God and the gifts of the Holy Spirit. In other words, ritual baptism modifies one's salvific situation by its social, ecclesial consequences. For it means that one may begin to share in the life of the Christian community as its member and through that sharing grow in the life of God.

But baptism modifies one's salvific situation only partially. After baptism the forces that are anti-Christ continue to shape the believer efficaciously as an experience. Ritual baptism does not, therefore, "take away original sin" by eliminating those forces altogether. It "takes away original sin" by changing the way in which those forces are experienced evaluatively. Prior to baptism they are experienced as merely sinful. After baptism they are experienced as "concupiscent." The term "concupiscence" was used at the Council of Trent to describe those forces in the experience *of the baptised* which are a consequence of sin and an inducement to sin without being formal, personal sin. Like "original sin," concupiscence is, then, a situational, Christocentric concept. Like "original sin," "concupiscence" designates forces within experience that are opposed to Jesus' redemptive work. Ritual baptism, then, "takes away original sin" by transforming it into "concupiscence."[16]

8. We are now in a position to begin to clarify two interrelated theological questions. They are related to baptism but have implications beyond baptism. They are: (1) What does it mean to say that baptism imposes an "indelible character"? and (2) What does it mean to say that the sacraments are endowed with salvific efficacy?

Catholic theology has traditionally held that three sacraments —baptism, confirmation, and orders—all confer a "character."[17] The precise meaning of this teaching has not always been clear. It certainly signals out these three sacraments as having special consequences. But what are those consequences? And what is this mysterious "character"? Similarly Catholic theology has also insisted that the ritual sacraments are in some sense efficacious and that they effect the grace that they signify. The meaning of this teaching has been the subject of both controversy and confusion among Catholics and Protestants. But an experiential approach to adult baptism helps clarify both of them.

The Christian community when it acts with authenticity proceeds in an attitude of faith-dependence on God. The same faith-dependence must characterise both the desire of an adult to enter the community and the process of acceptance. For the believing community has a responsibility to subject the desires of new candidates for membership to prayerful discernment in faith. It must test the truth and adequacy of the neophyte's understanding of Jesus and of His mission. It must test the neophyte's repentance of past sins and desire to experience the healing in faith of the present consequences of past faults. And it must test the neophyte's willingness to assume personal responsibility for the ethical consequences of a life lived in faith-dependence on God. In the early Church this period of testing and instruction was called the catechumenate. Ordinarily it lasted three years. Baptismal acceptance of adult candidates into the community presupposed, therefore, that the candidate already lived open in faith to God and showed signs of progress in the gifts of sanctification. Baptism was, therefore, a public "sealing" of the candidate's faith in the two-fold sense in which Max Thurian describes "sealing" by the Spirit: ". . . . the seal *(sphragis)* of the Spirit is a sign which by the tokens or fruits of the Spirit testifies here and now that God's faithful belong to Him, and which will be a testimony in their favor in the day of redemption; as a seal insures the integrity of an official act, the seal of the Spirit insures the integrity of the baptismal alliance, guarantees its perpetual validity, and holds both parties to fidelity: fidelity on the part of God to his promise, and fidelity on the part of the believer until the end."[18]

The ritual act of baptism "seals" the faith of the believer in this twofold sense: (1) it is a public certification that the one baptised "belongs to God" and that (s)he has nothing to fear on the last day and (2) it is a public and official sign of the new covenant. For it attests to the fact that the one baptised has indeed been called in faith to a wholehearted commitment to God in the image of Jesus. It is a commitment which finds expression in the personal sharing of the physical supports of life and of the gifts of the Spirit in the community of faith Jesus founded. But there is more. For the community to which the baptised person stands committed goes beyond the local community in which (s)he is baptised. The believer is called to a love that is, like Jesus' love, unrestricted in its scope. And true faith binds one to every other believer. The community to which the true convert stands committed is, therefore, not just some local church, but the universal Christian community. Finally, baptism is strictly initiatory. It inaugurates personal acceptance into the Christian community as a whole. Those sacraments which confer a "character" have, as we shall see, all three of these traits: (1) they are strictly initiatory. (2) they demand commitment to the Church universal. (3) they are the ritual "seal" of the believer's faith in the sense described above.

But to affirm the "sealing" power of a sacrament is to assert its ritual efficacy. Baptism is acceptance into the Church universal. One cannot be accepted into a community except by one empowered by that community to speak in its name. The word which the community pronounces over the adult catechumen in baptism is a kerygmatic word, a prophetic word, and an intercessory word. It is kerygmatic because it proclaims to the neophyte the good news about salvation in Christ Jesus and demands a Spirit-filled response. As we have seen, however, every authentic kerygmatic word is a transmutation of prophecy. The sacramental word is, therefore, prophetic in the sense that it is a confrontational word pronounced in the name of God, a summons to a deeper repentance and to a lifetime of pneumatic growth. Moreover, as a prophetic word it is efficacious of the divine judgment it proclaims. We are here at the heart of any sound understanding of the efficacy of the ritual sacraments.

"Judgment" is here understood in the Johannine sense of that term. In the gospel of John, God judges the world by the simple expedient of: (1) revealing in Jesus that He is absolutely committed to them in love and (2) demanding a similar response from men in return.[19] Jesus, therefore, in John's gospel passes judgment on no one but nevertheless efficaciously judges the world. For by faithfully proclaiming the message of salvation to humankind He forces the choice between death and life. One way or another, then, His word is efficacious: for it brings either salvation or damnation, either life in the Spirit or death in unbelief.

The sacramental word spoken in baptism and in the other sacraments is the same prophetic, judgmental word which Jesus spoke to men: repent, believe the good news, and be saved. It is spoken to humankind in the name of God and of the risen Christ, and with the authority of His Spirit. It is, therefore, endowed with the same prophetic, judgmental efficacy as Jesus' own word. This same insight came to expression in an earlier sacramental theology under two different rubrics. On the one hand, Trent taught that when a sacrament is received with proper dispositions it is efficacious of grace. And on the other hand, Catholic theologians have traditionally held that when a sacrament is received in mortal sin and without appropriate repentance, the reception is itself another mortal sin. One way or the other, therefore, the sacramental word effects what is signifies, for it promises either life or death according to the dispositions of the sacramental worshipper.[20]

The fact that the baptismal word is a "seal" of the believer's faith in the sense described above re-enforces its prophetic function. For once posited it cannot be undone. It is therefore an "indelible seal" which stands either in confirmation of a life lived in faith or as a testimony against religious hypocrisy. To the sealed apostate it stands as a reproach on the day of the Lord. For having acknowledged Jesus as his Lord in baptism, the apostate has chosen to return to the bondage of Satan.

Finally, one may recognize in the word of baptism a certain intercessory efficacy. It is a prayer for the neophyte's total transformation in the image of Jesus. That prayer is certainly efficacious in the sense that it is certainly in accord with God's salvific will and therefore certainly sanctioned by Him. It will, therefore, be answered provided the neophyte places no obstacles to God's saving action in the course of his or her religious development.

There is, then, nothing magic or automatic about the sacramental conferral of grace. The reception of grace through the mediation of sacramental worship is wholly contingent upon the dispositions of the sacramental worshipper. At the same time the ritual sacrament is endowed with prophetic and intercessory efficacy in the sense defined above. Moreover, what is true of baptism is true of all the sacraments. For in each sacrament the same word is pronounced: repent, believe the good news and be saved. When, however, the adult sacramental worshipper is properly disposed, the sacramental act does indeed, as Florence and Trent insisted, contain and effect the very pneumatic transformation it signifies. In the case of the adult it forgives personal sins because it is expressive of the neophyte's repentance in faith and in the strength of God's prior salvific commitment made visible in Christ and in the Church. That commitment comes to ritual visibility in the minister's sacramental proclamation of salvation.

9. We are now in a position to begin to reflect on the complex question of infant baptism.[21] It is a matter of some importance to those involved in the Catholic charismatic renewal for a variety of reasons. Many Catholics have a confused and inadequate understanding of the salvific efficacy of sacramental worship. Confusion about sacramental efficacy breeds a confused understanding of the meaning of infant baptism. For the two questions are, as we shall see, closely interrelated. Moreover, confused thinking about infant baptism has led more than one person involved in the charismatic renewal to seek re-baptism after receiving what in the renewal is called "baptism in the Holy Spirit." The problem is rendered even more complex by ecumenical contact with Protestant Pentecostals who speak of "water baptism" as a "purely external" and "inefficacious" ritual. Moreover, Protestant Pentecostals are themselves divided on the question of infant baptism. The majority reject the practice. But a significant minority practice it.

There are three distinct but interrelated questions concerning the practice: (1) Does it have Biblical justification? (2) What is the purpose of the practice? (3) What is a sound pastoral approach to the baptism of infants?

There is a strong patristic witness during the first centuries to the fact that the apostles themselves practiced infant baptism. But Protestants who reject infant baptism do so because they find no evidence for such an affirmation in Scripture itself. Oscar Cullmann and Joachim Jeremias have, however, suggested four arguments in support of belief in a New Testament witness to infant baptism. This is no place to reproduce their arguments in detail. But they encompass the following points. First, the practice of baptising entire households is mentioned more than once in Acts. Moreover, the word used for "household" designates a family whose membership includes small children. Second, by Jewish law, infants were circumcised on the eighth day. In its historical context, Paul's insistence that Christian baptism replaces circumcision can, therefore, be read as a theological justification for the salvific sufficiency of infant baptism. Third, the story of Jesus blessing the children is too trivial an incident to have been preserved scripturally were it not a theological justification for admitting infants into the community. Fourth, the practice of infant baptism is tacitly assumed by the biblical writers. Had baptism been restricted to adults, one would expect to find in the New Testament some evidence of the fact that Christian families were divided into community members and non-members. But no such evidence exists. On the contrary, Paul addresses the children in the community as members alone with everyone else.

There is, however, serious doubt that the question of infant baptism can be resolved by exegetical arguments alone. The mere fact that the apostles baptised infants does not in itself prove that the practice ought to be continued universally today. Moreover, underlying exegetical arguments for infant baptism or against it are a host of presuppositions about the meaning and purpose of sacramental worship which derive, not from Scripture, but from medieval and reformation theology. Until those presuppositions are faced as such and their inadequacies corrected, the argumentative citation of Biblical text and countertext is likely to bear as little ecumenical fruit in the present as it has in the past. It is, then, necessary to move beyond exegesis to a reflection of the purpose of infant baptism and the relative merits of the arguments for and against it.

Some possible "justifications" of the practice are manifestly inadequate. Infant baptism should not, for example be perpetuated simply in order to keep the churches numerically large. Some Christians certainly fear for a variety of practical and pastoral reasons that the discontinuation of infant baptism would result in reduced Church membership. But such fear is not a theological argument. The healthy expansion of the Church ought to be the fruit of conversion. Moreover, there are a number of serious pastoral considerations which would seem to call the practice of infant baptism into question. Of those baptised as children not a few abandon the Church in later life often for lack of commitment. Others

remain church goers but live at a primitive level of religious awareness. Some Protestant theologians have attempted to justify infant
baptism by portraying it as the ritual confirmation of some kind of
germinal faith in the infant. The argument is, however, far-fetched.
Nor has anyone ever provided a convincing explanation of what
such "infantile faith" might consist in.

But if some of the arguments in favor of infant baptism are
theologically questionable, so too are many of the arguments
against it. It has, for example, been urged that infant baptism be
abandoned because the sacramental ritual is a purely external rite
and devoid of salvific efficacy. Both affirmations are untenable.
The word which is pronounced over the child in baptism is identical with the word pronounced over the adult convert. As we have
seen, however, the sacramental word pronounced over the adult has
the efficacy of a prophetic judgment and an intercessory efficacy
that is contingent on the proper dispositions of the sacramental
worshipper. Both forms of efficacy attend the baptismal word spoken over a child. The fact that the child does not comprehend the
baptismal word at the time it. is spoken does not diminish its efficacy any more than the human incapacity of the infant Jesus to
understand the prophetic word of Simeon in the temple diminished
its prophetic efficacy. And truly, an event which changes an experience efficaciously is immanent to that experience, even though it
remains unconscious. Moreover, the efficacious impact of baptism
upon the life of a child is enormous. For it is creative of a matrix
of graced, lifelong relationships which are the only environmental
context adequate to nurture integral personal development in faith.
Moreover, the graces of baptism span a lifetime. Hence, while an
infant can pose no obstacle to grace at the time of baptism, it can
pose multiple obstacles in the course of a lifetime.

It has also been urged against infant baptism that no one can
be brought to baptism, because the sacrament must seal an act of
faith. And since the child is incapable of faith, it ought not to be
baptised. Such an objection is in fact an instance of the "essence
fallacy," for it presupposes incorrectly that the sacraments in each
instance mediate divine life in essentially the same way. The sacraments, as the old adage has it, mediate grace by signifying it. The
grace mediated is the grace signified. The mediation of grace in a

sacrament is, then, a function of the sacrament's meaning. And within any sacramental act there are three distinguishable levels of meaning: a common meaning, a situational meaning, and a personal meaning. The meaning common to all the sacraments is that described at the beginning of this chapter. A sacrament is an act of new covenant worship which, through the presence of an authorized minister engages the faith of the Church universal by challenging the recipient of the sacrament kerygmatically and prophetically to an appropriate response in faith to the graces ritually proclaimed and sought from God in the name of Jesus and in the power of His Spirit.

But besides this generic meaning, each sacrament has a core of meaning proper to itself. This second level of meaning is defined by the sacrament's symbolic relevance to a generic kind of human situation: to integral community initiation, to the need for spiritual and physical healing, to initiation into marriage and apostolic ministry, to the service of worship in a eucharistic covenant renewal. This second level of meaning differentiates one sacrament from another generically and defines the kind of grace proper to that sacrament.

But the full salvific meaning of a sacrament is not exhausted by these more or less abstractly definable characteristics. For a sacrament takes on concrete meaning only in its application to the life of a specific individual. This third level of meaning is constituted by the concrete tendencies operative in the salvific situation of the person who is the focus of the sacramental prayer.

This third level of meaning is proper to each emergent person in his or her concreteness. It cannot, then, be grasped by an abstraction applicable to all believers. It is not proper to any sacrament as such. Nor is it a trait common to all sacraments. The presence of personal sin in the adult is just such a concrete variable in his or her salvific situation. And it transmutes the total meaning of baptism when it is administered to the adult convert. Since the same variable is not present in the experience of the child at the moment of baptism, the total salvific significance of the sacrament is proportionally altered. Since, therefore, the sacraments effect grace by signifying it, baptism effects grace differently in the child and in the adult. In the adult it forgives personal sin by sealing personal repentance and conversion to faith in the triune God, and it removes original sin by introducing the adult into a charismatic Christian community of faith. In the case of the child it simply removes original sin, for it cannot signify the forgiveness of non-existent personal sins. In addition, the sacrament challenges the child to respond in faith during the course of its life to the graces which membership in the Christian community brings.

It has also been argued that the practice of baptising infants is indefensible because it is linked to an individualistic conception of the "infusion" of grace. But not every concern with personal salvation can be dismissed as "individualism." It becomes such when it seeks to divorce the reception of saving grace from its ecclesial and sacramental context. Far from seeking to effect such a divorce, however, the practice of infant baptism affirms the infant's salvific relationship with God to be a function of his or her developing relationship with the rest of the believing community. It is, then, the very opposite of soteriological individualism. In its earliest formulations, however, much Protestant theology gives evidence of having been tinged by such subjectivistic individualism. Grace was often portrayed as coming to individuals in the "inmost recesses" of the heart. Only subsequent to that transformation were "external" links established with the believing community. Such an approach to grace is open to serious question. For it describes grace in dualistic, philosophical categories that completely sunder the inner from the outer person, the individual from society, transcendence to God from transcendence into the community and the world.

An experiential approach to the process of conversion has, however, revealed that grace enters experience, not "within subjectivity," but, as an environmental impulse. Ordinarily it comes to visibility in symbolic words and deeds which are expressive of the saving presence of God in other persons. Even were God alone to act directly and efficaciously upon an individual, that activity could come to consciousness only through the believer's interpretative response to it. But the symbolic structures operative in that response are environmentally derived. There is, then, no such thing as a purely subjective, conscious experience of grace. If, therefore, a young child is to experience saving grace, that grace must be mediated socially and environmentally: through social contact with acts of faith which are expressive symbols of grace and through environmentally derived structures of interpretation which mediate assent to a direct pneumatic impulse.

There is evidence that a high infant mortality rate helped motivate the early practice of infant baptism.[22] To interpose the sacrament between a child and all but certain death has a clear and legitimate meaning. It is a prophetic gesture, like the prophetic gestures performed by Jesus and the Old Testament prophets. It is also the act of a community of faith which claims the dying child for God and proclaims in the teeth of death the victory of Jesus over the grave.

Infant baptism is, then, an act of mature adults: it is performed by Christian parents and by the mature members of the Church to which they belong. The test of whether they truly believe in infant baptism is whether they are willing to assume responsibility for the practical consequences of such an act. One may, then, argue that many Christian communions which defend infant baptism speculatively against communities which reject the practice give serious evidence of not really believing the doctrine they teach so forensically. For there is a problem with infant baptism. The problem is not its theoretical justification but its pastoral advisability. The Catholic Church has always taught in theory that infants should not be baptised automatically. Parents who bring their infants for baptism should show evidence of sufficient religious conversion in their own lives to justify such an act. They must be capable of providing a faith environment informed by the gift of the Spirit to a degree that is sufficient to nurture the child's growth in Christ. One could, then, envisage the official, temporary suspension of infant baptism in parishes which give evidence of being imbued with serious religious inauthenticity.

For the real problem with infant baptism is that the environments into which young children are actually received are often only nominally Christian. Moreover, graces mediated through a family environment charismatically open to the Spirit can be all too effectively undermined by the sinfulness of the larger believing community. When the child's early experience of parish worship is one of boredom and hypocrisy, when (s)he regularly encounters adults who praise God in church but stand indifferent to the ills of human society, when (s)he discovers a church in which bourgeois values inform the fabric of life rather than the gospel ideals of faith-sharing, unrestricted love, and atoning service in worship, is it any wonder that the efficacious impulse of grace initiated by baptism is in more than one instance distorted into an angry, adolescent repudiation of the Church and even of God? In the faith experience of such a child there are obstacles *(obices)* enough to grace.

The practice of infant baptism is, then, theoretically justifiable within limits. It should not be done automatically. Each case should be subjected to discerning scrutiny. Moreover, the practice need not in principle be mandatory. For sound pastoral reasons, it could be replaced by an extended catechumenate followed at the appropriate time by sacramental baptism. Ultimate decision in these matters is, of course, reserved to those in the community with authority to bind and loose in the name of Jesus.

10. We are now in a position to clarify the relationship between baptism and the gifts of the Spirit. As a ritual act, baptism is a kerygmatic and prophetic challenge to the Christian neophyte to respond in faith to the God who has revealed Himself in Jesus and to do so as a member of the Pentecostal community He founded. The sacrament is also an intercession that the neophyte will respond each day to the transforming presence of the Spirit until (s)he shares fully in the glory of the risen Christ. As Vatican II insists, therefore, the graces of baptism encompass a lifetime; and, unless one falls from grace, they are sufficient for salvation. But if the salvific consequences of baptism are in fact so all encompassing, why are there any other sacraments? This much is initially clear: the reason why there are other sacraments is not that the graces they mediate bear no relationship to baptism. On the contrary, every other sacramental act reaffirms and further specifies one's original baptismal covenant. The graces proper to baptism must, then, be understood reductively. They are not the graces proper to confirmation and the other sacraments. As we shall see, however, the other six sacraments are all intimately linked with the gifts of service. Reductively, then, the service gifts cannot be the proper grace of baptism.

The sacraments, as we have just seen, cause grace by signifying it. As rituals, moreover, their meaning is in part a function of the life situation which they address. Baptism is a rite of acceptance into the Church universal. And it speaks to the commitment that is demanded of any person publicly decided to live in the name and image of Jesus. The complete rite of Christian initiation has a double focus: belief in Jesus and belief in the transforming power of the Spirit. This is only appropriate; for the God whom Christians adore takes experiential shape in the twofold mission of the Son and of the Spirit.

When baptism is contrasted with the rite of confirmation, it is seen to be Jesus-centered. Besides faith in the triune God it demands the renunciation of Satan in the image of Jesus, the Spirit-filled founder of the new Israel. To renounce Satan in Jesus' image is, however, as we have seen, to stand open in faith to the Spirit who teaches us to put on the mind of Jesus. It is to stand committed to the ethical vision described in chapter II of this book. To grow in that vision is to grow in the gifts of sanctification. Since the graces of baptism span a lifetime and since, as we shall see, the service gifts define the graces proper to the other sacraments, among the basic graces mediated by the sacrament of baptism is lifelong docility to the Spirit in putting on the mind of Jesus: in other words, lifelong growth in the gifts of sanctification. Actual growth in the sanctifying gifts presupposes, however, that the believer place no obstacles to the sanctifying action of the Spirit. Chief among the obstacles which stifle the Spirit are, of course, lack of conversion at an affective, intellectual, or moral level.

11. The theology of confirmation is a tangle of thorny speculative problems. Recent exegesis has, for example, cast considerable speculative doubt on the classical biblical "proofs" employed by Catholic manual theology to establish the existence of confirmation as a separate sacrament in apostolic times. The classic "proof text" was, of course, Acts 8:4-24. The passage was even cited by the Council of Florence as an instance of the apostolic administration of confirmation. It describes the mission of Peter and John to the Samaritans whom the deacon Philip had evangelised and baptised, in order that the apostles might pray for them to receive the Holy Spirit. The text would, then, seem to describe the

post-baptismal administration of what today is called the sacrament of confirmation.

Florence's reference to the passage is more a doctrinal than an exegetical statement. The Council fathers simply noted that the qualitative characteristics which they had defined to be essential to the sacrament of confirmation can be found in the Lukan narrative: a post-baptismal invocation of the Spirit by the apostolic leaders of the community.[23] The citation in Florence is then, the invocation of a scholastic *auctoritas*, rather than a strict exegesis.

There are, however, serious problems with too naive an exegetical reading of the passage. As we shall see, historical evidence points to the fact that baptism and confirmation were not dissociated until long after the apostolic era. Luke seems, moreover, to present the mission and activity of the apostles to the Samaritans, not as a typical act of ritual worship, but as an extraordinary measure justified by a perplexing and exceptional pastoral situation. The text suggests that the Samaritans' failure to respond to the gifts of the Spirit even after baptism was rooted in their fascination with the magical practices of Simon. And the incident appropriately culminates in Peter's confrontation with Simon and in the latter's repentance. Rather than offering an account of typical sacramental practice in the early Church, therefore, Luke seems to be describing a pastoral anomaly.[24]

Until recent developments in Biblical criticism, Acts 8 offered Catholic sacramentology what seemed to be its strongest Biblical argument for the apostolic origin of the sacrament of confirmation. But once that argument was exegetically undermined, it became increasingly difficult to discover any other unambiguous Scriptural text to replace it.[25]

Liturgical theology has also raised some unanswered questions about confirmation. Investigation into the historical development of Christian initiation has refocused attention on the diversity of church disciplines surrounding this sacrament. Early Christian community initiations seem to have proceeded in three stages: first baptism, ordinarily by immersion; then, the laying on of hands and invocation of the Holy Spirit; third, first eucharistic communion. This primitive ritual pattern is preserved in the Christian Oriental tradition in both adult and infant initiation.

In the Western Church, the three stages of community initiation have become temporarily separated. The dissociation of ritual baptism from the invocation of the Spirit seems to have occurred largely for disciplinary reasons. Western Christians came to feel that the solemn invocation of the Holy Spirit was of sufficient importance to be reserved to the bishop. With time, the last two stages of the initiatory rite were postponed until the child was sufficiently mature to perform them intelligently.[26]

Within the Western Christian tradition, moreover, churches which hold for all seven sacraments have in some instances developed different ritual patterns in the administration of confirmation. The Anglican communion has preferred to postpone first communion until after confirmation, while Catholics allow for first communion before confirmation.

The questions raised by this disparity of ritual practice are many. Were the disciplinary departures from the original rite of initiation theologically justified; and, if so, on what grounds? Can one justify infant confirmation and infant first communion? If the separation of confirmation from baptism is ritually justified, must confirmation precede communion?

Dialectical developments within Christian sacramentology further complicate the attempt to reflect on confirmation. Since the Protestant reformation a significant number of Christian communions do not acknowledge confirmation as a sacrament instituted by Christ. Besides citing the lack of decisive biblical arguments to support the sacramental character of the ritual, many Protestants reject confirmation as a theological contradiction. It is absurd, they contend, to be initiated twice into the same community. Since, moreover, the Holy Spirit is given in baptism, they find it meaningless to affirm that He can be given again in confirmation. The ecumenical movement has inclined Catholic theologians to be more sensitive to such arguments than they have been in the past. As a result, a Catholic theology of confirmation stands at a bit of an impasse. One possible way out of the impasse is renewed insight into the purpose of ritual confirmation. To reach such an insight, one must situate the sacrament within the dynamics of a Christian conversion experience.

The global character of baptismal consent and its centrality to

Christian conversion sets it in a positive relationship with all other, graced pneumatic impulses. They either lead to or flow from baptism. It is this fact which makes baptism "necessary for salvation." The relationship of the other sacraments to baptism is not, then, static and essentialistic, but dynamic and genetic. It is analogous to the relation which exists between the sanctifying gifts and the gift of faith, between the gift of faith and the service gifts. For the other sacraments further concretize baptismal consent by integrating new decisive variables into the open ended faith-commitment of the Christian neophyte. They are, in other words, ritual transmutations of baptismal consent. And being sacraments, they effect this transmutation in the context of a solemn, public reaffirmation of one's baptismal covenant with God.

We have seen that the basic ethical structure of a developing Christian faith commitment demands that it come to sacramental expression. We have also seen that the decision demanded by sacramental baptism entails that one live in graced openness to the gifts of sanctification. Our analysis of the gifts of sanctification has also revealed, however, that one cannot consent authentically to them without consenting to being called by the Spirit to some form of ecclesial service. But, as we have also seen, consent to the gifts of sanctification must be distinguished from consent to this or that service gift. The distinction is once again best understood in genetic, rather than in static essentialistic categories. But it remains nevertheless real. The decision embodied in one's response to the gifts of sanctification is the decision to put on the mind of Jesus. It is common to all Christians. The service gifts are not common to all believers in this sense: that not everyone receives the same gift of service, even though all are normally called to receive some service gift. The service gifts, moreover, by personalizing and specifying the commitment of faith-dependence nourished by the sanctifying gifts endow the life of a believer with a specific sign-value. The service gifts, therefore, mediate the kind of visible transformation of a pneumatic faith-experience which the apostles underwent on Pentecost.

As the encyclical *Divinum illud munus* suggests, the Spirit did not descend on the apostles for the first time on Pentecost.[27] They could never have consented to Jesus as Messiah and risen Lord without being moved efficaciously to do so by the Spirit. The purpose of the Spirit's Pentecostal descent was, therefore, to inaugurate their visible pneumatic transformation in a manner that paralleled Jesus' visible transformation subsequent to His baptismal experience. The liturgical distinction between Easter and Pentecost is, therefore, grounded at the level of conversion in the distinction between consent to baptismal faith and the gifts of sanctification, on the one hand, and consent to the service gifts on the other. This insight takes on sacramental significance in the light of Church teaching concerning the sacrament of confirmation. The official pastoral catechesis has rejected the notion that confirmation is the sacrament of Christian adolescence, the sacrament of Catholic Action, or the completion of religious formation. It is, as the council of Florence teaches, the Pentecost of the individual Christian.[28] That is to say, in confirmation the sacramental worshipper professes personal willingness to be transformed visibly by the Spirit as the apostles were transformed on Pentecost. The ritual does not embody consent to any specific service gift. Rather it is the public profession of personal readiness to respond to whatever gift(s) of service the Spirit may choose to give in the course of one's development as a converted Christian.

A sacramental ritual ought to express the dynamics of a Christian conversion experience. Initiation into the Spirit-filled new Israel ought to include the explicit invocation of the Pentecostal Spirit on the neophyte; for Pentecost is the event which founds the Church as such, and lifelong openness to whatever service gift(s) the Spirit may give is the unavoidable consequence of integral conversion to Christ. But if the preceding reflections are sound, there is no single way of ritualizing that invocation. The separation of baptism from confirmation gives ritual expression to the fact that the initial consent of faith and consent to the gifts of sanctification is not simply identical with consent to this or that service gift. Their simultaneous administration dramatizes the fact that one cannot consent authentically to the triune God in sanctifying faith unless that consent includes a willingness to accept whatever gift of service the Spirit may choose to give. Similarly, growth in the gifts of sanctification is among the chief graces of baptism. To grow in the gifts of sanctification includes the desire to offer the

Father authentic worship and praise. Since the Christian community of worship is a eucharistic community, first holy communion crowns baptismal consent and is more directly related to it than to consent to this or that service gift. Hence, first communion prior to confirmation is justified by the dynamics of normal charismatic development, although confirmation prior to communion has the advantage of preserving the ritual order of the earliest baptismal celebrations of the Church. The infantile administration of confirmation is, moreover, justifiable on the same terms as infant baptism. But some form of the sacramental invocation of the Pentecostal Spirit is integral to full community initiation, even though like the word of baptism, it is a prophetic word and an efficacious prayer of the Church whose total pragmatic effectiveness is contingent upon the child's failure to place obstacles to the activity of the Spirit in the course of subsequent personal development. Hence, too, the pastoral advisability of infant confirmation is subject to the same qualifications as infant baptism.

It has been objected that the infantile administration of any sacrament would justify the infantile administration of them all. Such an objection falls victim, however, to the same "essence fallacy" noted above. It presupposes that there is a common essence to all the sacraments and that, as a consequence, what is predicated of one must be predicated of them all. But while the rituals of baptism and confirmation are relevant to the situation of an infant whom the Christian community desires to accept as its member and nurture in Christ, the rituals of marriage, orders, reconciliation, and anointing of the sick are not. That this is so should become clearer as we reflect more in detail on these other rituals.

The preceding reflections also cast light upon some of the exegetical perplexities which have surrounded the sacrament of confirmation. The reason why there are no clear biblical references to a separate rite of confirmation would seem to be that in apostolic times the rite had not yet developed into its present form. At the same time, Jesus' promise of the Spirit, His fulfillment of that promise in Pentecost, the community's experience of the different Pauline gifts as calls giving personal specification to the more general summons of the Spirit to "put on Jesus' mind," and the community's realization that committed openness to the reception of some service gift is integral to the commitment which mediates one's entry into the community—all these beliefs have ample biblical grounding and provide sufficient textual justification for the traditional teaching concerning the sacrament of confirmation: that it is a sacrament "instituted by Christ to give grace."

Those who deny the sacramentality of confirmation commonly do so on the grounds that one cannot be initiated twice into the same community and that the Spirit who was sent in baptism cannot be sent again in confirmation. But human communities commonly establish stages in the initiatory process. Moreover, with the possible exception of the anointing of the sick, every sacrament has some sort of initiatory significance. And even the sacrament of the sick involves the reaffirmation of one's baptismal covenant in the face of serious illness and possible death. Confirmation is initiation into personal public service in the community through lifelong openness to the Pauline gifts. Marriage is initiation into the specific responsibilities of Christian parenthood. Orders is initiation into official leadership in service within the Christian community. Sacramental reconciliation mediates re-initiation into the community after some serious fault has excluded one from full communion. First communion is the culmination of the initiatory process. The eucharist is the public re-affirmation of one's baptismal initiation. And viaticum is initiation into glory.

To say the Spirit cannot be sent to any individual more than once is another oversimplification. The sending of the Spirit cannot be restricted to the single moment of baptism or to the reception to a specific gift, like tongues. It encompasses the total pneumatic transformation of human experience. St. Thomas correctly observes that the sending of a divine person implies (1) a relation of divine origin in the Godhead and (2) the salvific transformation of human experience. Thus, the Spirit proceeds from the Father and Son from all eternity, but His sending is the salvific transformation of the Church. Aquinas correctly distinguished two aspects of the Spirit's mission: His permanent indwelling and His "surprises" (innovationes). The indwelling of the Spirit is His constant, pre-conscious presence to the believer as a sustaining and healing life-source. His "surprises" are the pneumatic breakthroughs He effects, especially by means of the gifts of service.[29] Every time a believer is visibly transformed by some new gift of service, one may, then, speak appropriately and meaningfully of a "new sending" of the Spirit. The sacrament of confirmation pledges the believer to stand in lifelong openness to the Spirit's surprises. And it affirms such openness to be binding on all who are covenanted to God in the image of Jesus.

When administered separately, therefore, confirmation ought to be understood as the second stage of initiation into the Church universal. Since the sacrament is strictly initiatory and affirms a new relationship to the universal Christian community by calling the believer to public, Spirit-led service, the sacrament "seals" the believer in the same special and solemn manner as baptism. That "sealing" is its sacramental "character."

In our argument so far, we have attempted to make the following points: (1) Any ritualization of Christian initiation is legitimate which is truly expressive of a consent of faith to the God who has revealed Himself in Jesus and in the Holy Spirit. Since however, induction into the Christian community is an act of the Church universal, the form of the ritual ought to express a discerning consensus of the entire believing community. (2) The consent of faith is inauthentic unless it includes consent to its consequences: i.e., to lifelong growth in the gifts of sanctification. Consent to lifelong growth in the gifts of sanctification is inauthentic unless it includes consent to its consequences: i.e., to lifelong willingness to accept whatever gift of service the Spirit chooses to give. (3) Since consent to the gifts of sanctification is a consequence of the consent of faith it is not simply identical with the consent of faith. Since consent to lifelong openness to whatever service gifts the Spirit may choose to give is a consequence of consent to the sanctifying gifts, it is not simply identical with consent to the sanctifying gifts. (4) Consent to lifelong openness to whatever service gifts the Spirit may choose to give is integral to the consent demanded by Christian initiation: its ritualization, whatever form it may take, is not optional and may be legitimately called "confirmation."

The graces of any sacrament can, of course, be given outside the sacramental system. The Spirit is not bound by ritual. But the mere fact that a grace is so given is no proof that it ought to be. For one cannot respond authentically in love to a grace that binds one in covenant to the Christian community while repudiating the ritual which embodies such a commitment. To consent to the gifts of service but remain closed to some legitimate sacramental sealing of that consent is, then, to introduce some element of inauthenticity into one's personal response to God.[30]

12. We are now in a position to evaluate critically some popular expressions of charismatic piety. The rhetoric of charismatic Christians is the language of personal faith; but it sometimes leaves something to be desired. One observes, for example, a penchant for a kind of God-talk that seems to obliterate concern with natural and human causes. As a consequence, "leave it to God" can on occasion degenerate into a variation on "let George do it."

The phrase "the baptism in the Holy Spirit" is also somewhat theologically abrasive. The problem is not with "baptism in the Holy Spirit" but with the article "the." For the article seems to tie Spirit-baptism to a single moment in human experience. In point of fact, Spirit-baptism is a lifetime process. It cannot be equated with any single graced experience, much less with the reception of any single service gift, like tongues. Jesus Himself did not enter into relationship with the Spirit for the first time on the Jordan. The virginal conception of Jesus proclaimed in the infancy gospels, whatever its full exegetical meaning, is in part an attempt by the evangelists to affirm that from the very first moment of conception, Jesus stood in a positive relationship with the Holy Spirit. Moreover, even after His Jordan experience, Jesus could say: "There is a baptism I must still receive, and how great is my distress until it is over!" If, then, the Spirit comes in order to conform us to Jesus, Catholic charismatics should be sensitive not to speak as though they enjoyed pneumatic privileges which Jesus Himself lacked. Jesus' Spirit-baptism was a lifelong transformation in the Spirit, culminating in His glorification. But He experienced a moment of decisive "charismatic" breakthrough in His messianic anointing. Every Christian is called to a Pentecostal moment analogous to Jesus' Jordan anointing. It consists in the initial reception of one or more of the service gifts. It effects the intensification and personalization of baptismal faith. It may be reached gradually or suddenly. But when it occurs it ought to change visibly a person's life into a public act of witness to Jesus.

Such a moment may also be legitimately designated "*a* baptism in the Holy Spirit," that is, a deeper plunging into the Spirit received in baptism. It may be called "an experience of Spirit-baptism." But it may not be called "*the* baptism in the Holy Spirit," for the simple reason that there is much more to "Spirit-baptism" than the experience of a Pentecostal breakthrough. The phrase "a fuller release of the gifts of the Spirit" may, however, be used to describe the Pentecostal moment in personal religious development, provided one does not imagine that all of the gifts of the Spirit lie latent in each believer waiting to be triggered.

Similarly, Catholic charismatics must stop using the term "Spirit-filled" or "Christian" in a restrictive sense. The only person who possessed the plentitude of the Spirit was Jesus; only He, then, was truly "Spirit-filled." A Christian who is growing charismatically is at best only "Spirit-led," whether or not (s)he attends prayer meetings.

The dramatic changes in people's lives effected by prayer for "Spirit-baptism" are instances of what Abraham Maslow has described as a "peak experience."[31] "Peak experiences" bring a sense of detachment from pedestrian concerns, a feeling of self-transcendence. They are self-validating experiences, whose value needs no proof for the one who has them. In a peak experience, one often loses a sense of space and time. One is enraptured by a sense of beauty, value. One feels oneself in contact with a reality which is eminently desirable. Peak experiences are more contemplative than ordinary experiences: peak experiences induce a certain passivity in the face of reality, a wonder, awe, reverence, humility, surrender. They also bring a diminishment of fear, anxiety, and inhibition. They tend to effect an enduring transformation in the one who has them. Peak experiences bring self-integration, freedom, the enhancement of creativity, and greater selflessness in one's action. In peak experiences one is intensely aware of being a person, not an object, and of bearing responsibility for one's self and one's life. Peak experiences engage the deeper motives which function in human experience. And they combine a proper evaluation of one's self with the ecstatic affirmation of values that go beyond oneself. Not every "peak experience" has an overt religious character. In religious peaks, however, one senses an assimilation to the divine. One encounters realities that go beyond this world. Moreover, in religious peaks, God is encountered in the concrete, in some person, experience, event which mediates a sense of the Holy.

If the service gifts are in fact rooted in the gift of faith, and if the gift of faith mediates the concrete personalization and interiorization of baptismal consent, is it any surprise that, when a baptised Christian reaches an initial moment of genuine charismatic breakthrough, it would tend to take the form of a peak experience? Here, however, several cautions are in order: (1) No one lives at a constant peak. Peak experiences give rise to plateau experiences and may evey be followed by a descent into the lower emotional depths. (2) The ability to have a peak experience is a function of one's emotional makeup. Not everyone peaks easily. Nor is the ability to peak a condition for receiving one of the gifts of service. The Spirit's call need not be dramatic; it can be a very pedestrian experience. (3) To covet peak experiences is to fall into "spiritual gluttony." It is a form of testing God. (4) Nonpeakers should not despise peakers. All things being equal it is better to peak than not to peak. Emotional inhibition can also block personal response to others and an integral response to grace.

There is, however, no necessity that any sacramental experience be a peak experience for it to be either a genuine covenant renewal or a grace-filled, Spirit-led act. There is no psychic necessity, for not everyone is a peaker. Nor can peak experiences be controlled manipulatively. There is no necessity on the part of God, since He is free to dispense His gifts to peakers and nonpeakers alike, whenever and however He chooses. There is no necessity in the gifts themselves, for one can consent authentically to a gift of the Spirit without peaking at all. Finally, because confirmation is initiatory, its graces like baptism's span a lifetime. The covenant commitment made in confirmation is to live in constant openness to whatever gifts and graces the Spirit may choose to give. And He may choose to give them long after the ritual is administered.

Hence, it makes no sense to seek re-baptism just because one has reached a charismatic "peak." It is understandable that one who has experienced an initial charismatic breakthrough might want as a consequence to renew his or her baptismal covenant. But there are rituals available for renewing one's baptismal commitment, and they may be appropriately embellished by those who are liturgically imaginative. The re-administration of baptism as such is, however, ritually confusing, for it seems to call into question the ritual efficacy of one's initial sacramental covenant. The practice is, therefore, doctrinally unsound and should be excluded from Catholic prayer groups.

Notes

1. Cf. Ernst Cassirer, *The Philosophy of Symbolic Forms*, translated by Ralph Manheim (3 vols.; New Haven: Yale, 1955) vol. II; Erich Neumann, *The Origins and History of Consciousness*, translated by R.F.C. Hull (Princeton: Princeton, 1954); Mircea Eliade, *Patterns in Comparative Religion*, translated by Rosemary Sheed (N.Y.: World, 1963).

2. Neumann, *op. cit.* pp. 220-256.

3. Cf. G.B. Caird, *Principalities and Powers* (Oxford: Oxford at Clarendon, 1956) pp. 1-23.

4. Cf. Charles Moeller, ed., *Satan* (N.Y.: Sheed and Ward, 1951) pp. 3-18. The attempt to completely demythologize devils has not been totally successful. For an insight into some of the controversy on this question, see: Ruth Nanda Anshen, *The Reality of the Devil: Evil in Man* (N.Y.: Harper and Row, 1972); Don Basham, *Deliver us from Evil* (Washington: Chosen, 1972); H.A. Kelly, *The Devil, Demonology, and Witchcraft* (N.Y.: Doubleday, 1968); "Demonology and Diabolical Temptation," *Thought*, XL (June, 1956) pp. 165-194; "The Devil in the Desert," *Catholic Biblical Quarterly* (April, 1974) pp. 190-220; Jeffry Russell, *Witchcraft in the Middle Ages* (Ithaca: Cornell, 1972); F.B. Welbourn, "Exorcism," *Theology* (1972) pp. 593-596; S. Vernan McCasland, *By the Finger of God* (N.Y.: Macmillan, 1951); Moeller, *op. cit.*

5. Caird, *Principalities and Powers*, pp. 31-37.

6. *Ibid.*, pp. 39-42.

7. *Ibid.*, pp. 43-54.

8. *Ibid.*, pp. 69-98.

9. Lk 4:31-37, 9:37-43, 13:10-17, 6:6-11, 10:17-20; Mt 1:21-28, 12:22-32, 16:21-33, 17:14-18, 19:1-8; Mk 8:31-33, 9:14-27; Jn 5:1-47.

10. Paul Ricoeur, *The Symbolism of Evil*, translated by Emerson Buchanan (Boston: Beacon, 1967) pp. 232-278.

11. Mircea Eliade, *Cosmos and History: The Myth of the Eternal Return* (N.Y.: Harper, 1954).

12. Ricoeur, *op. cit.*, pp. 211-231.

13. Cf. Henri Rondet, S.J. *Original Sin: Patristic and Theological Background*, translated by Cajetan Finegan, O.P. (Staten Island: Alba House, 1972); Zoltan Alszeghy, S.J. and Maurizio Flick, S.J. "Il peccato originale in prospettiva evoluzionistica," *Gregorianum*, XLVII (1966) pp. 201-259; "Il peccato originale in prospettiva personalistica," *Gregorianum*, XLVI (1965) pp. 705-732; Patrick Burke, "Man without Christ: An approach to Hereditary Sin," *Theological Studies*, XXIX (March, 1968) pp. 4-18; James L. Connor, "Original Sin: Contemporary Approaches," *Theological Studies*, XXIX (June, 1968) pp. 215-240; Bruce J. Molina, "Some Observations on the Origin of Sin in Judaism and St. Paul," *Catholic Biblical Quarterly*, XXXI (January, 1969) pp. 18-34; Piet Schoonenberg, *Man and Sin*, translated by Joseph Donceel, S.J. (Notre Dame: University of Notre Dame, 1965); Michael J. Taylor, S.J., ed., *The Mystery of Sin and Forgiveness* (N.Y.: Alba House, 1973) pp. 21-277; DS 222-223, 1312, 1314-1316, 1513.

14. Schoonenberg, *op. cit.*

15. DS 3896-3898; cf. Karl Rahner, S.J., "Theological Reflections on Monogenism," *Theological Investigations*, I, pp. 229-296.

16. DS 1515; the approach to "concupiscence" offered here differs in its philosophical presuppositions from that offered by Karl Rahner: Cf. *Theological Investigations* (Baltimore: Helicon, 1961) I, pp. 347ff.

17. DS 781, 1313, 1609, 1767, 1864, 2536.

18. Max Thurian, *Consecration of the Layman*, translated by W.J. Kerrigan (Baltimore: Helicon, 1963) p. 31.

19. Jn 3:22-23.

20. DS 1606.

21. For more recent controversy, see: Karl Barth, *The Teaching of*

the Church Regarding Baptism, translated by Ernest A. Payne (London: S.C.M. Press, 1965); Oscar Cullmann, *Baptism in the New Testament*, translated by J.K.S. Reid (Chicago: Regnery, 1950); Joachim Jeremias, *Infant Baptism in the First Four Centuries* (Philadelphia: Westminster, 1960); James McClendon, "Why Baptists Do not Baptise Infants," in *The Sacraments: An Ecumenical Dilemma* (N.Y.: Paulist, 1967) pp. 1-15; K. Aland, *Did the Early Church Baptise Infants?* (London: 1963); George Beasley-Murray, *Baptism in the New Testament* (London: Macmillan, 1963); O. Hallesby, *Infant Baptism and Adult Conversion*, translated by Clarence J. Carlson (Minneapolis: Augsburg, 1964); Michael Hurley, S.J. "What Can Catholics Learn from the Infant Baptism Controversy?" in *The Sacraments: An Ecumenical Dilemma* (N.Y.: Paulist, 1967).

22. DS 184.

23. DS 1318.

24. Cf. James Dunn, *Baptism in the Holy Spirit* (Naperville: A.R. Allenson, 1970); for a critique of Dunn's position on Spirit-baptism, see: George T. Montague, S.M. "Baptism in the Spirit and Speaking in Tongues," *Theology Digest*, XXI (Winter, 1973) pp. 342-361.

25. Cf. Kilian McDonnell, O.S.B. and Arnold Bittlinger, *The Baptism in the Holy Spirit as an Ecumenical Problem* (Notre Dame: Charismatic Renewal Services, 1972); Raymond E. Brown, S.S., "We Profess One Baptism for the Forgiveness of Sins," *Worship*, XL (May, 1966) pp. 260-271.

26. Cf. Charles Davis, *Sacraments of Initiation: Baptism and Confirmation* (N.Y.: Sheed and Ward, 1964); Adalbert Hamman, *Le batème et la confirmation* (Paris: Desclée, 1969); Lutfi Laham, "Der penumatologische Aspekte der Sakramente der Christlichen Mystagogie (oder Initiation)," *Kyrios* (1972) pp. 97-106.

27. *Divinum illud munus*, 20-21.

28. DS 1319.

29. *Summa Theologiae*, I, Q. XLIII, see especially, a. 3.

30. For a discussion of the position of Protestant Pentecostals on Spirit-baptism see: Walter Hollenweger, *The Pentecostals: The Charismatic Movement in the Churches* (Minneapolis: Augsburg, 1972); Frederick Dale Brunner, *A Theology of The Holy Spirit* (London: Hodder and Stoughton, 1971); James Dunn, *op. cit.*; John Hardon, S.J. *Protestant Churches of America* (N.Y.: Image, 1969) pp. 169-185; Kilian McDon-

nell, O.S.B., "The Ecumenical Significance of the Pentecostal Movement," *Worship*, XL (December, 1966) pp. 608-629; Herbert Schneider, S.J., "Heiligung und Geisttaufe: Herkunft und Ziele der Pfinstbewegung," *Stimmen der Zeit* (December, 1972) pp. 426-428; Emmanuel Sullivan S.J. "Can the Pentecostal Movement Renew the Churches?" *Study Encounter* VIII (1972) pp. 1-16; Simon Tugwell, O.P., "Reflections on the Pentecostal Doctrine of Baptism in the Holy Spirit," *Heythrop Journal* (1972) pp. 402-414.

31. Abraham Maslow, *Religions, Values, and Peak Experiences* (N.Y.: Viking, 1964).

VI
Marriage and
Celibacy

1. An experiential approach to Christian marriage ought to be rooted in an understanding of the normal patterns of human psycho-sexual development.[1] Children begin normal sexual growth in discovering their own bodies. Little boys discover that they are different from little girls; and they learn that the difference is visible in the shape of their genitalia. Little girls discover that they are different from little boys, that they do not have the same kind of externally visible sex organs. This initial discovery can trigger a variety of emotional reactions. The boy's feelings may be colored by anxiety: he may fear that his genitalia may somehow be mutilated or taken away. The little girl may feel that she has been short-changed, that she is in some way inferior. In both cases the child's emotional reactions to these early sexual discoveries can lead to a strong emotional identification with the parent of the opposite sex. When it occurs, this identification tends to be only temporary. It is eventually repressed and replaced by a strong emotional identification with the parent of the same sex.

The physical changes of puberty signal the onset of adolescence. In the pre-adolescent, they enter consciousness in vague body sensations and in mingled apprehension and eagerness as the child looks forward to personal sexual maturity. The period of full pubescence is marked by rapid physical development. These physical changes enter consciousness initially as emotional turmoil. And they help ground the adolescent's proverbial emotional instability. The emotional storms of early adolescence are symptomatic of a need to integrate evaluatively into experience the new biological variables which puberty brings.

In early adolescence, sexual feelings, repressed in childhood begin to surface, triggered by the child's rapid emotional and physiological development. Childhood attraction to the parent of the opposite sex may re-enter consciousness, tinged by feelings of guilt and hostility. The young adolescent manifests intense embarrassment if personal toilette is interrupted by the parent of the opposite sex. Childhood feelings of hostility emerge and help motivate a growing desire to be free of parental authority.

These physiological and emotional changes cause the disintegration of the familiar social relationships of childhood. The pubescent child begins to develop emotional distance from nurturing family relationships. The young adolescent copes with this disintegration in a variety of ways. Often (s)he finds emotional escape in a frenzy of activity. For such activity forestalls the need to face a tumult of feelings (s)he cannot fully understand or evaluate. Through exploratory dating, the emerging adolescent begins to create an alternate set of social relationships. Early heterosexual contacts are tentative, however, and marked by periodic withdrawal into more familiar forms of childhood behavior.

The rapid physical growth of adolescence enters conscious experience as intense body-awareness. The adolescent is concerned often to the point of anxiety with physiological processes. Adolescents worry about acne, about excessive sweating. They become intensely narcissistic and introspective. Adolescents of both sexes feel the need to expend large amounts of physical energy, often in sports. Adolescent sports also provide an important outlet for unresolved feelings of resentment and hostility. And sports in turn feed physical growth.

Adolescence also initiates intellectual awakening. The emerging young adult manifests a new capacity for abstract thinking. Interests and activities broaden. There is a conscious re-evaluation of childhood beliefs. And when this re-evaluation touches the religious sphere it can trigger a "crisis of faith."

With growing maturity, the adolescent is under increasing social pressure to assume the responsibilities of adult life. This often comes as a bit of a threat. Gradually initial rebellion against parental authority begins to assume a more generalized form. In middle adolescence, the emerging young adult tends to deepen in a fearful, felt sense of the inadequacies and inconsistencies present in the adult world (s)he is about to enter. The maturing adolescent becomes more critical of adult values, first in word but increasingly in action. Strong identification with one's peer group provides a social half-way house between the family of one's childhood and the world of adult responsibility toward which one is moving.

As psycho-sexual maturation proceeds, erotically colored feelings of guilt and anxiety continue to surface. In early and middle adolescence, young people spend a great deal of time fantasizing. And their fantasies are often erotic in tone. Masturbation tends to be statistically common especially among males. With time, mere sexual fantasies give way to a more realistic image of oneself as sexually mature.

As the young person moves toward late adolescence, heterosexual contacts begin to grow in complexity and depth. Late adolescence is ordinarily marked by growing religious and moral idealism, by a greater sureness of oneself and of one's ability to assume a functioning role in adult society, and by a greater clarity about the character of that role. Rebellion against the authority and values of one's parents takes on an increasingly social character. In late adolescence young people are apt to become politically involved in idealistic protest movements. They engage in active public criticism of the social, economic, and political "establishment."

In late adolescence, young people also begin to "play" with a certain seriousness at being an adult, but without actually assuming very many adult responsibilities. This role-playing functions as a kind of emotional dry-run for the impending serious business of life. The dry-run can include erotic factors, among them such behavior as the genital expression of craving and of affection outside of marriage.

In late adolescence, the emerging young adult manifests increasing independence of parental control. At the same time, peer friendships deepen. There is growing occupational self-definition, greater clarity about the role one will play in adult society. And there is the growing stabilization of the values which will function in subsequent adult decision making.

The resolution of adolescence is marked by final separation from parental control, by the establishment of an adult sexual identity, and by vocational commitment. The balanced young adult is capable of lasting friendship and of giving and receiving tender, sexual love. After a time of personal independence, the young adult ordinarily re-establishes a new relationship with his or her parents, one of relative equality. Finally, the young adult is assimilated more or less creatively into the social establishment from which the experience of adolescence had provided temporary alienation.

The preceding genetic analysis of adolescent growth and development conforms to the analysis of the transmutation of experience attempted in the first chapter of this book. The development of primary and secondary sex characteristics during puberty are the product of physical changes which result from the child's creative interaction with its environment. Part of that environment is the child's own developing body. Puberty changes the child's physiological makeup. And these new environmental changes enter conscious experience initially as vaguely felt emotion.

As the initial emotional tumult of adolescence develops, vague psycho-sexual feelings are transmuted into more or less conscious physical purposes. At first these physical purposes are more or less blind. They lack conceptual clarity and explode without a clear sense of direction. But as growth proceeds, erotically tinged physical purposes are transmuted into increasingly complex beliefs about oneself and the role one ought to play in society. These beliefs provide the evaluative ground for integrating the changes of adolescent growth into the emergent self. As a consequence of these physical and evaluative processes, there is a shift in one's nurturing environment. One's personal perspective on the world expands. There is a gradual redefinition of one's relational stance toward the persons and realities which function, first, in one's immediate family environment and, eventually, in one's larger social environment. One begins to derive one's life increasingly, then more or less exclusively, from other sources than one's childhood home. But in the normal processes of growth one eventually re-incorporates one's immediate family evaluatively into one's new emergent environment. In the process, family relationships are transmuted evaluatively into a different kind of experience. The entire process of adolescent growth is experienced as a process of self-transcendence, of novel self-definition through the re-evaluation of one's stance toward new and old variables operative in one's total emergent environment. The new subsistent relational reality which emerges from the process is the young adult.

What then ought to be the relationship between normal adolescent development and the experience of personal self-appropriation mediated by an integral, fourfold conversion?

2. The dynamics of normal adolescent growth might at first glance seem to force a moral conversion. In shifting from the world of childhood to adult existence, the adolescent is certainly forced to re-evaluate his or her stance toward childhood attitudes and values. But moral re-evaluation is not necessarily expressive of moral conversion. One is free in adolescence to substitute for passive moral dependence on one's parents passive moral dependence, first, on one's peer group and, then, on the institutional directives and authority figures one encounters in the adult world. Many adolescents are authoritarians in the making. But authentic moral conversion is rooted in personally responsible sensitivity to all of the legitimate human values which function in a given situation, not in craven submission to peer pressure or the voice of authority.

Similarly, adolescent growth tends spontaneously to give rise to some sort of faith crisis. The ideal resolution of such a crisis ought to be a personal religious conversion in which the emerging young adult assents with an adult mind and heart to a God whom he or she has encountered personally. But once again, there is no automatic assurance that conversion will occur.

Moreover, intellectual awakening during adolescence gives no automatic guarantee of producing a genuine intellectual conversion. The emerging young adult may cling in insecurity to the thought patterns of childhood by accepting blindly from any surrogate parental authority theoretical norms for what is true or false, valuable or valueless, emotionally satisfying or unsatisfying. But if the young adult is to achieve integral personal maturity, he or she must learn to assume personal responsibility for the formation of personal beliefs and for their theoretical and practical consequences. To do so, however, is to experience intellectual conversion.

Finally, the adolescent will surmount the emotional crisis of puberty successfully if he or she comes to a balanced evaluative insight into the feelings which early childhood experiences have shaped and into the emotions which accompany sexual maturation. Once again, however, the conversion process will not occur automatically. The emerging young adult may be overwhelmed by erotic impulses or by the conscious surfacing of feelings of hostility, fear, and repressed guilt. Or he or she may remain mired in the excessive narcissism that marks adolescence. Clearly, then, the emotional developments of adolescence can be surmounted successfully, only if the emerging young adult can be brought to face every feeling evaluatively without fear and take the appropriate means to insure balanced emotional growth. To assume such a stance is, however, to experience affective conversion.

Clearly, then, the failure to resolve the crisis of adolescence in an integral, four-fold conversion cripples young persons as they move into the world of adult reflection and decision. For without conversion at every level, the young adult must attempt to cope with problems of a complexity which transends the simplistic emotional, interpretative, and evaluative habits of both childhood and adolescence.

3. If, however, integral conversion is the goal of adolescent growth and if, as we have seen in the preceding chapters, adult commitment to God is mediated by docility to the gifts of the Spirit, then how ought the gifts of sanctification to function in the emergent experience of a Christian adolescent? If our analysis so far has in fact been sound, the gifts of sanctification ought ideally to provide the emerging young adult with a stable ethical context within which to evaluate the complex physical and emotional developments of pubescence. That evaluative integration will, needless to say, be a process of considerable complexity. We can, therefore, only indicate in passing a few of its more obvious traits.

Faith-sharing is the most basic fruit of growth in the gifts of sanctification. Docility to the sanctifying gifts ought, then, to enable the adolescent to look upon pubescence as creating new possibilities for authentic Christian sharing in faith. But the adolescent's freedom to do so will be a function of pneumatic growth in a number of other attitudes. To begin with, in adolescence, one must come to regard one's own body, not simply as a personal possession, but as a gift of God given to be shared in faith and love with others. Among the things Christians share as an expression of faith-dependence on God are the spatio-temporal, environmental supports of life. The human body itself is chief among those supports.

Moreover, the human body functions within experience as an efficacious symbol of the self. Sharing which is mediated by bodily activity is, therefore, both efficacious and symbolic. It is never purely efficacious, never purely symbolic. For one cannot have an efficacious impact on the conscious experience of another without one's act assuming significance within the other's evaluative response. That response will moreover be a more or less adequate interpretation of the meaning expressed by one's act.

In different bodily acts, however, efficacy may predominate over symbolic significance and vice versa. The construction of a bridge is, for example, a complex act of many human beings. But the product effected is less symbolically significant than the Beethoven Ninth. As a result, the symbolic meaning of bridges and other artifacts needs to be speculatively or artistically evoked through further symbolic acts, like a historical study of the bridge's construction, or like poetry and the visual arts.

The Christian adolescent must, then, learn to be concerned that the efficacious use of his or her maturing sexuality be charged with salvific meaning. Since mature sexual organs create a capacity both for personal, romantic involvement with another and for the physical creation of the human life impossible for the child, the adolescent whose pubescence is informed by the ideals of gratuitous sharing in the image of Christ will be concerned that personal use of these new capacities will in fact be expressive of the mind of Jesus.

By thus deepening in the adolescent a mature concern to act responsibly towards others in sexual matters and by informing the process of physical maturation with altruistic ideals of Christ-like sharing, the gifts of sanctification ought also to serve as an effective antidote to the morbid self-preoccupation which normally accompanies adolescent growth. Through growth in holiness, the emerging young Christian must learn to experience evaluatively the possibility of sexual intercourse and foreplay not merely as the egocentric satisfaction of narcissistic needs, but rather as acts whose experienced personal satisfaction is ultimately rooted in the fact that they are acts of self-sharing which express the same quality of atoning love for others as was embodied in the Lord Jesus.

The love of God for us revealed in Christ is, however, a creative love, in the sense that it not only summons human beings to integral conversion, but in the process it frees them to consent to the ethical demands of the new covenant. It follows, therefore, that the only completely authentic use of sex morally possible for a Christian is one which is not only rooted in integral personal conversion but one which is also evocative of an integrally converted response in one's sexual partner. And this lesson too the emerging Christian adolescent must learn from charismatic openness to the Spirit.

Docility to the gifts of sanctification ought also to root the Christian adolescent's evaluative response to puberty in an attitude of faith-dependence on God. The pubescent child ordinarily experiences the onset of sexual maturity with mingled feelings of fear and anticipation. But if the preceding analysis is sound, docility to the gifts of sanctification ought to mediate the healing of such fear. The Christian adolescent ought, therefore, to experience the collapse of the familiar world of childhood as an exodus event, as a liberation from childish illusions and as motivation to trust all the more in a divine fidelity that encompasses every moment of human life and growth.

Growth in the gifts of sanctification ought to mediate the adolescent's increasingly mature love and appreciation for his or her own body. As we have seen, in the initial discovery of bodily differences between the sexes, a child can be plagued by feelings of physical inadequacy, of fear, and of resentment. Such feelings can color one's attitude towards one's body later in life. One cannot, however, share authentically in love what one does not value. The sanctifying gifts ought, then, to mediate the healing of unresolved feelings of shame, fear, or anxiety about one's physical sexuality. For until such feelings are healed, one is not fully free to engage as an adult in self-sharing through the genital expression of human love.

The adolescent must also integrate into his or her emerging

experience a host of novel social relationships. As we have seen, the adolescent's sense of alienation begins as a repudiation of parental authority that is colored by feelings of guilt and anxiety. In normal growth such alienation is gradually transmuted into social, political and religious idealism. Growth in atoning, Christlike love ought to transmute both of these experiences. It ought to free the adolescent to forgive in Christlike atonement whatever inauthenticities may exist in his or her personal past, in an adult world marred by hypocrisy and compromise, or in the equally inauthentic world of adolescent frustration and immaturity.

Moreover, by grounding the emerging young adult's rejection of injustice and hypocrisy in the vision of Jesus rather than in personal hostilities, frustrations, and guilt feelings, the gifts of sanctification can gradually mediate the transmutation of the natural rebellion of youth into authentic Christian prophecy.

Docility to the sanctifying gifts ought also to provide the adolescent with an ethical alternative to blind assent to parental authority on the one hand, and to moral acquiescence in peer pressures, on the other. It should orient the adolescent's moral growth toward an ultimate and unconditioned consent to the ethical demands of the new covenant as the only set of political and social ideals worthy of absolute moral commitment. The ethical vision of a Christian adolescent ought, then, to be informed by Jesus' own vision of an open, classless community of free-sharing and of worship in mutual atoning love. And it is that vision which ought to orient personal attitudes and values toward prophetic opposition to all those social and political forces which are anti-Christ.

At the same time, the young adult's growth in the gifts of sanctification ought either to facilitate mature reconciliation with his or her parents or render it unnecessary. It will facilitate it when parental conflicts have developed to the point that they demand some formal act of mutual forgiveness in the image of Christ. Growth in the sanctifying gifts prevents such reconciliation when the emergent young Christian is sufficiently advanced in the process of sanctification to have forgiven in advance whatever limits or inauthenticities have been operative in parental relationships.

Finally, the experience of adolescence ought also to be transmuted by the ideal of Christian service. Adolescence is an explosion of physical, human energy. That energy is initially diffused and only gradually channeled into creative activity through the evaluative processes that ground an integral four-fold conversion. The vocational choice which eventually integrates the emergent young adult into the adult "establishment" will fail to express such a conversion and will effect nothing more than a moral acquiescence in the *status quo*, unless that choice is an authentic response to a genuine service gift.

But if the Christian adolescent can reach adult maturity only through openness to the gifts of sanctification, it follows that the only community which is capable of providing an adequate environment for such charismatic growth is a faith-community that is open to all of the service gifts. For only through the operative presence of all of the gifts in the worshipping community can its members attain full self-awareness in the knowledge that it is summoned to put on the mind of Jesus. By the same token, diminished charismatic awareness in the faith-community from which the adolescent emerges will restrict the adolescent's freedom to grow in the mind of Christ, and will tend to reinforce a sense of religious and social alienation.

Here there are several points worth noting. First, human sexuality cannot be adequately understood as governed by mechanical laws. In an experiential approach to human development, there are no sexual mechanisms. There are only sexual organicisms of varying degrees of spontaneity and freedom. As a result, it is possible within limits to decide the kind of sexuality one will enjoy.

The professional football player, for example, experiences his muscular-skeletal structure differently from the bookish scholar. That experiential difference is a function of the divergent evaluative stance both have taken toward their bodies in the course of their personal development. There are obvious biological limits to such differences. Both scholar and quarterback have generically the same kinds of organs and bodily functions. But there are concrete dynamisms and capacities for activity in both of their bodies which make them clearly different in kind. The quarterback in disciplining his body to serve the exigencies of sport has developed a strength and agility to transcend the powers of the scholar. The scholar for his part has disciplined his body to serve the exigencies of reflection and research. In so doing he has acquired a physical endurance of his own. The hours he spends in patient scholarly research transcend the concrete powers of the mere quarterback to engage in similar activity. Moreover, the very physical appearance of the scholar and of the quarterback tends to be expressive of the evaluative stance each has taken toward his personal physical makeup.

What is true of human muscular strength and agility is analogously true of human sexuality as well. The conscious and unconscious evaluative decisions taken toward one's own sexuality give incremental definition to the psycho-sexual dynamisms which characterize the emergent self. Those dynamisms come to expression in human activity. Activity which engages one psychosexually is in turn an expressive symbol of the emergent self.

It should be fairly clear that not every use of human sexuality is expressive of the mind of Jesus. If the preceding analysis is fundamentally sound, no act which engages one psychosexually will express the mind of Jesus which is: 1) expressive of neurotic fears, anxieties, or morbid self-preoccupation; 2) rooted in hatred of one's own body; 3) expressive of the self-reliant desire to dominate and control others rather than of the desire to share of oneself in authentic faith and love; 4) grounded in a lack of integral, fourfold conversion.

When the human use of sex is not grounded in an integral fourfold conversion, it can moreover, be expressive of a variety of concupiscent attitudes. The intellectually unconverted individual will be inclined to fix his or her sexual beliefs and attitudes by blind submission to external authority or to peer pressure, by personal dogmatisms, or by mere esthetic preference. (S)he will be victim not only to misleading personal and social taboos, but also to unconscious fears and anxieties. Lack of affective conversion can also condition the expressive symbolic character of human sexuality. Some uses of human sexuality are clearly expressive of emotional confusion and of psychic illness: impotence, frigidity, sadism, masochism, exhibitionism, scotophilia, voyeurism. Lack of moral conversion in sexual matters transforms sexuality into an expressive symbol of irresponsible egocentricity. It inclines one to use other people, whether maliciously, aggressively, or experimentally for one's personal growth and selfish satisfaction. It produces the Don Juan, the prostitute, group sex. Lack of religious conversion transforms the use of human sexuality into an expressive symbol of sinful self-reliance. Such self-reliance comes to expression in the vain cultivation of sexual prowess, in the ego-centric and manipulative use of sex to control, dominate, and hurt others. The Christian adolescent's ability to cope with these and similar obstacles to personal growth will, then, be a function of the extent to which the environment which nourishes personal development is efficaciously expressive of the Spirit's charismatic presence.

4. Another serious obstacle to balanced psycho-sexual development is misunderstanding concerning the meaning of love. Too often in the past, catechesis concerning human love has been marred by a misleading spirit-matter dualism derived, not from Scripture, but from Greek philosophy. Augustinian theology had profound impact on the Christian ascetical tradition. But it described the movement of love as inward and upward. Love draws one away from the body and from physical sensory experience. It leads one through subjective solitude to the contemplation of eternal and immutable truth. When love is equated with love of the immaterial, however, the genital expressions of love tend to be devalued as decadent and illusory. A Christian Aristotelian account of love is marred by operational dualism. It locates love in the spiritual faculty of the will. Love's task is, as a consequence, to subject the "lower, sensible faculties" to the "higher, spiritual faculties. In practice, such a theory of love breeds schizophrenia. It inculcates suspicion of one's feelings and of emotional spontaneity. It leaves one trapped in a quasi-Stoic cultivation of rationalistic, voluntaristic self-control. There is, then, need to articulate a theology of Christian love which avoids the pitfalls of philosophical dualism. One possible approach to the problem is that suggested by Otto Bird.[2]

Human love is personal commitment to another person as a person. Experience becomes consciously personal through conversion. For conversion is an act of self-appropriation. Through conversion, I grasp myself consciously and evaluatively as capable of self-understanding and responsible decision. In the process I differentiate myself evaluatively from other selves and from the environmental forces which shape me. Authentic personal love ought, then, to be the fruit of conversion. By the same token, it ought to seek to lead others to the freedom which is born of an integral, fourfold conversion. Human relationships which are not shaped by such love are oppressive and manipulative.

Like any human decision the commitment of love is shaped by environmental and evaluative forces. As decision, love binds me to the concrete: to persons, to situations. The quality of my love is, however, the result of the emotions and beliefs which motivate it. One may distinguish three simple forms of human love. The simple forms of love are distinguishable and irreducible modalities of loving. They may be present in varying degrees in any act of love. They are: gift love, appreciative love, and need love. Gift love is atoning love. It frees one to suffer personal diminishment and even death so that the beloved might grow and live. Atoning love is gratuitous, unmerited, unmeritable, because it is always simply there. It creates love in the beloved. Appreciative love, on the other hand, is ecstatic, contemplative love. It is born of "peak experiences" in which one is possessed by the vision of realities and values that are personally enthralling. Contemplative love does not change the beloved but rejoices in the beloved's beauty. Need love is born of personal deficiency and limitation. It is the love of dependence. Gift love came to its purest human embodiment in Jesus: "Greater love than this no one has: to lay down one's life for one's friend." Appreciative love finds its purest human expression in the mystical marriage. Need love that is untouched by self-sacrifice or appreciation is concupiscent love. It is marred by self-pity, egocentricity, manipulation. It comes to expression in erotic tendencies which have yet to be transformed by an integral, fourfold conversion.

As human relationships develop, the simple forms of love blend and intermingle. As deficiency needs are fulfilled, one develops a growing capacity for appreciative love. The experience of gift love creates the capacity to respond with a similar gift of self. The love we call "affection" is primarily a blend of gift love and of need love. It is born of situations in which familiarity breeds a tolerant contempt. Its most common environment is the family; its most familiar exemplification, parent-child and sibling relationships. Affection is embodied in acts of self-sacrifice that nurture growth in those whose needs are greater than one's own and in the beloved's gestures of grateful response to such love. Friendship, on the other hand, is primarily a blend of gift and appreciative love. Unlike affection, friendship is love between equals; and equality breeds a freedom and mutual independence which· is less dominant in other forms of love. Friends have deep appreciation for one another. They make sacrifices for one another and stand by one another in moments of need. But their love is born of shared enthusiasm and shared interest rather than of craving or of abiding personal deficiencies. Craving, on the other hand is primarily a blend of need love and of appreciative love. It is romantic love. Young lovers need one another deeply, idealize one another, and remain notoriously blind to one another's faults.

Authentic Christian charity is a harmonious blend of need, appreciative, and.gift love. It transmutes need love into an expression of a gift love that is in turn rooted in a contemplative appreciation of the divine atoning love embodied in Jesus and sealed in

DIAGRAM 4: The Dynamics of Loving, according to Bird

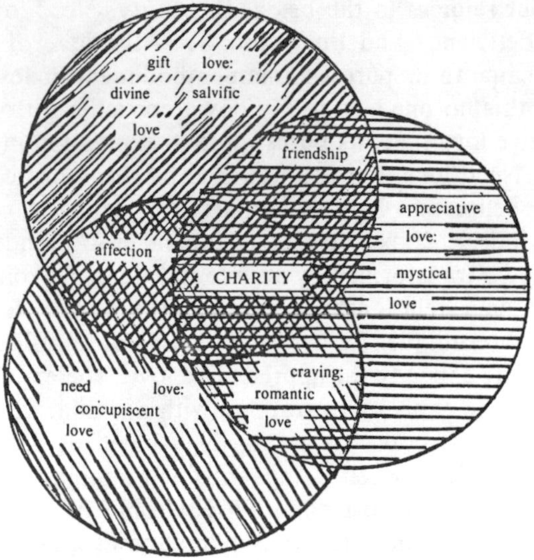

the sending of the Spirit. Let us reflect on how this occurs. The converted Christian has faced personal weakness and sinfulness but has been freed by the loving forgiveness of God revealed in Christ to acknowledge that weakness before others. But for such a person, the very act of accepting the ministry of others is a way of giving oneself over to them in love. Thus, in authentic Christian love, even need love is transmuted into an expression of gift love. This transformation is, moreover, mediated by the graced contemplation of the gift of divine love embodied in Jesus. Moreover, as one's deepest personal needs are healed through the gift love of others, one discovers power in the Spirit to begin oneself to minister to other persons with the same atoning love of Christ. As a Christian, I must, then, root the practice of love in a frank acknowledgement of my need to love and be loved. But I must also reject any expression of eroticism which is rooted exclusively in deficiency needs. For mere eroticism is concupiscent love untouched by an integrating vision of faith and unhealed by atoning self-sacrifice.

5. The redemptive transformation of Christian love is effected by personal growth in the gifts of sanctification. Moreover, the sanctifying gifts are, as we have seen, among the chief graces of Christian baptism. Docility to the Spirit in the healing of erotic concupiscence is, then, an important aspect of lived fidelity to one's baptismal covenant. But fidelity to the gifts of sanctification also demands, as we have seen, that one follow the lead of the Spirit in deciding the precise form of ecclesial service to which one will dedicate one's life. Among the Spirit's service gifts are, however, marriage and celibacy. No converted Christian can, therefore, enter authentically into Christian marriage except as a response to the Spirit's summons. If, however, to be authentic, Christian marriage is indeed grounded in a service gift, then two important consequences follow. First, it is clear that when it is authentically responded to, the gift of marriage enhances the collective public faith witness of the Christian community. Hence, it is also clear that an inauthentic response will detract from that shared, public witness. Second, since response to the gift of marriage engages the collective witness to which the Christian community is called by God, the authenticity or inauthenticity of one's call to service is

subject to communal discernment. And the community includes its official apostolic leaders. Accordingly, the Council of Trent declared Christian marriages to be invalid unless contracted in the presence of an ordained apostolic minister who had authorization to preside over the ceremony.[3] The decree makes sense as an attempt to establish canonical safeguards against contracting a sacramental marriage without adequate discernment and communal confirmation. The publication of marriage bans is also a formalistic and fairly empty legal reminder that the discernment which ought to precede Christian marriage is ecclesial in character. But when a marriage is discerned and sanctioned by the believing community and its ordained apostolic leaders, the contracting marriage partners confront one another in faith not merely in the name of the God who has called them together but also in the name of the Church universal.

The establishment of canonical, legal impediments to marriage should also be re-evaluated in the light of a sound theology of gift.[4] In discerning the charismatic basis of a proposed marriage, pastors need negative principles for deciding when a given union gives evidence of not being from God. Such principles should be rooted in sound teaching and should facilitate the attempt to decide whether a given marriage is truly grounded in a charismatic call of the Spirit. Once one begins to think in such terms, however, the pastoral inadequacy of the existing list of impediments becomes patent. Needless to say, there would seem to be no reason for perpetuating in these days an impediment like spiritual affinity. But such obvious and fairly trivial problems aside, one finds in the present list of marital impediments an almost total absence of ascetical criteria for evaluating the charismatic authenticity of a Christian marriage. The Catholic hierarchy takes much more care in discerning the vocation of its priests than of its married people. It subjects seminarians to years of scrutiny and has elaborated a fairly detailed set of ascetical norms for judging the authenticity of a charism of apostolic service. But when it comes to the discernment of the layman's charism of married service, present pastoral practice is too often content with the perfunctory legal examination, a Cana conference, and the posting of bans.

If, however, the only authentic reason for entering into Christian marriage is that one has been called to such ecclesial service by the Spirit of Jesus, then the only sound pastoral approach to marriage is one which subjects the proposed union to serious ascetical scrutiny. Does the young couple give evidence of genuine growth in the gifts of sanctification? Are they integrally converted? Is their relationship charismatically grounded and informed by the mind of Jesus? Do they give evidence of sufficient growth in the gift of faith? For if their union is to be authentically Christian, they must experience it as a way of giving public Christian witness. Most important of all, do both parties experience their attraction for one another as more than mere romantic involvement? For mere romantic attraction is insufficient to ground a Christian marriage. The Christian couple must recognize the finger of God clearly and unmistakably in their desire to be one, although their awareness of God's call can grow and deepen within marriage itself. But prior to marriage they must acknowledge in their consciences that their marriage is a response to the call of the Spirit; and in the rite of marriage they must consent to one another in virtue of that call, once it has been discerned and confirmed by the community.

If the couple fails to meet these tests of discernment, sound pastoral practice should prevent them from binding themselves to a sacramental marriage covenant they may subsequently regret. For marital consent in response to a service gift transforms from within the ethical character of human marriage. Baptism commits one to love every person with the atoning love of Jesus Himself. Growth in the gifts of sanctification mediates growth in the understanding and practice of such love. Marriage transmutes the baptismal love of a Christian by focusing it on a specific individual. Normal romantic love is exclusive. Extreme exclusivity in romance easily breeds the aberration of jealousy. When the exclusivity of romantic love is transmuted by an atoning, forgiving, Christ-like love, it becomes a monagamous and indissoluble commitment. For it demands in addition to exclusivity that Christian married love embody the atoning love of Jesus and that as a consequence it be unrestricted in its conditions and in its consequences. Love that is unrestricted in its conditions is love that is simply there. Like the love of God made visible in Jesus, it does not ask to be merited. It is there before any response of love is expressed; it is even creative of that response.

Love that is unrestricted in its consequences forgives in advance any fault. It forgives before betrayal, during betrayal, after betrayal and prior to repentance, just as we have all been forgiven in Christ.

A marriage commitment which is expressive of the quality of love demanded by authentic openness to the gifts of sanctification cannot, then, as the Council of Trent saw, be rescinded by the spouses themselves because of the personal sinfulness and infidelity of one's partner. In an authentic Christian marriage all such offenses are foreseen in advance and forgiven. The individual who is neither morally nor emotionally capable of maintaining and sustaining such a commitment should not proceed to Christian marriage.

According to traditional Catholic teaching, for a Christian marriage to be legally valid it must be *ratum et consummatum*.[6] A marriage is *ratum* when it is entered into as a response to a service gift that has been subjected to communal discernment and confirmed by the believing community acting in solidarity with and through its ordained apostolic leaders.[7] Because the marriage contract is a response to the charismatic anointing of the Spirit of Jesus, it is made in Jesus' name. Because the gift has been publicly discerned and confirmed by the community, it is also made officially in the name of the community. Because it is done in faith, the act is an act of worship. By focusing baptismal love on a specific individual, marriage transmutes one's baptismal covenant. As consent to a specific gift of service it transmutes one's confirmation commitment.

Christian marriage is, then, much more than a private act of devotion. For it is an official public act in which each spouse confronts the other both in the name of Jesus and in the name of the Christian community. Moreover, marriage is more than a repetition of the believer's sacramental covenant of initiation. For it transmutes that earlier commitment by endowing the spouses with rights and obligations which go beyond the more generic covenant commitment made in baptism and confirmation. In thus transmuting the believer's initiatory covenant, marriage endows the Christian couple with a status in the Church analogous to orders. That status is not, however, an "order" in the strict sense, since it is not an expression of the charism of community leadership as such. Nor does it confer a "character." For while it is initiatory, it does not embody a commitment to the Church universal as such. One marries, not the Church, but one's spouse.

Marriage is like the apostolate, however, in being rooted in a gift whose function is to transform from within a pre-existing institutional structure. Jesus did not begin the institution of marriage. But He instituted marriage as a sacrament by His ethical teaching on the indissolubility of marriage and by grounding Christian marriage charismatically through the mission of His Spirit.

Clearly, then, one cannot affirm the charismatic basis of Christian marriage without implicitly conceding that it ought to be a sacrament in the strict sense. For a sacrament is, as we have seen, an official public act of new covenant worship in which an official spokesman for the community confronts a Christian worshipper in Jesus' name, reminds the worshipper of Jesus' unconditioned, redemptive love, and demands of the worshipper an appropriate response to faith. Two Christians cannot consent to marriage in response to a gift of the Spirit which has been officially confirmed through communal discernment without ministering to one another in just such a manner. For if authentic, their mutual consent in love is an expression of the atoning love of Christ. Because it is a consent made in response to the Spirit, it is done with the authority of Jesus. Because it has been discerned and confirmed by the community acting in and through its apostolic leaders, it is done in the name of the Church universal. It is made in the context of a public renewal of one's baptismal and confirmational covenant, a renewal which gives further ethical specification to the concrete terms of that covenant. Clearly, then, anyone who concedes the charismatic character of marriage but denies its sacramentality has introduced elements of inauthenticity into his or her understanding of Christian marriage.

At the same time the preceding analysis casts some light on the pastoral dilemma of many divorced Catholics. A marriage is not ratified *(ratum)* until it is discerned and confirmed by the community. A judgment of discernment is, however, fallible. Its truth or falsity must evaluated in the light of the care with which it was reached and of its experienced consequences. If the discernment process preceding a marriage was in fact perfunctory, if the partners entered into a sacramental union without a clear sense of God's call, and if subsequent to the marriage contract there is serious reason to doubt that the union was in fact originally rooted in a gift of the Spirit, then it is in the competence of Church authority to declare such a union void for want of an adequate charismatic basis. For only a marriage which is rooted in a gift is fully sacramental *(res et sacramentum)*. The Church may ratify a charism; but only the Spirit can give a charism.[8]

If the judgment which confirms a marriage is fallible, the judgment which reverses an earlier discernment is, however, no less fallible. Like every judgment of discernment, it is bound to the concrete and resists facile regulation by universal laws. If, then, marriage courts are to proceed with justice, their proceedings must be founded on more than abstract legalities. Their decisions must be rooted in a personal knowledge of the parties involved and of the spirits that move them. And such decisions must be prayerfully as well as rationally reached. Marriage cases should, then, be pastorally handled as much as possible at a local level.

Moreover, the consummation of a marriage would seem to be best understood, not as a single act of intercourse, but as the founding of a family through the generation of offspring. The mere fact, however, that the marriage is unconsummated in this sense does not automatically justify its dissolution. For if the Spirit really is calling two people together He will sustain them in that call despite the difficulties they encounter and despite the absence of children to bless their union. The care of orphans is, moreover, a basic Christian apostolate. Adoption is, then, a real possibility for many who are prevented from having children through intercourse.

Finally, we may conclude on the basis of the preceding analysis that there is a serious need in the Church for a renewal of Christian betrothal. The period of betrothal should be an official period of communal public discernment in which the spiritual maturity and personal call of the betrothed are prayerfully tested and confirmed by the community. For only by rescuing sacramental marriage from the romantic individualism with which secular society has surrounded it can young Christians be protected from entering into an indissoluble union without having been called to it and strengthened for it by the Spirit of God.

6. The preceding reflections also cast light on the Biblical basis for affirming the sacramentality of Christian marriage: (1) *The teachings of Jesus:* Jesus did not inaugurate marriage as an institution. But there is solid Biblical evidence that He denounced the divorce practices of His contemporaries. His teaching on the indissolubility of marriage gave decisive shape to the early catechesis of the Church concerning Christian marriage.[9] (2) *Pauline catechesis concerning marriage:* Paul developed his teaching on marriage in the context of his overall theology of the gifts. The Lord's love for the Church as His own body comes to expression, Paul believed, in the salvific action of the Spirit. The gifts of the Spirit are, as a consequence, visible signs of the unalterable love of the Divine Bridegroom for His bride the Church. Among the Spirit's gifts are marriage and celibacy. Moreover, Paul regarded the human body as an instrument to be used either for the works of light or of darkness. He compares it on occasion to a military weapon to be used against the forces of darkness. Moreover, for Paul, pagan sexual license was one of the clearest proofs that the gentile world had closed its heart to the saving action of the Spirit.[10]

These Pauline insights provide the speculative background for understanding the cryptic theology of marriage articulated in the letter to the Ephesians. Jesus, the Divine Bridegroom, reveals His love for His own body, the Church, by sending it the Spirit, who through His charismatic gifts builds up the body of Christ to the fulness of life and of holiness. The divine love thus revealed in the death and glorification of Jesus is an unconditioned, atoning love. Since marriage is rooted in a gift of the Spirit, the Christian's use of physical sexuality must be expressive of the ethical demands of the new covenant, and not of mere human impulse or sinful desire. Indeed, the entire relationship of husband and wife in marriage must be transformed by that ethical commitment. It must embody the qualities of mutual atoning service in love which Jesus exemplified in His death and glorification. That service is, moreover, a reaffirmation of the spouses' baptismal covenant. The sign that a husband loves his wife "as his own body" in the image of Jesus is that his love effects the wife's charismatic transformation and sanctification. The sign that a wife loves her husband in the Spirit is that her love for him expresses the same quality of love as is demanded by the Christian baptismal covenant. By thus embodying the new covenant in their relationship with one another, the Christian husband and wife transform their marriage into a "great mystery," an event which reveals the meaning of the redemptive mission of Jesus and of the Holy Spirit.[11]

One of the traits of Pauline theology is its patriarchal, rabbinic rhetoric. In speaking of marriage, Paul speaks, for example, of Christ as the head of the Church, and of husbands as the head of their wives. In approaching Pauline teaching, it is important to recognise the plurality of theologies present in the New Testament. There are elements in Pauline thought which express the shared faith of first generation Christians. There are other elements which are peculiar to the apostle's manner of preaching and theologizing. It has been the perennial temptation of fundamentalists to confound the two. Paul's theology of marriage goes far beyond the use of the metaphor of the "husband-as-head." It is, then, unfortunate that some of the lay leaders in the charismatic renewal have fastened upon the phrase to lend pseudo-religious sanction to the patriarchal suppression of women in marriage. This misguided teaching reflects the sexist, patriarchal attitudes of American Catholics in general. Nor is it the first time that Christians have abused the word of God to lend divine sanction to the social oppression of women. Such abuse remains a source of scandal in the charismatic renewal and in the Church as a whole. Far more central to Pauline teaching on marriage is, however, the reciprocity of Christlike love demanded of Christian spouses.[12] That reciprocity is meaningless unless it comes to expression in the integral sharing of parental responsibilities. Rather than confining women to home and hearth so that hubby may busy himself in the marketplace, Christian husbands need to learn how to share in the burdens of homekeeping and childrearing so that their wives too may contribute in creative ways to the development of human society.

(3) *Johannine theology.* The gospel of John develops the theme of the Divine Bridegroom somewhat differently from Paul.

A Johannine theology of "signs" endows the fourth gospel with a tight theological unity. In John's gospel, the first sign which Jesus gives His disciples is that He is the Divine Bridegroom. It is given at Cana. The sign at Cana is full of theological complexities which are not directly revelant to the theology of marriage. It would seem, however, that the key to the meaning of the sign is the enigmatic exchange between Jesus and His mother. Mary, on discovering that there is no wine, informs Jesus of the fact. Jesus replies literally: "Woman, what to me and to you?" The phrase is a colloquialism indicating mild disagreement with what had just been said. It has been variously translated. But one of the most theologically suggestive renderings would seem to be: "Woman, of what kind of wine do you speak?" Having expressed His disagreement, Jesus then adds: "My hour is not yet come."[13]

The hour of which Jesus speaks is the hour when He will be lifted up in glory. In that hour He will give the living water, the Spirit of life which He would promise both to the Samaritan woman and to the pilgrim crowds on the feast of Tabernacles. But the hour of Jesus is also the moment when He will give the new wine of His blood, the blood of the new covenant that is sealed in water and the Holy Spirit. This, then, is the meaning of the blood and water which flows from His pierced side upon the cross. Through Jesus' death the new messanic wine of the covenant promised at Cana is given to men along with the living water of the Spirit. For the new wine is, of course, also the eucharistic wine promised in the bread of life discourse.[14]

Clearly, then, in the gospel of John, the human experience of marriage is transformed imagistically into a complex religious symbol of the new covenant sealed in the blood of the Lamb. It is an image which will recur with power in the book of Revelation, which describes the final wedding of Jesus and His Church.[15] John's use of marriage as a religious symbol complements Pauline thought by associating it more closely with the eucharist. Paul's application of the image of the Divine Bridegroom to Jesus complements a Johannine theology of marriage by associating it and a Christian theology of marriage with a theology of gift. For Paul, Jesus is revealed to be the divine bridegroom in the charismatic activity of the Spirit, Who by His gifts builds up the Lord's own body. The same insight is, however, implicit in John's insistence that Jesus' full revelation as the Divine Bridegroom coincides with the "hour" when He breathes forth the Spirit, Who will glorify Him by conforming the words and deeds of His followers to those of Jesus himself.

The institution of a sacrament is always the act of the risen Christ. Even the eucharist derives its full sacramental significance from the death and glorification of Jesus and the mission of the Spirit. As we have seen, Jesus' disciples seemed to have administered a proselyte baptism like John's; but it is the risen Christ who sends His disciples into the world to baptise in the name of Father, Son, and Spirit. Moreover, it is Pentecost which reveals the purpose of Christian baptism to be baptism in water and the Holy Spirit. A similar process is at work in the divine institution of marriage as a sacrament. By His teaching on divorce, Jesus transformed the ethical terms and religious significance of human marriage. Then, by sending the Spirit He grounded Christian marriage in a service gift which is in need of public communal discernment and official confirmation. In so doing He transformed Christian marriage charismatically into a transmuted reaffirmation of the Christian sacramental covenant of initiation. The ethical structure of such an act fills all of the conditions for a ritual sacrament in the strict sense of the term. It is a covenant act, but more than a mere repetition of one's initial Christian covenant commitment. For it transmutes that commitment by binding one to specific moral obligations that are not consequent upon one's baptismal covenant. As covenant worship, however, Christian marriage is an act in which a minister, that is, one who speaks with full authority from the community, confronts a sacramental worshipper in the name of Jesus and demands an appropriate response of love to the God made visible in Jesus and in the pneumatic act of covenant worship itself. For the spouses in matrimony administer the sacrament to one another in virtue both of their gift and of the approval and sanction of the believing community.

7. Official pastoral catechesis has, however, also linked the theology of marriage with that of celibacy. In so doing, it has followed and reiterated Pauline teaching of the subject. It is important, however, not to misinterpret the meaning of Tridentine teach-

ing that celibacy is "better and more blessed" than marriage. Paul himself was forced to qualify his own teaching on that subject in such a way as to make it clear that he claimed no absolute advantage to celibate existence.[16]

We can begin by excluding some obvious misinterpretations of the advantages of celibacy. To say that celibacy is "better and more blessed" than marriage does not mean that celibates are necessarily holier than married people. One can respond to a gift of celibacy inauthentically. Nor does it mean that those who marry are second-class citizens in the Church. It does not mean that married Christians would be celibates but for the fact that they are oversexed. Nor does this teaching mean that sexual intercourse is itself tainted, suspect, and better to be avoided. Celibacy is in fact in greater need of ethical justification than marriage. For one can seek celibacy for a variety of motives that are devoid of ethical significance. One can flee marriage for reasons of moral cowardice or psychosexual inadequacy. Needless to say, such a decision would be incompatible with an integral fourfold conversion. Nor would it be authentically expressive of a gift of the Spirit.

To be authentically Christian, the decision to lead a celibate life must transmute the ethical commitment mediated by the gifts of sanctification and of faith. It must be expressive of a decision to live in faith dependence on the Father in the image of Jesus by reaching out in atoning love and service to others. It must also be expressive of a desire to witness publicly as a person of faith to the mercy and goodness of God.

Authentic Christian celibacy must, then, be charismatically grounded. It must be rooted in a positive response to the love of God and of one's fellow men. Such a response must be expressive of the gifts of sanctification and of faith. But it transmutes both by being in addition a response to a specific call to ecclesial service. The fact that celibacy is charismatically grounded is what endows it with positive value. For of itself the renunciation of marriage is the rejection of something genuinely valuable. Such a renunciation takes on justifiable moral significance when it is motivated by other values which are touched with ethical absoluteness and ultimacy. For the converted Christian, this can occur only when the choice of celibacy as a way of life is in the first instance an expression of the faith-dependence on God that is mediated by the sanctifying gifts. But to choose to live a life in faith-dependence on God is to do so in responsive sensitivity to the divine call. It is, then, the call to celibacy, seen as a transmutation of the gifts of sanctification and of faith, which for the Christian transforms it into a "ought," an ethical value.

To be honest, however, the devout Roman Catholic must acknowledge that the occasional irrational fervor with which spiritual writers have in the past attempted to justify celibacy against the attack of "heretics" and "sensual worldlings" has sometimes blinded them to the fact that, if there is a sense in which it is better and more blessed to be celibate than married, there is also a sense in which it is better and more blessed to be married rather than celibate. A normative insight into celibacy reveals that in its basic decisional structure it is a call to give counterwitness to marriage in a Christian community whose corporate faith witness is authentically mediated only by its openness as a community to all of the service gifts.

As we have seen, marriage is in part a sacrament because it is rooted in a service gift. The charismatic grounding for Christian marriage justifies the right of the spouses to confront one another in the name of Jesus in the ritual sealing of their marriage. The official discerning approbation of their act by the believing community acting with and through its ordained leaders transforms them into sacramental ministers capable of confronting one another in the name of the Church universal.

Nevertheless, the focusing of love upon a single individual and on the children which will be the fruit of one's marital union is of itself a circumscription of the scope of the love to which all men are called in Christ. For the Christian in baptism stands committed to a love that is unrestricted in its scope. A love demanded by the covenant of Christian initiation is better described as "unrestricted" rather than as "universal," in its scope. The term "universal" suggests "abstract." But Christian love reaches out to concrete living persons, not simply to abstract ideals. Nevertheless, Christian love is unrestricted in the sense that it excludes no one in principle from its concern. Baptismal love is also situational rather than individual in its orientation. It is content to function within the concrete limits of any given situation unless there is some clear indication that the demands of love and the call of the Spirit forces one to seek a change in one's situation. But within any situation, baptismal love seeks to reach out to those especially who seem to be most in need. More specifically, the unrestricted character of Christian baptismal love comes to concrete experiential visibility in the attempt to reach out to those who are commonly excluded from the love of others: the outcasts of society, the poor, the weak, the needy, the confused, the despairing, the lonely, the bewildered, the oppressed, the alienated, the resentful, the violent. It seeks to touch such people by offering them a love that is simply there, which does not ask to be earned, and which forgives in advance any offense or rejection.

Where the Christian community's collective witness to baptismal love is limited to its charismatic embodiment in marriage, the unrestricted scope of Christian love would come to imperfect, quasi-sacramental visibility in the shared life of the community. For the dynamics of the love-commitment embodied in a Christian call to marriage focus it with a certain exclusivity upon a specific group of persons: one's spouse and children.

Needless to say, within the context of Christian marriage there is ample scope for growth in gift-love and in authentic baptismal charity. Children are incredibly needy, and the love of parents for them must be simply there, despite the child's inability at almost every stage of development to appreciate such love or to respond to it appropriately. Spouses too must grow in mutual forgiveness, if they are to grow in love.

But marital and parental responsibilities can easily circumscribe one's concrete ability to reach out beyond the immediate circle of the family. And they certainly preclude in most instances making such activity the exclusive and central focus of one's life. The celibate is one who is called to just such an extra-familial witness to love. And he or she is called to it precisely as a counter-witness within the total charismatic community. For the celibate is called to witness to the fact that the scope of Christian love is not exhausted by a call to marriage.

When a marriage-commitment is lived in fidelity to the Lord it witnesses in a special way the fact that Christian love ought to be mutual and personal. A commitment of married love, even though it is unrestricted in its conditions and consequences, is made in the strength of a response of love from one's spouse. And its irrevocability binds the two persons together for life.

The celibate's love commitment, when it is lived in earnest, reaches out actively to those in the Christian and human community who are in greatest need. It involves the celibate, therefore, primarily in self-giving to those who are least capable of responding adequately in love. Celibate love, therefore, when lived, witnesses by its inner dynamic more obviously to the gratuitous character of Christian love then does Christian marriage. And by reaching out to the dispossessed, it witnesses more visibly to the unrestricted character of Christian love.

If then celibate love is "better and more blessed" in so far as it witnesses in a special way to the gratuity and unrestricted scope of Christian love, Christian married love is "better and more blessed" in its witness to the mutuality and concretely personal character of Christian love.

Needless to say, neither vocation has a corner on any modality of love. Gratitious gift-love, reciprocity, concrete personal commitment, and loving service to the dispossessed can and ought to function in the faith-experience of both married persons and celibates. But in the authentic living of a call to Christian marriage, reciprocity in commitment to specific persons tends to be valued up, gratuity and the unrestricted scope of Christian love tends to be valued down. In the authentic living of celibacy, the gratuity and unrestricted scope of baptismal love are valued up, reciprocity, and a commitment to a specific person valued down. The two calls serve, therefore, complementary, not contradictory, functions in the collective charismatic witness of the Christian faith community.

We have argued these positions in more detail in *Discerning the Spirit*. There is no need to repeat those arguments here. It suffices to call the reader's attention to them, should it be helpful to pursue them further.[17] It is, however, useful to note the connection between these earlier reflections on the religious life and the present analysis. Not every gift of celibacy need be a call to the religious life. One may be called to a life of celibate service outside of a vowed community. A call to the religious life transmutes the gift of celibacy into a call to assist the hierarchy in their call to leadership in service and within the Christian community. We shall attempt to explore some of the complexities of a call to apostolic service in the following chapter.

Notes

1. Group for the Advancement of Psychiatry, *Normal Adolescence* (N.Y.: Mentor, 1933).

2. Otto Bird, "The Complexity of Love," *Thought,* XXXIX (June, 1964) pp. 210-220.

3. DS 1803-1804, 1816.

4. *Ibid.*

5. DS 1798-1799, 1805, 1807.

6. For a discussion of the development of Christian teaching on marriage, see: Eduard Schillebeeckx, O.P., *Marriage: Human Reality and Saving Mystery* (2 vols.; N.Y.: Sheed and Ward, 1965). See especially: I, pp. 19-20, 84-85, 108ff., 234-244, 284-301.

7. Until Vatican II, official Catholic teaching on marriage failed to insist on its charismatic basis. Protestant and Orthodox theology were less slow in doing so. Cf. *Lumen gentium,* 11; *Apostolicam actuositatem,* 11; Karl Barth, *On Marriage* (Philadelphia: Fortress Press, 1968); Paul Evdokimov, *Sacrement de l'amour* (Paris: Editions de l'épi, 1961); George Crespy, Paul Evdokomov, Christian Duquoc, *Marriage and Christian Tradition,* translated by Agnes Cunningham (Techny, Ill.: Divine Word Press, 1968).

8. There has been a growing concern in Catholic circles to discover a rationale for dissolving Christian marriages more easily without attenuating the ethical demands of a marriage entered into as an expression of the Christian covanant. An acknowledgement of the charismatic basis of marriage would seem to provide a way out of the dilemma. Those not called by the Spirit to marriage should not be held to a Christian marriage contract. Jon P. Alston, "Evaluation of Church Officials' Attitudes Toward Making Divorce Easier and Toward Three Kinds of Intermarriage," *Journal for the Scientific Study of Religion* (1972) pp. 282-286; Aloysius Am-

brozic, "Indissolubility of Marriage in the New Testament: Law or Ideal?" *Studia Canonica* (1972) pp. 269-288; G. Chikopela, "Marriage Commitment," *African Ecclesiastical Review* (1972) pp. 327-331; Bernard M. Daly and Patrick Keran, "Christian Marriage: Is it Possible?" *America* (February, 1973) pp. 160-162; M. Desdouits, "La dispense de marriage non consommé," *Esprit et vie* (1972) pp. 617-620; Sean Fagan, "Divorce: A Possibility for Catholics," *Doctrine and Life* (1972) pp. 625-635; Excelso Garcia, O.P. "Indissoluble Marriage and Divorce," *Philippiniana Sacra* (1972) pp. 54-88; Edward J. Kilmartin, S.J., "When is Marriage a Sacrament?" *Theological Studies*, XXXIV (June, 1973) pp. 275-286; Theodore Mackin, S.J. "Consummation: of Contract or of Covenant," *Jurist* (1972) pp. 213-223; David McAndrew, "Pastoral Ministry to the Invalidly Married," *Homiletic and Pastoral Review* (1973) pp. 26-30; James T. McHugh, "No-fault Divorce Laws: An overview and Critique," *Catholic Lawyer* (1972) pp. 237-242; William J. Nessel, "The Catholic Divorcee: A Pastoral Approach," *Homiletic and Pastoral Review* (1973) pp. 10-16; John T. Noonan, *Power to Dissolve: Lawyers and Marriages in the Courts of the Roman Curia* (Cambridge: Harvard, 1972); G. Pelland, "Le dossier patristique relatif au divorce," *Science et Esprit* (1973) pp. 99-120; Peter J. Riga, "Divorce and Remarriage in the Catholic Church," *U.S. Catholic* (March, 1973) pp. 18-20.

9. Cf. Quentin Quesnell, "Made Themselves Eunuchs for the Kingdom of Heaven," *Catholic Biblical Quarterly*, XXX (July, 1968) pp. 335-358; Aiden Mahoney, C.P., "A New Look at the Divorce Clauses in Mt 5, 32 and 19,9," *Catholic Biblical Quarterly*, XXX (January, 1968) pp. 29-38.

10. 1 Co 6:12-20, 12:1-3, 7:32-40; Rm 1:18-32, 6:12-23, 7:1-6, 8:31-39.

11. Ep 5:21-23.

12. John Navone, S.J., "Love in the Message of St. Paul," *Worship*, XL (August-September, 1966) pp. 437-444.

13. Jn 2:3-4, 4:11-15, 7:37-39.

14. Jn 19:30-37, 20:19-23.

15. Rv 21:1-4.

16. DS 1810; 1 Co 7:1-40.

17. Donald L. Gelpi, S.J., *Discerning the Spirit: Foundations and Futures of Religious Life* (N.Y.: Sheed and Ward, 1970) pp. 57-109.

VII
Apostolic
Ministry

1. Jesus is presented consistently by New Testament writers
as having confronted other persons with authority.[1] The basis of
that authority is, moreover, always described as personal. The
religious claims He made did not depend for their binding force
upon the sanction of any existing civil, human, or religious institution. His claims were, rather, rooted exclusively in His unique relation to the Father.

Jesus' sense of standing in a privileged relationship to the Father is, moreover, presented in the gospels as the conscious ground
of His messianic mission. That mission was inaugurated visibly by
His public ministry, but it culminated in His death and glorification, and in the sending of the Spirit. The full revelation of Jesus'
authority is, then, identical with the total incarnational process by
which He was revealed to be messiah and Lord. It is the same process viewed under distinguishable but related formalities.

If, however, the basis of Jesus' messianic authority is completely personal and therefore unique, the revelation of His authority can only be described as pneumatic. For His visible transformation in the Spirit begun at the Jordan culminated in His Paschal
revelation as the Lord who sends the Spirit to enlighten men and
women concerning His person and authority. This revelatory process was, from beginning to end, Spirit-led, Spirit-effected.

The Synoptics all portray Jesus' baptism at the Jordan as His
messianic investiture, the inauguration of His pneumatic revelation
as messianic Son of God. Jesus' baptism at the hands of John
would seem to be historically incontestable. The fact that the lead-

er of another religious movement had baptised the founder of Christianity was probably a polemic issue between Jesus' and John's disciples and even an embarrassment to the first Christians. It seems unlikely, therefore, that the community would have preserved an account of the event unless it functioned in some significant way in the inauguration of Jesus' public ministry. And, as we have seen, the event took on clear symbolic significance in the light of Easter and of the baptismal practices of the first Christians.

The fact that Jesus was drawn to undergo John's baptism suggests that Jesus was moving in the same religious circles as the Baptist himself. The ministry of the Baptist, however, proclaimed a vibrant eschatological hope. Johannine baptism was a prophetic gesture whose apparent purpose was to gather together a faithful remnant of believers who lived in expectation of a decisive salvific intervention of God in history. Subsequent to His own baptism, Jesus is portrayed in the gospels as having engaged in a ministry similar to the Baptist's in a number of respects. Not unlike the Baptist. Jesus preached the imminent arrival of the "reign of God." He seems to have taught, or at least allowed, His disciples to practice a proselyte baptism similar to John's. In all likelihood, that baptism too was a prophetic gesture, whose purpose was to gather about Him a community of people who desired to live in eschatological hope and expectation of the coming reign of God. The moral conditions for membership in such a community would seem to have been willingness to live a life of gratuitous sharing, of unrestricted love, and of service in the worship of atonement. Jesus' parables of the kingdom and His prophetic and eschatological statements provided, then, the religious context for interpreting His ethical teaching. But His ethical teaching provided pragmatic clarification of His vaguer parabolic, prophetic, and eschatological utterances.

In addition to preaching, Jesus is portrayed in the gospels as having exercised a ministry of faith healing. The gospels all portray these healings as integral to Jesus' ministry. Moreover, in the face of unbelief, Jesus is depicted as reluctant to heal. In the synoptics, Jesus heals in proof of His power to proclaim the forgiveness of sins, in justification of His right to ignore the minutiae of sabbath law, and as a revelation of His power over Satan.[2] Johannine theology approaches Jesus' sabbath healings somewhat differently. The fourth gospel portrays them as signs of the glory of God being revealed in Jesus, and, therefore, as judgmental acts which force a choice between light and darkness.[3]

Moreover, as C.K. Barrett has correctly observed, it is through Jesus' pneumatically inspired ministry of teaching, of faith healing, and of exorcism that His authority *(exousia)* to confront others in the name of God was historically and pneumatically revealed. In the synoptic tradition, the term *"dynamis"* can signify a miraculous deed of power. At times it is a reverential periphrasis for God. It is on occasion a divine attribute ascribed to God in doxologies. It also designates cosmic power and the power to work miracles. Finally, *dynamis* designates power that is exerted through the Spirit of God. It is Luke, as one might expect, who tends especially to associate the term "dynamis" with the revelation of the Spirit. In Mark, it has more of an eschatological ring. Nevertheless, it is clear that for the synoptic writers the deeds of power which God worked in Jesus when He healed and cast out demons were a pneumatic revelation of His messianic authority, or *exousia.* Barrett observes: "We have seen that the word *dynamis* is frequently used in the synoptic gospels to describe the mighty activity of God, especially as it was revealed in things done by Jesus of Nazareth. It has a sense close to that of *energeia* (cf. Eph 1:19ff); that is, it is not merely the power of God, but the power of God in action, force doing work. In comparison with this kinetic energy, as it were, *exousia* corresponds to potential energy; it is the divine authority which may at any moment become manifested as power, *dynamis,* through the impulse of God's will. This contrast between *dynamis* and *exousia* is, of course, not peculiar to biblical Greek, but is involved in the proper meaning of each word. For this reason, *exousia* could be used for an office, or magistracy, which afforded authority, the capacity for wielding *dynamis.* This *exousia* belongs to a stage of effectiveness which lies behind *dynamis,* which *dynamis* reveals and on which *dynamis* depends; although as we shall see, there are cases in which *exousia* is used in substantially the same sense as *dynamis.*"[4]

It was in the course of a ministry whose authority was confirmed by divine deeds of power that Jesus chose the Twelve to be

His co-workers. Long before Pentecost, they are an established fixture in the community of disciples. Their number is, moreover, clearly symbolic. With Jesus they begin the New Israel. The gospels portray Jesus as having associated the Twelve with Him in His ministry of proclamation and of faith-healing. And He is also portrayed as having evoked from them, in the person of Peter, a confession of the messianic character of His mission.[5]

Subsequent to Peter's confession Jesus is also described as having engaged in an on-going struggle with the Twelve concerning the political character of His mission and of the reign of God. He himself resisted all popular attempts to make Him king. Even in the triumphal entry into Jerusalem, He accepted the messianic accolades of the crowd (if we are to believe the gospel of John) only after the political forces in the nation had clearly aligned themselves against Him. And He was careful to counter the enthusiasm of the crowds with a prophetic gesture that made it clear that the true purpose of His ministry was not political, but the religious purification of the temple of God.[6]

Jesus is, then, portrayed in the gospels as having apprenticed the Twelve to a ministry of service in His image. He had taught them that in order to be the greatest in the kingdom, they must make themselves the least of all, the servants of all. They must become like little children. The Twelve were forbidden power politics. They were forbidden the path of political compromise. They had to learn to follow the servant of the Lord, even when His steps led to Calvary.[7]

Clearly, then, Jesus' personal sense of mission as it is sketched in the gospels provides the basis for a unitive insight into the kind of service exercised by the Twelve in the post-resurrectional Church. For as community servants subject to Jesus during the latter's ministry of atonement, the scope of the post-resurrectional ministry of the Twelve derived its on-going, concrete definition from Jesus' own developing ministry. The Twelve are portrayed in the gospels as having had to learn by word and deed to share in His labor of proclaiming the good news of atonement: the reconciliation of men to God in a divine forgiveness that cannot be earned because it has always been there from the beginning. They had to learn not only to announce that forgiveness in word, but they also had to witness to it by a life of gratuitous sharing, unrestricted love, and mutual service in the worship of atonement. Finally, they had to learn to heal and cast out demons in Jesus' name as an efficacious sign of the reconciliation with God which they were sent to proclaim.[9]

Some exegetes question whether the Twelve engaged in a ministry of healing prior to Jesus' resurrection. The problem is, however, merely factual. It is a question of historical dating, not of the purpose of the apostolate as a charismatic impetus in the Church. Sufficient for a normative insight into the purpose of the apostolate is that the faith-healing eventually practiced by the apostles would have been experienced both by them and by the Christian community as an extension of Jesus' own healing ministry. For by their post-Pentecostal healing ministry, the apostles were revealed as sharing in the same pneumatic authority *(exousia)* as Jesus himself, since their word ministry was blessed by the same signs of divine power *(dynamis)* as Jesus' own ministry.[10]

The dark night of the apostolate coincided with the passion and death of Jesus. For it was in the passion and crucifixion that Jesus embodied fully and completely the atoning love which He had preached and which the apostles were called to exemplify in the community. In the last supper, Jesus is portrayed as prophesying the eschatological significance of the ordeal He was about to face and as enjoining His disciples to repeat the prophetic ritual in memory of Him. In His trial before the Sanhedrin, He is described in the Synoptics as finally acknowledging in public His messianic claims, but under the qualifying image of the Son of Man. And by His death, He fulfilled the prophecy of the suffering servant.[11]

The Easter experiences of Peter and the Twelve are portrayed by New Testament writers as mediating between the experience of Jesus during His ministry and their own personal pneumatic transformation in His image. For it was only in the Pentecostal outpouring of the Spirit effected by the risen Christ that the Twelve came to realize the full scope of their calling.[12]

With the arrival of the Spirit, the Twelve began, in Paul's phrase, to "put on the mind of Jesus." For the first time, it seemed, they understood the meaning of their personal mission and of His message. Not only did they experience a decisive out-pouring of the sanctifying gifts, but the gift of faith was given them as well to free them to bear courageous personal witness to the Lord. The Spirit's descent on the apostles was, moreover, portrayed in Acts as their initiation into Jesus' own Jordan anointing. The same Spirit who empowered Jesus to confront others prophetically in the name of the Father, had now come to empower them after the resurrection, to confront others prophetically in Jesus' name. And as the Spirit had confirmed Jesus' ministry and authority with signs and works of power, so too did He confirm the ministry and the authority of the Twelve.[13]

From the gifts of sanctification and of faith, therefore, the apostolate derived its extra-communitarian impulse. As men sent to proclaim the universal salvation revealed in Jesus, the Twelve summoned others to repentance and to baptism with pneumatically sanctioned authority. By ritual initiation, they loosed men from the bondage of Satan and of sin. And their ministry of proclamation was confirmed by their ministry of healing.

2. The place and scope of the apostolate within the community was, however, also illumined by the Pentecostal outpouring of the service gifts. First, it revealed the apostolate to be only one of the gifts by which the Spirit builds up the Christian community. For the Spirit came to transform, not merely the apostolate, but the community as a whole by an outpouring of all of the service gifts.[14]

There is a second sense in which the outpouring of the service gifts on the entire Christian community illumined the purpose of apostolic ministry. For it clarified the purpose of Christian initiation. By doing so. it implicitly clarified the purpose of any charismatic, apostolic witness. For the arrival of the Spirit made it clear that Jesus' baptism was more than a proselyte baptism of repentance like that of John. Once the Spirit had initiated the visible, charismatic transformation of the community by pouring out His gifts on all believers, initiation into the Christian community could only be interpreted as initiation into a pneumatic, charismatic community of faith. To summon others to repentance and to baptism is, then, to summon them to open their hearts to the Spirit who alone can teach them to put on the mind of Jesus and who by

His charisms summons believers to mutual service in Jesus' name.

Moreover, repentance, like conversion, is a lifetime process. Having proclaimed the word pneumatically to the community with an authority *(exousia)* derived from the Spirit of Jesus, the apostles also found themselves faced with the responsibility as servants of a charismatic community to challenge and correct any impulse in the community that contradicted Jesus' teaching or which gave evidence by its consequences, of being inspired by some other spirit than the Spirit of Christ.[15]

In other words, the Pentecostal transformation of the community revealed in its consequences not only what it meant for the apostles to exercise the power to "loose" from the bonds of sin, law, and death by initiating new members into a pneumatic, charismatic community, but also that that power brought with it the responsibility to "bind" by excluding from the same community those who gave evidence of having closed their hearts to the anointing of the Spirit.[16]

Moreover, the apostles' ministry of proclamation was inseparable from their ministry of healing. And their exercise of authority to bind and to loose, which crowned their ministry of proclamation was an aspect of their healing ministry. For as we have noted, the most basic form of healing effected by a word ministry is conversion. And binding and loosing mediates communal healing. For the act of binding, of excluding someone from the community, is a prophetic gesture summoning the one bound and those in the community who feel and think the same as (s)he to repentance and conversion to God. When the binding effects what it intends, it is, then, efficacious of a healing whose authenticity is confirmed when the re-converted pentitent is loosed and re-admitted into the community.[17]

Clearly, then, the outpouring of the service gifts on the community revealed the purpose of the apostolate to be the evocation and discernment of gifts in the community through the exercise of a kerygmatic ministry whose authority came to revelatory visibility in the conversions, healings, and miracles which accompanied their ministry of proclamation and in the loosing and binding of men in the name of God. Hence, in the very efficacy of its exercise, the apostolate was also revealed to be only one possible source of authentic healing, instruction, and leadership within the community. For among the gifts poured out by the Spirit upon the community were gifts of prophecy, teaching wisdom, teaching instruction, healing, miracles.

In pouring out word gifts even on ordinary believers, the Spirit revealed that the scope of the community's total ministry of teaching extends beyond the teaching ministry of the apostolate. For, as Avery Dulles has noted, any tested and approved gift of prophecy and of teaching is integral to the total magisterium of the Church, even though final responsibility in justice and in love for the correct pastoral evaluation of such teaching lies with the official apostolic leaders.[18]

3. The outpouring of the service gifts illumined too the scope and limits of the apostolate in yet another way. For the Spirit effected not only the authoritative empowering and revelatory transformation of the apostolate, but also its charismatic diversification.

Even though the apostolate was inaugurated as an institution by Jesus and by Jesus alone, it is impossible to point to any specific moment in Jesus' ministry when He clearly defined the "legal scope" of the apostolate. Rather, He inaugurated the apostolate by associating Twelve men in a special way with Himself and His public ministry. He thus designated them as pillars of the new Israel. He shaped them and their ministry gradually in the course of their personal association. And in His risen glory He transformed their ministry and endowed it with pneumatic power and authority through the sending of the Spirit. It is in this sense that He may be said to have instituted the "sacrament of orders," and with it, the healing ministry of the apostles.

Scripture scholars are correct in distinguishing two different kinds of apostles in the writings of the New Testament: the Twelve and missionary apostles. They also correctly note the absence of any Scriptural evidence that the Twelve passed on their specific apostolic office to others. They are correct too in affirming that Paul grounded his authority for the exercise of his missionary apostolate in his gift rather than in any sanction of the Twelve. Paul's gift was, however, confirmed and approved in its exercise by the community as a whole, a community which included the Twelve as its ultimate court of appeal. And Paul was careful to exercise his apostolate in solidarity with the Twelve.[19]

As official ambassadors of the community with tested and approved gifts, the missionary apostles participated in a pneumatic authority *(exousia)* which, like that of the Twelve, was grounded in their gift. Moreover, there is evidence that as in the case of the Twelve, it was in many instances an authority which was confirmed and communally approved by the signs of conversion, healing, exorcism, and miracles which accompanied it; or else it was a mission sanctioned officially by the community and by those who exercised approved apostolic authority.[20]

The charismatic differentiation of the apostolate took a variety of forms. The establishment of the diaconate effected the first clear division of official responsibility in the community's leadership, although, as Raymond Brown has noted, the purpose of the first deacons was probably further removed than is sometimes supposed from the diaconate as we know it today. The establishment of resident leaders in the community founded by the missionary apostles effected a further charismatic specification of apostolic responsibility. And, as Brown has also noted, the practice transmuted the missionary apostolate into the episcopacy.[21]

Clearly then, the notion of the transmutation of gifts suggested in chapter three has important implications in any analysis of the charismatic basis of the sacrament of orders. In an experiential problematic, it is the transmutation of experience, rather than immutable principles of being, which grounds analogical resemblance. For through the process of transmutation an experience both is and is not changed. It is not changed to the extent that at least some of the same variables function within it as did prior to the transmutation. It is changed to the extent that the integration of one or more novel variables effects the adjustment of the total relational structure operative in the experience. An art object is a useful analogue. The addition of a new patch of color to a painting does not eliminate the pigmentation on the rest of the canvas. But the addition does so affect the interrelation of colors within the painting that it transforms its total impact as felt.

If the preceding analysis is sound, the gift of the apostolate received its initial genetic definition through the association of the

Twelve with the ministry of Jesus. It was subsequently transmuted in the charismatic empowering of the Twelve on Pentecost. It was still further transmuted through the emergence of the diaconate, which mediated the expansion of apostolic service to include community leaders who serve in solidarity with the Twelve. It was transmuted yet again through the emergence of missionary apostles, who shared in virtue of their charismatic anointing in the *exousia*, or authority of the apostles, and whose ministry led them to proclaim the good news to the ends of the earth. Although the Twelve as a group are not portrayed in Acts as having initially functioned in the community as missionary apostles, there is evidence that Peter did so function as the community expanded. If so, the dichotomy between the Twelve and the missionary apostles may not have been as absolute as some recent exegesis sometimes suggests. The final definitive transmutation of the apostolic ministry emerged with the establishment of the presbyter/bishops, resident community leaders who exercised their ministry in solidarity with the missionary apostles.

In the transmutation of a gift certain constants remain despite the integration of new variables into the call. Among the constants which characterize any authentic exercise of the gift of the apostolate are: (1) the call to sanctification in faith and love by putting on and embodying the mind of Jesus within a charismatic community of worship and mutual service; (2) the call to leadership in the loving service of atonement; (3) the call to witness to Jesus by proclaiming in His name the word of God to all and by summoning them to repentance and to baptism in water and the Holy Spirit; (4) the exercise of a ministry of proclamation with an authority that is charismatically grounded, ecclesially confirmed, and effective of faith-healing: i.e., of conversion, of the transformation of suffering into grace, of physical healings, and in more extraordinary instances of miracles; (5) the right in virtue of one's ecclesially confirmed apostolic call to confront the community in acts of binding and loosening which are performed both in Jesus' name and in the name of the Church universal, since the Church universal by ordination, has approved one's official apostolic acts, provided they are performed for the good of the Church; (6) the obligation to exercise such a ministry to the community in collegial solidarity with all of those who share officially in a similar calling; (7) the obligation to conduct such a ministry in responsive openness to the authentic impulses of the Spirit which emerge in the community; (8) the obligation to challenge the community constantly to a greater charismatic openness to the Spirit of God and to the gifts He brings; (9) the obligation, implicit in the right and responsibility to bind and loose, to discern which charismatic impulses come from God and which do not; (10) the obligation to reach such a discernment in openness to all the authentic gifts operative in the collective and apostolic leadership of the community and in the Church universal; (11) the obligation not to suppress the Spirit, since anyone who exercises a gift authentically confronts the community in the name of God; (12) the responsibility for discerning the impulses of the Spirit in light of the universal salvation offered all men by God in the Jesus/Pentecost event; (13) willingness in the light of all the preceding responsibilities to assume a share in the collegial leadership of the Church universal and not simply of some local congregation or parish.[22]

For no true apostle can limit the scope of his or her concern to a local prayer community. To do so would be to abandon one's call to proclaim the gospel to all creatures. It would also be to exercise one's ministry heretically, by closing one's heart to the voice of the Spirit as it comes to expression in the Church universal. Integral to the apostolate is, then, the responsibility to challenge both individuals and local communities to concern for the entire Christian and human community.

Moreover, as the Second Vatican Council has noted, the Church universal encompasses in some sense all communions of truly baptised Christians, despite their present divisions and misunderstandings.[23] To exercise one's apostolic ministry while remaining closed to the authentic manifestations of the Spirit in Christian communions other than one's own is, therefore, to act irresponsibly and to run the risk of serious inauthenticity in one's own ministry.

The variables which function in the transmutation of the apostolate are the different ecclesial contexts within which such a ministry comes concretely to be exercised. There are three contexts in which this gift has been exercised historically: in the missionary apostolate, in a local resident apostolate, and in a "conciliar" context of shared deliberation and discernment about questions of common interest to the community. Consensus concerning the purpose of the apostolate is the first ecumenical step toward a mutual recognition of ordained ministries.

4. It should be clear that the thirteen constants which characterise ordained apostolic ministry are unintelligible outside of a charismatic context. For only by openness to the sanctifying gifts can one grow into a true vision of the mind of Jesus, a vision which one is called, as an ordained minister, to proclaim in faith by word and deed to all people. Nor can one exercise such a ministry effectively without mediating charismatic healing in some form, and even, on occasion, God willing, miraculous healing.

The charismatic character of the apostolate grounds its authority and its scope. It grounds its authority, for only one called by the Spirit can confront the Church universal in the name of God. And only one whose call to apostolic leadership in service has been confirmed by the call of the Church through the action of its approved leaders can confront believer and nonbeliever alike in the name of the Christian community as such. Nor is one's call from the Spirit experientially clear until it is ecclesially discerned and confirmed. Moreover, the authentic exercise of an apostolic ministry is also impossible outside of a charismatic context. For the authentic apostle must exercise a ministry in faith by responsiveness to the impulses of the Spirit which emerge in other ordained ministers and in the people of God as a whole.

The preceding analysis also vindicates the fact that one can respond authentically to an apostolic call only if one does so sacramentally. Ordination to apostolic ministry is an act of official covenant worship which engages the faith of the Church universal. It is official because it is done by the Christian community as an expression of the faith and love which unites all true believers everywhere. Since the ordaining community is not just the local community, but the universal Church, ordination to apostolic ministry must be performed by one who confronts the ordinand in the name of the Church as such, that is, in the name of all believing Christians throughout the world, not simply in the name of some local congregation. The ordaining minister's function is twofold: 1) it is to summon the ordinand officially and prophetically to minister to others as the apostles did and 2) it is to invoke the Spirit upon the ordinand in a prayer whose salvific meaning and fruits are certainly sanctioned by God irrespective of the personal worth of the minister. In the ordinand's authentic response to that summons, the covenant of grace revealed in the Jesus/Pentecost event is renewed. Here several points need to be noted:

First, it is impossible to exercise an apostolic ministry in the strict sense unless one's call is ecclesially confirmed. Ecclesial confirmation of the call is not, therefore, extrinsic to the call, but integral to it. For a call to apostolic ministry is a call to minister to men in the name of Jesus and of the Church universal. One cannot minister in the name of a world-wide community unless that community consents to one's ministry. At the same time, if one's call is from God, then the community has no right to refuse its consent. As in the case of laymen gifted to serve the community in a special way, those called to apostolic service have the "right and duty" to exercise their gift in the community.

Second, the official "sealing" of an apostolic call is an act of covenant worship. It is expressive of the faith of the Church universal, of the commitment to God mediated in the gifts of sanctification and of faith. In it, the ordinand reaffirms his or her baptismal faith. (S)He also reaffirms the commitment to the Church universal which came to visible expression in baptism and confirmation. But (s)he does so in a context which brings with it a host of specific leadership responsibilities not present in a more generic baptismal and confirmational commitment. For in ordination, reaffirmation of belief in God and of willingness to serve in the community occurs in a new ecclesial context that is defined by one's personal gift of service. And that gift is a call to prolong in space-time the charismatic impulse of the first apostles.

Third, because an authentic apostolic ministry is grounded in the free gift of the Spirit, the sex of the ordinand is irrelevant. To exclude women arbitrarily from the ministry in the Church is, then, to run the serious risk of certainly suppressing the Spirit.

Fourth, the public confirmation of a call to apostolic ministry is done by the local community in the name of the Church universal. The call to apostolic service differs from other calls to Christian leadership precisely by the universality of its scope. Those with non-apostolic service gifts minister by virtue of their personal call alone to some local community of faith. The apostle by contrast to these non-apostolic ministries assumes collegial responsibility for leading the whole Church in responsiveness to the Spirit.

The confirmation of a call to minister to the Church universal must be effected by the Church universal. And the Church universal can act as such only if there are those within it with the authority to confront others in its name. Hence, the official confirmation of an apostolic call can only be confirmed by another apostle, or by one empowered to speak in the name of the apostolic college. The act of ordination ought, moreover, to be truly expressive of the confirming discernment of the believing community.

The confirmation of an apostolic call demands, therefore, the establishment of criteria for discernment accepted throughout the Church universal. They are implemented concretely within some local community. But when the discernment of an apostolic vocation is carried on in solidarity with the rest of the Church and with its leaders throughout the world, its confirmation is an act which engages the Church universal as such. It is, therefore, also appropriate that the public, ritual confirmation of an apostolic vocation be reserved ordinarily to one who bears ultimate responsibility for discernment in the community and in the Church universal as a whole. Such responsibility rests upon the bishops.

Fifth, the act of the bishop within ordination is a kerygmatic and prophetic act. In publicly and officially sanctioning the communal discernment of the community, the ordaining prelate proclaims the salvation revealed in Jesus. (S)he affirms it to have been an efficacious force in the life of the ordinand. And (s)he challenges the ordinand to fidelity to the call which the ordinand has received from God to serve the community in the image of Jesus and as a successor to the apostles.

Sixth, ordination is also an act of worship. It is public praise to God for the work of grace He has effected in the life of the ordinand, and it is a prayer that the ordinand will remain faithful to the call (s)he has received. That prayer is sacramentally efficacious in the senses discussed in chapter five. It will also be pragmatically effective if the ordinand not only is truly called by God but also places no obstacles to the action of the Spirit in the course of his or her ministry.

Clearly, then, the ordination ritual is the culmination and confirmation of a call to apostolic service much as the sealing of the marriage contract is integral to and the culmination of the charismatic call to marriage. But as in the case of marriage, the ritual alone cannot guarantee the ordinand's charismatic call, since the Spirit, not the community, is the ultimate source of the call and since the discernment that grounds the ritual is fallible. One cannot create a service gift by ritual or legal fiat.

Nevertheless, there is no doubt that even the ordinand whose call has been fallaciously discerned is authorized by the ritual of ordination to administer the sacraments truly and "validly" to the Christian community. Here it is important to recall that in order to function as a "valid" sacramental minister, one need not enjoy the gift of the apostolate. One need only have authority to act in the name of the Church universal and to administer the sacraments according to the Church's understanding of their meaning. Even an unbeliever can function as an extraordinary minister of baptism if (s)he is willing, in baptising, to do what the Church does.

The "validly" ordained minister, in virtue of his or her ordination, certainly enjoys the authorization to function officially in sacramental situations, even should the discernment of his or her call prove subsequently to have been fallacious. For at the time of ordination both (s)he and the discerning community believed the ordinand to have been authentically called.

5. The scope and purpose of an apostolic gift is illumined by comparing and contrasting it with marriage and with the sacraments of community initiation. Ministerial ordination resembles marriage in that both rituals express the charismatic transformation of pre-existing institutions. Jesus discovered marriage as a fact and a ritual in human social experience; but He transformed it sacramentally by His teaching and by sending the gift-giving Spirit to make marriage into a Christian calling. Jesus himself, however, created the institution of the apostolate by setting aside certain men to be His close associates in His ministry of leading others in the service of atonement. But Jesus also transformed the apostolate He had thus "institutionalized" by sending the gift-giving

Spirit to effect its charismatic illumination diversification, and historical transmutation.

Marriage and ministeral ordination are similar too in that both sacraments ought to be the culmination and official sanction of a prior process of communal discernment. In both sacraments the ritual gives public, official sanction to an authentic charism, or call, *(res)*, but is unable of itself *(sacramentum)* to substitute for the charismatic action of the Spirit by a mere legal or ritual fiction.

But marriage and orders differ radically in the scope of the love commitment they embody. In Christian marriage, there is a narrowing of the love commitment made in baptism. In married consent, one's baptismal love is focused upon one's spouse and on the children who will be the fruit of married love. In orders, one's sacramental commitment is to the Church universal as such, to assuming responsibility for its public leadership in the service of atonement. Marriage, then, transmutes one's baptismal and confirmational commitment by focusing and circumscribing it. Orders transmutes and intensifies one's baptismal and confirmational commitment without circumscribing it in any way. It intensifies it by integrating a new variable into one's original Christian faith commitment. As an apostle, one is publicly committed to do more than serve God as a Christian. One is in addition officially committed to public leadership in service, by seeking to set an example of service for all believers while fulfilling the responsibilities of apostolic office.

Because its love commitment is universal in scope, ordination, like baptism and confirmation, confers a character. Hans Küng is correct in insisting that the "character" conferred by orders cannot be adequately interpreted in purely legal or in outdated metaphysical terms. Unfortunately, he seems also to imply that there is no other way to understand the meaning of the sacramental "character." As we have seen, the three sacraments which have been traditionally described as conferring a character have the following traits in common: they are initiatory sacraments in the strict sense and they all "seal" a faith-commitment to the Church universal as such. Baptism and confirmation initiate one into full Church membership. Orders initiates one into the college of those responsible for the official leadership of the universal Church.

No other sacraments can be similarly described. Marriage is strict initiation but restricts the scope of one's love commitment. The sacrament of reconciliation involves commitment to the universal Church; but it is re-initiation, not initiation in the strict sense. The anointing of the sick looks to individual and personal healing rather than to initiation. First communion is not initiation itself, but the celebration and fruit of a completed baptismal initiation. And the eucharist is the communal reaffirmation of an initiatory commitment already made. Finally, the consent of faith mediated by baptism, confirmation, and orders redefines the believer's relation to the Church universal and does so in an unrepeatable act. For an act of strict initiation cannot happen more than once. It is, then, appropriate that the image of a "seal" be applied in a special way to such an act. For by publicly inaugurating a new relationship with the universal Church, such sacraments have special redemptive significance and give a decisive re-orientation to the believer's life.

6. The preceding analysis also allows us to distinguish the gift of apostolate from the gifts of leadership, administration, official service, and helping. The apostolate has an affinity for all these gifts. The apostle is a leader: as chief discerner (s)he has ultimate responsibility for decision-making in matters that touch the community as a whole. Hence, (s)he cannot avoid administrative responsibilities. By ordination, (s)he exercises official authority. And, like the helper, (s)he seeks to facilitate shared group activities.

These other charismatic gifts differ, however, from the apostolate in their scope and in their potentially ephemeral character. They differ from the apostolate in their scope because by their inner dynamic they look, not to the service of the Church universal, but to the service of some local community. They do not, therefore, require discerning confirmation by the entire Church, but only by some local community.

Any impulse to ordain sacramentally after confirmation one who has experienced an ordinary charismatic call to serve some local community would, then, be theologically misguided. Confirmation itself is ordination to non-apostolic community service.

There is no college of non-apostles in the Church; hence, there is no need to initiate members into it.

The action gifts like leadership, administration, helping, differ also from the charism of apostolate by being potentially ephemeral. Such calls are potentially ephemeral because they are restricted in their conditions and consequences. A call to minister to a particular prayer group does not involve an absolute commitment. The Spirit moves where He wills, and He may well call a local group leader, a local administrator, a local official elsewhere and to some other form of service. But the apostolic commitment is not abolished by a change of residence nor need it be reconfirmed as one moves from place to place. For it is a commitment, not to serve some local group, but to serve the Church universal.

The apostolate, moreover, like marriage, demands a love commitment to God and to the Church universal that is unrestricted in its conditions and consequences. Such a commitment cannot be revoked by the one who makes it. Those, therefore, who feel an allegedly temporal vocation to the priesthood give evidence of being called to administration, official service, local leadership, or community facilitation rather than to the apostolate. In other words, not every call to Church ministry need be permanent, but the call to apostolic service is. For, like marriage, once it is made, it cannot, being an unconditioned love commitment, be personally revoked by the ordained minister without sin.

The call expressed in the non-apostolic action gifts also differs from both marriage and the apostolate in that the former are task oriented. They are by their proper dynamic a call to perform a certain kind of practical activity of benefit to some local community. Such tasks can, as we have seen, be dissociated in their exercise from Christian love. Both orders and marriage are, by contrast, calls to embody a certain quality of love. The tasks which both calls impose are only consequences of that love. Married love is, however, restricted in its scope. Apostolic love, like the redemptive love of Christ, reaches out to all persons. It becomes all things to all people to win all to Christ. The love of the apostle ought, then, to be proportioned to the universal scope of the apostolic call to proclaim the good news to every creature and to exercise leadership in service for the Church universal. As in the case of celibacy, then, apostolic love comes to concrete expression in acts which reach out to those in the human and Christian community who are in greatest need.

The apostle's call to leadership in the service of atoning love endows the gift of apostolate with a strong affinity for celibacy. For the celibate too, as we have seen, is called to embody just such a love. In other words, one cannot respond authentically to marriage, to celibacy, and to the apostolate without being sanctified in the love of Christ, although, as Paul warns, one may respond to the other gifts of service without growing in love. But celibacy and apostolate are not identical. One may, then, be called simultaneously to the apostolate and to marriage. The reason why these calls are compossible is that while marriage restricts, it does not annul the baptismal call of every Christian to put on the mind of Christ. And baptismal love, like apostolic love, is unrestricted in its scope. Still, anyone called to both marriage and the apostolate is apt to experience serious personal tensions as a consequence of both calls. And one of the tests of their authenticity will be a certain freedom in the Spirit to bring them to effective personal integration. By the same token, however, to make celibacy a condition for ordination is to run a serious risk of certainly suppressing the Spirit.

The preceding analysis also sheds light on the meaning of apostolic succession. It is ecumenically fashionable to speak today of functional rather than historical succession to apostolic ministry. Functional succession implies that one may succeed to the ministry of the apostles without being sacramentally authorized to do so by a member of the apostolic college. Historical succession demands such authorization. There is a truth present in both theories.

The insight struggling to expression in the notion of functional succession is that the call to apostolic service entails charismatic constants wherever that call exists. The notion of functional succession also underscores the fact that the official, ritual confirmation of an apostolic call alone is not itself creative of the call it confirms. The call comes from the Spirit; it is only confirmed efficaciously by the Church in the sense of sacramental efficacy described in chapter five.

One may, then, enjoy a calling to apostolic service prior to its final ritual confirmation, as is the case with ordained clergy prior to ordination. One may also have one's ministry confirmed by a local community prior to its final confirmation by the Church universal; and such local confirmation is an important phase in the discernment of an apostolic call. It is this fact which in part legitimizes minor orders. For there is a primordial sacramentality operative in any apostolic ministry prior to its final ritual confirmation. The Spirit of Jesus comes to experiential visibility in the ministering words and deeds of the candidate for official apostleship. Without such experiential visibility the call would never be discerned.

The truth which comes to expression in the notion of historical apostolic succession is that a call to apostolic service comes to integral completion and full, experiential, sacramental visibility only when it is confirmed by the Church universal acting through the action of its ordained apostolic leaders.

Clearly, then, the evil consequences which follow upon the rending of the Church through heresy and schism have their parallel in the rending of the apostolic college. For just as Christians who are separated doctrinally and sacramentally cannot to that extent share effectively the gifts and fruits of the Spirit, so too is an apostolic college rent by heresy and schism to that extent spiritually impoverished by its inability to share effectively in the gifts of the Spirit operative in other communions and in their apostolic leaders. The ecumenical problems become more complex when one is confronted with a variety of Christian communions endowed with an ordained apostolic ministry who mutually excommunicate one another while simultaneously claiming to represent the Church universal.

If the preceding analysis is sound, the gift of the apostolate may indeed be operative in different Christian communions; but those enjoying the gift will be able to function as apostles with full charismatic and sacramental visibility only when they have resolved the divisions which separate them in some formal act which acknowledges the collegial solidarity of their apostolic ministry. On the face of it, there would seem to be no reason why such a reconciliation could not take the form of the mutual recognition of the orders operative in different communions without sacramental reordination. Such recognition would presuppose, of course, that serious doctrinal incompatibilities concerning the scope and purpose of official pastoral ministry have been resolved. If so, however, the historical validation of the orders of a communion other than one's own is a theological red herring.

7. The preceding analysis also casts light on the difference between a charismatic and a hierarchical ministry of teaching. The difference does not lie in the fact that the ordained minister is called to teach while the unordained charismatic teacher is not. Each has a personal gift; and each in virtue of that gift confronts the community in God's name, when, that is, each teaches authentically. Nor does the difference between these gifts lie in the concrete act performed. Both may teach identically the same doctrine. But there is a difference in the ecclesial context in which a hierarchical and a non-hierarchical ministry of teaching is each exercised. And that difference entails special responsibilities for the ordained apostolic preacher.

For the ordained preacher, in virtue of the scope of the apostolic call and of its official confirmation through ritual initiation into the apostolic college, confronts the community on those occasions when (s)he teaches officially, not merely as one personally gifted by God, but as an official spokesman for the Church universal. In such situations (s)he stands under obligation to proclaim only those doctrines which express the shared, evolving faith of the community. (S)he cannot substitute for such doctrinal instruction merely private personal opinions, even if (s)he believes them to be from God.

The ordained apostle can, however, enjoy other gifts than that of apostolic ministry. One may in addition to an apostolic call have a personal, charismatic gift of teaching that sets one apart from other apostles and which mediates new personal insights into divine revelation. These insights may eventually come to be accepted as authentically expressive of the shared faith of the Church universal. But when the ordained minister uses such a personal gift, (s)he speaks as an individual, not as an official spokesman for the whole Church.

When functioning unofficially, as a charismatic teacher, the ordained apostolic minister, like every charismatic teacher, has the obligation to reflect on the meaning of the evolving, shared faith of the Christian community. But (s)he does so in a way that draws creatively on a personal belief system. The charismatic teacher seeks, then, to enrich the shared faith of the community through novel personal insight. But in official, public teachings, the apostolic teacher has an obligation to be personally self-effacing. Official apostolic teaching seeks merely to interpret the common evolving faith of the Christian community by proclaiming its accepted meaning. It is the proclamation of a consensus.

These insights lend charismatic grounding to Avery Dulles's distinction between the role of the official pastoral magisterium and that of creative theological reflection.[24] For it roots both forms of teaching in different gifts. Unofficial charismatic teaching bears the chief responsibility for expanding the community's understanding of divine revelation. Official pastoral teachers have the responsibility of proclaiming what is common doctrine and of setting down adequate and flexible norms for teaching, worship, and shared Christian living. An ordained apostle with a personal charismatic gift of teaching ought, then, to avoid confusing these two teaching roles in ministering to others.

But if a personal, charismatic gift of teaching differs in its ecclesial exercise from an apostolic ministry of teaching, prophecy must a fortiori similarly differ. For the prophetic message is confrontational and concrete. It speaks to a specific person, community, or situation. It is in fact, as we have seen, an initial, abductive, pneumatic interpretation in faith of the salvific meaning operative in the concrete order of human society. As the interpretation of a concrete situation prophecy is different from the creedal professions of the Church universal, which are by contrast the expression of a consensus which prescinds from local situations and local beliefs. Needless to say, the shared faith of the community, if it is to be a living faith, will illumine and direct the faith-experiences of local communities. And apostolic teachers are under serious obligation to enrich the faith of local communities by leading them to an understanding of the practical, situational consequences of the creedal profession which binds them to other Christians. But such teaching is logically deductive; it explicitates the consequences of premises communally held. Prophecy, as we have seen, is a charismatic abduction.

As a charismatic abduction, prophecy is in need of doctrinal evaluation. It must be measured against the shared faith of the community. Hence, prophecy can never lay claim to being spoken initially in the name of the Church universal. The prophet confronts the community in virtue of a personal gift, or call. As gifted, (s)he speaks in the name of God. The community as a whole may subsequently endorse a prophecy as authentically expressive of its shared faith. But until it is so endorsed, prophecy, like non-apostolic teaching, remains a personal act rather than an official pronouncement. This is why there can be no such thing as apostolic prophecy. Apostles may also be prophets. But when they teach prophetically, they teach as individuals personally gifted by God, not as spokesman for the Church universal. Moreover, if the analysis of the relationship between prophecy and interpretation proposed in chapter three is sound then what we have just said about prophecy applies to an interpreted tongue as well. For an interpreted tongue is in its impact on the community the equivalent of prophecy.

Moreover, as we also saw in chapter three, healing is the ordinary concomitant of an effective ministry of teaching. If, then, the ecclesial context of apostolic teaching is radically changed through ritual ordination, so too is the ecclesial context of an apostolic ministry of healing. For the apostolic healer does more than the charismatic faith-healer. The charismatic faith-healer speaks to others personally, in the name of God, as one individually called to such a ministry. The apostolic faith-healer when acting officially as an apostle confronts others as a consequence of official ordination also in the name of the Church universal. The official healing ministry of the ordained apostle engages the Church universal in two obvious ways. First of all, in its official exercise, an apostolic ministry of faith healing has as its object the healing of the community as such. Not that an apostolic ministry of faith healing does not seek to effect the healing of individuals. Rather it seeks to effect the healing of individuals by challenging them to a public reaffirmation of their commitment in faith to the universal Christian community. Apostolic faith-healing must, therefore, be invoked when the healing of an individual is impossible without such a formal act of communal reconciliation. This will be the case when the one in need of healing has performed some act that is so seriously incompatible with a Christian faith commitment that it equivalently places the penitent outside the community. The healing of such sinful acts engages the power of binding and loosing, for only by official loosing in the strict sense can their consequences for their author and for the community as a whole be healed.

Similarly, the invocation of apostolic authority in the healing of the physically ill is appropriately restricted to those cases which ought to be the special concern of the community as a whole, namely, those whose need for physical healing is most extreme. The ecclesial scope and context of an apostolic ministry of physical healing thus provides a practical, pastoral division of labor between hierarchical and charismatic faith-healers. The charismatic ministry of faith-healing is appropriately exercised in those instances in which the kind of healing required does not involve or concern seriously the Church universal as such.

Second, an apostolic ministry of faith-healing transmutes a charismatic ministry of faith-healing by transforming it into a public act of covenant worship. Ordained apostles may pray privately and unofficially for healing. But in the official exercise of a healing ministry, the apostle does not confront the one in need of healing simply as a charismatic individual. (S)he confronts the other in the name of the Church universal. As a consequence, the apostle's healing ministry, in its public, official exercise, challenges those in need of healing to renew their personal commitment to the Christian community as such. To renew such a commitment is to reaffirm one's baptismal covenant in transmuted form, as an expression of repentance after initial conversion.

Clearly, then, the apostolic exercise of faith-healing fulfills all the conditions for sacramental worship in the strict sense.[25] As a consequence of the presence of the apostolic minister, it becomes an official act of covenant renewal which engages the faith of the Church universal. The official exercise of an apostolic healing ministry occurs in the context of an official, apostolic proclamation of the good news. In challenging charismatically and prophetically the one in need of healing to turn to the Lord in faith, the apostolic faith-healer also demands an official, public renewal of that personal baptismal commitment which unites the believer to Christians everywhere. In invoking the healing power of the Spirit, the apostolic faith-healer, in the official exercise of his or her ministry, prays not simply in the name of God but also in the name of the Church universal. As a consequence, in the worshipper's public response to the apostolic faith-healer's ministering word, the baptismal covenant is officially and publicly renewed.

There is, then, both similarity and difference between the apostolic administration of the sacrament of reconciliation and a charismatic ministry of psychic "healing of memories." They are alike in that both seek to effect the healing of attitudes rather than of the physical forces within experience over which one has little or no evaluative control. Both challenge the sick person to a renewal of faith. Both look to God rather than to the minister to effect the needed healing.

But a charismatic ministry of psychic healing is not a sacramental ministry, for the simple reason that the charismatic faith-healer is not an ordained apostle. (S)He does not confront the one in need of healing officially, in the name of the Church universal as such. (S)He has no authority to lead one in need of healing in an official act of covenant renewal.

What is true of a ministry of psychic faith-healing is also true of the charismatic ministry of physical faith-healing. The ordained apostle functions sacramentally in such situations for the same reason that (s)he functions sacramentally in praying for a healing of attitudes.[26] And the charismatic faith-healer functions non-sacramentally for the same reasons as govern the authentic exercise of a charismatic ministry of psychic healing.

In an experiential problematic, what is healed, of course, is not just bodies and souls, but selves. The emergent self is, however, defined both by the physical, environmental forces which function in personal experience and by its evaluative attitudinal response to them. The distinction within experience between these two genetic moments in personal development legitimizes a distinct ritualization of sacramental prayer for attitudinal healing and sacramental prayer for physical healing. Reconciliation looks primarily to attitudes; the anointing of the sick to physical, environmental disorder. But in the official pastoral catechesis, these two forms of healing have, quite correctly, never been completely dissociated. The sacramental prayer for physical healing has always been regarded as a prayer for total healing: physical, psychic, spiritual. Similarly, the sacramental prayer for attitudinal healing has always presupposed repentance; and repentance is the conscious renunciation of past disordered decisions which enter present experience as physically grounded attitudes. Moreover, as the Council of Trent saw, the sacramental healing of attitudes seeks to effect, not only the social forgiveness of past disordered decisions; but it presents them to God in order that He might effectively heal their "consequences," their physical impact on the subsequent development of an emerging faith experience. We shall return to this point in discussing the Lord's supper.

8. The preceding reflections cast light, then, on the complex scope of an ordained, apostolic ministry. There has been a certain amount of discussion in recent years concerning the identity crisis of the Catholic priest in a post-Vatican Church. The discussion has suggested that in more than one instance, the concrete identity assumed by some priests has been a false one, rooted in motives that are clearly inauthentic when measured against an integral four-fold conversion. These motives might include the absence of intellectual and affective conversion; beliefs derived from an individualistic, Jansenistic asceticism; inordinate attachment to the trappings of clerical culture or to the comforts of bourgeois living, and inadequate theological understanding of priestly ministry. At the same time, many priests involved in the charismatic renewal have insisted that they have discovered their identity as priests with such freshness in the course of ministering to charismatic communities that it almost seems as though they have discovered themselves as priests for the first time.

If the approach to the apostolate suggested in these pages is sound, then such a discovery should scarcely come as a surprise. For the scope of the ordained apostolic ministry cannot be restricted to legal, sacramental, bureaucratic functions. The ordained apostolic minister, as the official spokesman in the local community for the Church universal, bears the ultimate responsibility for evoking and discerning the gifts of the Spirit. In proclaiming the revelation of God by example as well as by word, in season and out of season, (s)he is summoned by God to keep the community constantly turned to the Spirit who alone can teach them the mind of the Lord or lead them to the anointed service of the brethren to which the Father calls them. Such a ministry engages the power of binding and loosing and therefore culminates in sacramental moments. When it touches the unbeliever, it can lead to baptism. When it touches the inauthentic Christian, it can lead to sacramental reconciliation. When it touches the seriously ill, it can lead to sacramental anointing.

But while the ordained apostolic leader is called to embody the sanctifying gifts and to be faithful to the service gifts (s)he has personally received, (s)he is not called to embody all the service gifts in his or her own person. The ordained minister may possess no other service gift then a personal call to the apostolate. (S)he needs no other. For the success of an apostolic ministry within the community will be measured, not by the number of gifts the apostle personally posseses, but by the apostle's ability to evoke from the community the charismatic gifts of faith, prayer, tongues, prophecy, teaching, healing, miracles, discernment, practical service, celibacy, and marriage which any believing community needs in order to grow collectively in the mind of Christ. In other words, the true apostle is not the one who ministers personally to every single member of his or her congregation, except in those sacramental situations in which official public ministry is required. Rather (s)he is one who opens a believing community to the gifts of the Spirit so that the Lord himself may teach the members of that community to minister spiritually and charismatically to one another.

Let the ordained leader who imagines that such a ministry will leave the apostle with nothing to do try it. For experience shows that the more a community of believers opens charismatically to God, the more they are in need of ordained apostolic ministry. That ministry is correctly described by Vatican II as involving three key elements: 1) sound teaching; 2) discernment and decision, especially in cases which touch the community as a whole; 3) providing an adequate social and ecclesial context for charismatic and sacramental worship within the community.[26]

But if there is a sense in which the ordained minister evokes authentic openness to the gifts by the exercise of a gift of apostolate, it has also been the experience of many an apostolic minister that in serving a truly Spirit-led Christian community, the community ministers to its own apostolic leaders. It not only supports its ordained minister in prayer, in word, and in deed; but it summons its ordained leaders prophetically to lived fidelity to their apostolic calling. And through the activity of the gifts in the community it complements and in some instances corrects the ordained leader's ministry of proclamation, healing, discernment, and active service.

But the ordained apostolic minister is also the chief discerner of gifts. This is not a place for a detailed discussion of the inauthenticities which can attend the exercise of each of the service gifts. But some indication of the pastoral implications of the preceding reflections is in order. For they cast light on the meaning of an authentic exercise of apostolic ministry.

The absence of affective conversion can lead in any community to excessive emotional preoccupation with tongues, or with any other gift. It can breed the manipulative use of prophecy: the prophet's self-deluded attempt to foist his/her neuroses or psychoses on others in the name of God. It can motivate "scotosis" in teachers: the neurotic inability to face specific problems or novel insights. It can lead to morbid preoccupation with physical healing or to futile quests for "miraculous" solutions to neurotically motivated problems as an escape from facing one's neurosis squarely. It can lead to manipulative discernment: the attempt to use discernment as a means of forming others into one's own neurotic image. And it can lead to mindless conflict in the exercise of a practical ministry in the community.

The absence of intellectual conversion can motivate a fundamentalistic interpretation of tongues or of any of the gifts. It can lead to the attempt to endow one's prophecies with "objective self-evidence." It can dupe the teacher into substituting pet personal biases for the word of God or into proclaiming simplistic, fundamentalistic, and historically naive explanations of God's word. It can lead the faith-healer to subvert his or her own ministry by inauthentic teaching. It can mislead the discerner into the rigid application of speculatively inadequate criteria within the discerning process. It perverts the action gifts by endowing them with a rigidity and inflexibility of viewpoint.

The absence of moral conversion can lead the tongue speaker to dissociate the praise of God from the practical service of others. It can blind the prophet to the social and moral abuses to which (s)he is called to speak. It can lead the teacher to dissociate theoretical insights from their practical and socio-ethical consequences. It can blind the healer to the social causes of human ills and to society's need for healing. It can deprive the discerner of the ethical criteria needed to evaluate movements in the community. And it can divert the activities of those with action gifts into channels that are devoid of socio-ethical significance.

In addition to the inauthenticities which are rooted in the lack of affective, intellectual, and moral conversion, there are two other major sources of inauthenticity in the exercise of the gifts. The first is the dissociation of the exercise of one's service gift from the gifts of sanctification. The second is the dissociation of the exercise of one's service gifts from the other gifts operative in the Church universal.

The tongue speaker who does not embody the mind of Jesus turns glossolalic utterance, as Paul warns, into mere noise. The prophecy, teaching, discernment, or shared activity which is not expressive of the mind of the Lord subverts shared commitment to God in Christ rather than builds up the community.

The second religious source of inauthenticity is the exercise of one's service gifts in isolation from the gifts operative in the Church universal. We have already discussed this point in speaking of the ecclesial impact of the service gifts. If the argument there proposed is sound, then no one can grow authentically in the mind of Christ and in the service gift (s)he has received, if (s)he remains closed to the operation of the Spirit throughout the entire Christian community. It is this realization which has always led the great mystics and visionaries to submit their experiences in writing to the discernment of the believing community as a whole and of its ordained apostolic leaders.

The fact that one can exercise a service gift inauthentically does not necessarily deny the reality of one's call to service. The

Christian who so acts may be truly called by God to a ministry of tongues, interpretation, prophecy, teaching, healing, discernment, or active service. By dissociating one's response to that gift from the mind of Christ, one renders its exercise salvifically insignificant from a personal standpoint and potentially harmful in its consequences to the community. The apostolic leader who summons another to repentance should, then, challenge that person, not to a denial of his or her gift, but to its authentic exercise.

It may, moreover, be useful at this point to relate the analysis of the dynamic interrelation of the gifts undertaken in chapter three to an observation concerning the Pauline gifts in Vatican II. *Apostolicam actuositatem* teaches that anyone who possesses a gift of the Spirit has the "right and duty" to exercise it in the community provided (s)he does so for the good of the whole community and in solidarity with and submission to its ordained leaders. The doctrine is one of the most theologically pregnant statements concerning the gifts made at Vatican II. Rights and duties have traditionally been regarded as correlative. What is significant in the Council's teaching is its insistence that the Christian's ecclesial rights and duties are in part charismatically grounded.

Rights follow duties: one has the right to perform something one is morally obliged to do. At the basis of the Christian's ecclesial obligations is the call of the Spirit, as the Council fathers saw. The believing community in solidarity with its leaders can confirm or repudiate a given call. But it does not issue the call. The Spirit does. In other words there is a true sense in which every Christian truly anointed by the Spirit to perform an ecclesial service confronts the community *ex sese et non consensu ecclesiae* (i.e., of oneself and not by the consent of the Church). (S)he acts *ex sese* because every authentic service gift is personal. Hence, every authentic exercise of a service gift is also personal. (S)he does not act *ex consensu ecclesiae* because (s)he acts in response to a charismatic impulse that is ultimately grounded in the Spirit, not in the discerning community. At the same time, the pragmatic test of the pneumatic grounding of one's service gift is one's willingness to submit its exercise to the discernment of the community and of its ordained leaders.

9. The ordained apostolic minister is only a human being.

And (s)he is as subject to the lack of affective, intellectual, and moral conversion as any believer. The affectively unconverted apostle will be apt to foist personal neuroses on others and to do it in the name of God and the Church universal. The intellectually unconverted apostle will in the exercise of an official ministry be apt to be rigidly dogmatic and intolerantly closed to the anointed teaching of other members of the community. Or (s)he may lapse into doctrinal dilettantism. The morally unconverted apostle will stand hardened to the social plight of those in the community whose needs and claims are often the most pressing. And (s)he will be apt to rationalize such selfishness and spiritual tepidity in an ingenious variety of ways. The apostle who fails to seek the Spirit in prayer in order to grow daily in insight into the mind of Christ will be inclined to pursue a self-reliant apostolate. (S)He will trust human insight and initiative more than the Spirit of God. Such an apostle's ministry, if it succeeds at all, will evoke little more than bland humanitarianism. (S)He will be stingy with personal possessions and spiritual gifts, unconcerned to share with those in need. (S)He will be apt to set arbitrary and disordered conditions on commitment to the apostolate and (s)he will refuse to serve God and others unless those conditions are met. Such a minister will seek to coerce others rather than to embody for them the atoning love of Christ.

Finally, the apostle who remains closed to the Spirit's voice as it comes to expression in the local community and in the Church universal quickly transforms apostolic ministry into heresy. Not that the apostle need be a formal heretic. Karl Rahner is correct in insisting that in an increasingly pluralistic society, heresy is often only implicit: a serious inauthenticity in faith rather than a canonical act of defiance. But the consequences of such an inauthenticity can be nevertheless disastrous for one's self and for the people one touches.

There are, of course, checks to the inauthenticities which plague an ordained apostolic ministry. First, there is the relentless pursuit of the Spirit of God who touches the conscience of any person who is in any way open to His promptings. Second, there is the collegial character of ordained apostolic ministry. That collegial character is the consequence both of its original institution by

Jesus as a "college" of twelve and its subsequent charismatic diversification in the Pentecostal era.

Moreover, the collegial character of an ordained apostolic ministry has some important consequences for its authentic exercise. It means, first of all, that the true apostle is co-responsible with other ordained apostles for the leadership and service of the Church universal. The exercise of an apostolic ministry which fails to acknowledge such co-responsibility is to that extent suspect and questionable in its binding force upon the community. For one cannot act authentically in the name of the Church universal, if one closes one's heart to the voice of the Spirit as it comes to expression throughout the Church universal. One can hear the Spirit's voice as a Christian apostle, therefore, not by retiring into some monastic, Neo-Platonic, or bureaucratic solitude, but by discerning dialogue with one's fellow apostles and Christians and by sensitivity to every authentic charismatic voice in the community.

But if every ordained apostle shares co-responsibility for leading the community in Christian service, in the decision-making process the buck stops with the bishop at a local level and with the college of bishops in conciliar decrees or in other joint official decisions in matters that concern the Church universal. For the episcopal college bears ultimate responsibility within the community for deciding correctly in the Spirit issues that affect the universal Church.

But the authentic exercise of episcopal authority is impossible if bishops are insulated bureaucratically from their people and from their priests. Indeed, there is nothing that undermines ecclesiastical authority more quickly then its inauthentic exercise. For the bureaucratically isolated bishop acts in a vacuum that renders official decisions irrelevant to the needs of God's people and to the impulses of grace operative among them. The intellectually, morally, religiously, or affectively unconverted bishop can, then, easily and unwittingly transform what ought to be the service of God's people in atoning love into an act of religious oppression.

Nevertheless, as in the case of the charismatic gifts, every ordained apostle in the authentic personal exercise of an apostolic gift confronts the community *ex sese et non ex consensu ecclesiae* in the sense explained above. For the apostle's call to service is also personal and Spirit-grounded, even though its authentic exercise is a function of personal willingness to minister to others in collegial co-responsibility with other apostles.

For if the heretical use of a non-apostolic gift grounds a Gnosticism of the left, the heretical use of an apostolic gift grounds a Gnosticism of the right. A Gnosticism of the left opposes the "inner light" of the individual believer to the rest of the community and to its authentic institutions. A Gnosticism of the right opposes rigidly the "inner light" of the ordained leader to the Spirit operative in the community and to its authentic institutions. Moreover, the rightist Gnostic takes easy refuge in political intrigue, parliamentary maneuvers and institutional inertia in order to impose disordered personal desires upon others.

10. The preceding reflections cast light on the debate over papal infallibility.[26] In the charismatic transmutation of the apostolate over the years, the "Petrine trajectory" discernible in Scripture has evolved into an important and necessary principle within the episcopal college.

The charismatic grounding of the papal office entails that the pope, like every authentically gifted Christian, confront the believing community in the authentic exercise of his gift *ex sese et non ex consensu ecclesiae*. As in the case of the ordinary Christian, the phrase describes correctly the origin of papal rights and duties in the community without providing an adequate set of criteria for discerning the authentic exercise of the papal gift. But the phrase assumes special connotations when applied to the papal ministry. Those connotations derive from the peculiar responsibilities of that ministry, namely, the exercise of a unifying leadership function within the apostolic college.

If the preceding suggestions are sound, then the authentic exercise of papal ministry will be one which seeks to insure the effective exercise of co-responsibility in the apostolic college through the shared exercise of the gift of the apostolate. It will be open in prayerful discernment to the voice of the Spirit as it comes to expression in the Church universal. It will exemplify for the whole Church practical openness to the gifts of sanctification. And it will be expressive of an integral four-fold conversion.

Clearly, then, the functions of the papacy in the Church cannot be adequately grasped in purely legal terms. Any attempt to reduce a doctrinal account of the papacy to a legal definition of canonical papal jurisdiction must, then, be rejected as doctrinally inadequate and therefore as potentially misleading.

Nor can the function of the papacy in the Church be adequately defined by acquiescing blindly in the existing structures of the Vatican bureaucracy. The papal charism is wholly personal. It is not, then, shared by any Roman ecclesiastical official, not even those with an authentic gift of official service. Pope Paul has in fact acted more vigorously than any of his recent predecessors in demanding the reform of Roman bureaucratic structures: and for his attempts at reform he has on occasion earned the open criticism of the very bureaucracy he sought to change.

Equally inadequate will be any theological approach to papal infallibility which is derived exclusively from the First Vatican Council. For a variety of historical reasons, Vatican I described papal infallibility in terms that abstracted from the role of the episcopacy in the Church, from a generalized theology of gift, and from reflection on the indefectibility of the Church as a whole. To designate a doctrinal problematic inadequate is not to declare it false. Problematics are neither true nor false, for they are neither affirmed nor denied as such. They are the context within which verifiable and falsifiable affirmations and denials are made.

Nevertheless, to refuse to reformulate an inadequate problematic is to court serious inauthenticity in one's religious beliefs. For an inadequate problematic prevents one from reflecting on realities and values to which one must attend if one is to come to a correct resolution of any given question.

An experiential approach to papal infallibility demands that one distinguish carefully between logical and theological infallibility. Logical infallibility is the characteristic, not of a proposition, as Hans Küng has suggested, but of a deductive inference properly conducted. Here two points should be noted.

First, logical infallibility is characteristic of the deductive argument, not of the mind that constructs the argument. That is to say, in deductive reasoning, once specific premises are granted within an adequately defined, logical frame of reference, certain logical conclusions follow necessarily, i.e. infallibly. The mind which attempts to draw such conclusions may, however, labor under a fatigue that blinds it to its own blunders. It may be guilty of misunderstanding or oversight. Moreover, the infallibility of a given deductive conclusion does not necessitate the adoption of the frame of reference in which it occurs.

Second, logical infallibility is not the characteristic of either abductive or inductive reasoning. In the formulation of an hypothesis, one has no assurance prior to deductive clarification and inductive verification that one's hypothesis is the correct one. In the inductive verification of a deductively clarified hypothesis, one has no *a priori* assurance that new facts will not turn up that will call one's inductive conclusion or one's frame of reference into question.

But if no inductive inference can be regarded as logically infallible, nevertheless, in inferences about historical realities certain inductive conclusions can be regarded as both infallible and true. Such conclusions follow necessarily from premises in a given frame of reference and are applicable to human experience.

When an inference is both infallible and true in the sense just defined, it does not follow that every human attempt to apply it to experience will be true. The inference may be misinterpreted, or it may be correctly interpreted but incorrectly applied to experience. Rather, an inference which is both infallible and true is capable of being correctly and interpretatively applied to human experience, provided one accepts the frame of reference from which it is derived with deductive necessity.

In defining papal infallibility, Vatican I addressed itself to none of these logical issues. In defining theological infallibility, the Council gave no evidence of seeking to canonize any specific logical theory. In subsequent theological discussions of papal infallibility, however, logical and theological issues have been all too often confounded. Such muddle-headed thinking could be symptomatic of the lack of intellectual conversion. For one of its most common signs is the inability to distinguish speculatively between distinct and logically unrelated frames of reference. The doctrine of papal infallibility enunciated at Vatican I is, then, a theological not a logical doctrine. Moreover, the doctrine is a faith affirmation. It affirms God as the ultimate guarantee of authentic papal teaching, not the pope.

In discussing the limits of the exercise of papal infallibility, conciliar teaching has been consistently vague. The original definition of infallibility affirmed that the pope enjoys that kind of infallibility "with which the Divine Redeemer wished his Church to be instructed in divine doctrine about faith and morals." But it failed to specify what concretely the Divine Redeemer's intentions were or how one would possibly come to an adequate understanding of Jesus' mind on the subject.

Moreover, while restricting the use of papal infallibility to *ex cathedra* statements, the First Vatican Council failed to provide an adequate set of criteria for deciding when a statement is *ex cathedra*[27] and when it is not. The Council's teaching that in an *ex cathedra* statement, the pope speaks *ex sese et non ex consensu ecclesiae* cannot be taken as an adequate criterion. For, as we have seen, while the phrase describes correctly the personal character and pneumatic grounding of the papal (or of any other authentic) charism, it fails to provide a set of concrete rules for evaluating the authentic exercise of the papal (or of any other authentic) charism.

But if the preceding analysis has been sound up to this point, certain criteria can be excluded as inadequate for evaluating the authentic exercise of the papal ministry of teaching. First, the mere personal intention to define infallibly is insufficient to guarantee the infallibility of any papal teaching. Intentions do not change facts, and papal definitions must conform to the historical data of revelation. Second, any appeal to a papal "inner light" is an inadequate criterion. For it confounds an heretical with an authentic exercise of the papal charism. Such confusion is symptomatic of a Gnosticism of the right. Third, any appeal to papal authority will also be inadequate which fails to acknowledge the need for papal teaching to be expressive both of the mind of Christ and of an integral fourfold conversion.

Moreover, both Karl Rahner and Hans Küng would seem to be moving in the right theological direction in suggesting that the truth coming to inadequate expression in the teaching of Vatican I concerning papal infallibility is that the Church as a whole is indefectible. To profess belief in the indefectibility of the Church is an expression of confidence in God's saving fidelity. It is more a profession of trust than a perception of hard fact.

Clearly, then, there are serious reasons for thinking that the speculative problematic articulated at Vatican I should be abandoned, not as false, but as inadequate. It is not false because it yields a genuine insight into the personal and pneumatic character of the papal charism. But it is inadequate in that it fails to relate the exercise of papal authority to the collegial character of the apostolic office. It also fails to provide an adequate set of criteria for evaluating the authentic exercise of a papal charism. And it fails to distinguish adequately between logical and theological infallibility. There are also practical motives for acknowledging the problematic of Vatican I as inadequate. In an ecumenical age, "infallibility" is a red-flag word that engages the deepest irrationalism of Catholic and Protestant alike.

At the same time, Küng's doctrinal reformulation of infallibility, like the philosophical presuppositions which ground it is also inadequate. Küng's position rests on an inadequate propositional logic. And it seems to set up an arbitrary, dualistic opposition between the activity of the Spirit and of the hierarchical, institutional Church.

A reformulation of the doctrine of infallibility goes beyond the scope of this study. The preceding reflections do, however, cast light on the shape which such a systematic reformulation might take: (1) It would affirm the fidelity of God revealed in the Jesus/Pentecost event as the ultimate ground for belief in the indefectibility of the Church. (2) It would acknowledge human fallibility and human sinfulness as variables in our salvific situation which tend to undermine the Church's indefectibility. (3) It would acknowledge the need for the authentic teaching to be expressive of: (a) an integral, four-fold conversion; (b) growth in the gifts of sanctification; and (c) the dynamic interplay of the authentic movements of the Spirit charismatically operative in the Church universal. (4) It would discover the salvific fidelity of God practically expressed in the power of the Spirit to raise up prophets, teachers, and ordained apostolic leaders in every generation of the Church and in sufficient numbers to prevent the community of believers from ever completely abandoning its Savior or from so adulterating the Word of God in theory and/or practice as to wholly obscure the divine saving action. (5) It would acknowledge the unique responsibilities of ordained apostolic leaders within the community in problems which touch the good of the Church universal. (6) It would acknowledge the importance of papal leadership within the apostolic college as a principle of unity within a faith community concerned to preserve and foster legitimate human and charismatic diversity. (7) It would acknowledge the personal character and pneumatic grounding of any authentic service gift, including the papal charism. (8) It would acknowledge the need to elaborate an adequate criteriology for the authentic exercise of any service gift, including the papal call to service. (9) It would articulate such a criteriology and implement it in an ongoing critical evaluation of the authenticity of different papal teachings.

11. Finally, some Protestants may hesitate to subscribe to the suggestion that the apostolic minister assumes responsibility for leading and representing the Church universal. How, one may ask, can any individual do such a thing? No individual can, of course. The assumption of apostolic leadership responsibilities is a personal act. But the apostle is committed, not to individual but to collegial leadership of the Church universal. It is a responsibility exercised, not in isolation, but in shared solidarity with other ordained apostles. An ordained apostle teaches in the name of the Church universal by contributing responsibly to the formulation of official consensus statements on doctrine and by disseminating them officially within the community. An ordained apostle represents the universal Church in sacramental worship by interpreting the sacrament to believers in accordance with the official creedal stance of the believing community.

For the truth of the matter is that any human community which lacks official spokesmen cannot come to full consciousness as a community. The official formulation and revision of a creedal consensus on important issues ought, of course, to enlist all the best gifts operative in any community of belief. But official documents crystallize consensus in a way that the mere sharing of gifts cannot. Constitutions and laws crystallize shared political consciousness. Official creeds crystallize shared faith consciousness. As a consequence, it is only through critical reflection on authoritative creedal statements that a faith community can grow efficiently as a community to a full understanding of its history and destiny. One of the chief responsibilities of the ordained apostle is, then, to facilitate the process of official creedal development. It is, perhaps, the chief contribution of the gift of apostolate to the creation of a Christian community consciousness.

Such an interpretation of the apostolate places, however, a strong imperative on the ordained ministries of different Christian communions to move effectively toward a unified apostolic ministry. For only in the final reunion of all Christians will the ordained apostolate truly be able to give official voice to the evolving faith of the universal Church. Hence, until the apostolic colleges of different Christian communions are united, the faith consciousness of the Christian community as a whole will be proportionately diminished.

Notes

1. Mk 1:22ff, 2:1-12, 28, 4:41ff; Mt 5:20ff., 8:8ff., 9:1-8, 17, 17:24-27, 21:23-27; Jn 5:29-30; Lk 5:17-26.

2. Mt 4:23-25, 8:1-13, 9:28-34, 9:1-8; 11:1-15, 12:9-14, 12:22-32, 15:21-28; Mk 1:21-28, 32-34, 2:1-12, 5:1-20, 6:53-56, 7:24-37, 9:14-29; Lk 4:31-44, 5:12-26, 6:6-11, 8:26-56, 9:37-43, 11:14-22, 13:10-17.

3. Jn 3:1-21, 5:1-47.

4. C.K. Barrett, *The Holy Spirit and the Gospel Tradition* (London: S.P.C.K., 1947) pp. 32-33.

5. Mt 10:1-42, 16:13-20; Mk 2:13-19, 6:7-13, 8:27-30; Lk 6:17-19, 9:1-6, 10-21.

6. Mt 16:21-28, 18:1-4, 20:24-28, 21:1-16; Mk 8:31-33, 9:33-37, 10:41-45, 11:1-19; Lk 22-26,46-48, 19:28-40, 45-46; Jn 11:45-54, 12:12-19.

7. Mt 10:37-39, 18:1-4; Mk 8:34-35, 9:33-36, 10:15; Lk 9:23-24, 46-47, 18:17.

9. Mt 4:18-22, 10:37-39, 20:24-28; Mk 6:7-13, 10:28-31, 35-45; Lk 9:1-6, 23-26.

10. Act 2:43, 5:11-12.

11. Mt 26:26-29; Mk 14:22-25; Lk 22:19-20.

12. Mt 28:16-20; Lk 24:44-49; Jn 20:19-23; Act 1:1-11.

13. Act 2:1ff; 4:18-22.

14. Act 2:15-21.

15. Act 8:18-24; 15:1-29; 1 Co 5:1-13.

16. Mt 18:15-18; 16:19-20; Jn 20:21-23, 21:15-18.

17. Cf. Karl Rahner, S.J., "Forgotten Truths Concerning the Sacrament of Penance," *Theological Investigations*, translated by Karl Kruger (Baltimore: Helicon, 1963) II, pp. 135-174.

18. Avery Dulles, S.J., *The Survival of Dogma* (N.Y.: Doubleday, 1973). For a somewhat different handling of similar themes, see: Bernard Lonergan, S.J. *Doctrinal Pluralism* (Milwaukee: Marquette University, 1971).

19. Gal 1:11-2:21.

20. Cf. Raymond E. Brown, S.S., *Priest and Bishop* (N.Y.: Paulist, 1970). See also: Bernhard W. Anderson, "Ordination to the Priestly Order," *Worship*, XLII (August-September, 1968) pp. 431-441; A. Gelin, P.S.S., "The Priesthood of Christ in the Epistle to the Hebrews," in *The Sacrament of Holy Orders* (Collegeville: Liturgical Press, 1957) pp. 31 ff.

21. Brown, *Priest and Bishop*, pp. 47-86.

22. Cf. Louis Bouyer, S.J., "Ministère ecclesiastique et succession apostolique," *Nouvelle Revue Théologique*, XCV (March, 1973) pp. 241-252; Daniel J. O'Hanlon, S.J., "A New Approach to the Validity of Church Orders," *Worship*, XLI (August-September, 1967) pp. 406-421; Dom B. Botte, O.S.B., "The Collegiate Character of the Presbyterate and the Episcopate" in *The Sacrament of Orders* (Collegeville: Liturgical Press, 1957) pp. 76-77; Clement Dillenschneider, *Christ the One Priest, We His Priests*, translated by Sr. M. Renelle (St. Louis: Herder, 1964); *The Holy Spirit and the Priest: Toward an Interiorization of our Priesthood* (Baltimore: Helicon, 1965); J. Lecuier, C.S.Sp., "The Mystery of

Pentecost and the Apostolic Mission of the Church" in *The Sacrament of Orders* (Collegeville: Liturgical Press, 1957) pp. 131 ff.; Yves Congar, O.P., "The Church and Pentecost," "The Holy Spirit and the Apostolic Body," in *The Mystery of the Church* (Baltimore: Helicon, 1960); Hans Küng, S.J., *Why Priests?*, translated by John Cumming (N.Y.: Collins, 1972), *The Church* (N.Y.: Sheed and Ward, 1967) pp. 150-203; John L. McKenzie, *Authority in the Church* (N.Y.: Doubleday, 1966).

23. *Unitatis redintegratio*, 1-3.

24. Dulles, *Survival of Dogma*, pp. 79-137.

25. Cf. Bernhard Poschmann, *Penance and the Anointing of the Sick*, translated by Frances Courtney (Freiburg: Herder, 1964); Karl Rahner, S.J., "Forgotten Truths Concerning the Sacrament of Penance," *Theological Investigations*, translated by Karl Kruger (Baltimore: Helicon, 1963) II, pp. 135-174; H. Staffner, "What is Wrong with the Sacrament of Penance?" *Clergy Monthly* (1972) pp. 362-373; Karl Rahner, S.J., "The Meaning of Frequent Confession," *Theological Investigations* (Baltimore: Helicon, 1967) pp. 177-189; John Gallen, S.J., "General Sacramental Absolution: Remarks on Pastoral Norms," *Theological Studies*, XXXXIV (March, 1973) pp. 114-121; Clarence McAuliffe, S.J., "Penance and Reconciliation with the Church," *Theological Studies*, XXVI (March, 1965) pp. 1-39; George McCauley, S.J., "The Ecclesial Nature of the Sacrament of Penance," *Worship*, XXXIV (March, 1962) pp. 212-222; Eduard Schillebeeckx, O.P., *Sacramental Reconciliation* (N.Y.: Herder and Herder, 1971); Jerome Murphy-O'Connor, O.P., "Sin and Community in the New Testament," in *The Mystery of Sin and Forgiveness*, (N.Y.: Alba House, 1973) pp. 55-89; Paul Anciaux, O.S.B., "The Ecclesial Dimensions of Penance," in *The Mystery of Sin and Forgiveness*, pp. 155-165; David Kirk, "Penance in the Eastern Churches," *Worship*, XXL (March, 1966) pp. 148-155, Robert O'Connell, S.J., "The Sense of Sin in the Modern World," in *The Mystery of Sin and Forgiveness*, pp. 3-21; Karl Rahner, S.J., "Guilt and Remission: The Borderline Between Theology and Psychotherapy," *Theological Investigations*, translated by Karl H. Kruger (Baltimore: Helicon, 1963) II, pp. 265-282; David Belgum, *Guilt: Where Religion and Psychotherapy Meet* (Englewood Cliffs: Prentice-Hall, 1963); James F. Filella, S.J., "Confession as a Means of Self-Improvement," in *The Mystery of Sin and Forgiveness*, pp. 167-180; Donald L. Gelpi, S.J., "The Ministry of Healing," in *Pentecostal Piety* (N.Y.: Paulist, 1972) pp. 3-58; Kevin F. O'Shea, C.Ss.R., "The Reality of Sin: A Theological and Pastoral Critique," *Theological Studies*, XXIX (June, 1968) pp. 241-259; Dennis Linn and Matthew Linn, *Healing of Memories* (N.Y.: Paulist, 1974); F. Martin, "Healing of Memories," *Review for Religious*, XXXII (May, 1973) pp. 488-507.

26. Poschmann, *op. cit.*, pp. 233-257; Arnold Jurgens, M.H.M., "The Sacrament of the Sick," *African Ecclesiastical Review* (1972) pp. 337-340; Larry Maddock, "Anointing of the Sick," *Today's Parish* (January-February, 1973) pp. 24-25; Richard Trutter, "Communal Anointing," *Today's Parish* (September-October, 1972) pp. 9-12; Sr. Maureen Cleary, B.V.M., "The Anointing of the Sick," *Religion Teachers Journal* (February, 1973) pp. 38-41; Francis McNutt, O.P., *Healing* (Notre Dame: Ave Maria, 1974); DS 3065-3074; Charles Davis, *A Question of Conscience* (N.Y.: Harper and Row, 1967); Gregory Baum, *The Credibility of the Church* (N.Y.: Herder and Herder, 1968); Most Rev. Francis Simons, *Infallibility and the Evidence* (Springfield, Ill.: Templegate, 1968); Hans Küng, S.J., *Infallible? An Inquiry*, translated by Edward Quinn (N.Y.: Image, 1972) pp. 29-57; Avery Dulles, S.J., "*Infallible? An Inquiry*, The Theological Issues," *America*, CXXIV (April 24, 1971) pp. 427-428; Michael A. Fahey, "*Infallible? An Inquiry*, Europe's Theologians Join the Debate," *Ibid.*, pp. 429-431; George A. Lindbeck, "*Infallible? An Inquiry*, A Protestant Perspective," *Ibid.*, pp. 431-433; Avery Dulles, S.J., "Infallibility Revisited," *America*, CXXIX (August 4, 1973) pp. 55-58; Raymond E. Brown, Karl P. Donfried, John Reumann, eds., *Peter in the New Testament* (N.Y.: Paulist, 1973).

27. For those unfamiliar with Catholic legal jargon, *"ex cathedra"* is a phrase used to characterize papal teaching which explicitly invokes the full power of the papal office.

VIII
The
Supper
of Blessing

1. For centuries eucharistic theology has been a major theological cockpit for Catholics and Protestants alike. But one can find certain areas in which minimal agreement is possible. One doctrinal affirmation to which all Christians agree is that the eucharist is in some sense a communal act of recall. In it the saving act of God effected in the missions of His Son and Spirit is remembered and publicly proclaimed as a common object of faith. One question which needs to be raised, then, is this: what is the difference between a eucharistic act of remembering and recalling a dental appointment?

One obvious point of difference is that the eucharistic remembrance is an act of praise. To recall the saving action of God in Jesus and in the Spirit is to bless Him. To bless and praise God in faith is to reaffirm one's commitment to Him in the power and strength of His prior commitment to us in saving love.[1]

To reaffirm one's commitment to the God of Scripture is to renew one's covenant with Him.[2] Since that covenant demands a commitment to others in the name of Jesus, a Christian covenant renewal comes to full experiential visibility in symbolic acts of mutual commitment. Since such acts engage personal faith in Jesus and in the power of His Spirit, the eucharistic act of recall is more than a personal act of piety. It is the act of the Christian community as such, assembled in faith to proclaim before God and one another the divine saving action that binds them together as a community.

As an act of the Christian community, the eucharistic act of recall must, then, be more than an act of private devotion. In fact, it is not unlike taking an oath in civil court. The meaning and consequences of testifying under oath are prescribed by law. One who performs such an act in court is not free to decide that what (s)he has done has another meaning and other consequences than those legally prescribed. The meaning of the eucharistic action is not fixed by legal fiat. But it is fixed by the meaning of the historical events of salvation which are recalled. In an act of eucharistic covenant renewal, one must, then, either be willing to say "yes" to the meaning of those events and to the practical, lived consequences of such an assent or one must refrain from participating in the eucharist.

Those who seek to participate in the eucharist without consenting to the meaning of the events of salvation which the eucharist recalls and proclaims should be excluded from community worship until they are ready to participate in good conscience. In biblical terms, they must be bound so that they can be loosed. In canonical terms, they must be excommunicated so that they can be truly reconciled to God and to the Church.

Clearly, then, a community can celebrate the eucharist in good conscience as a community only when it has reached basic agreement about the religious significance of the salvific events being recalled. It is, then, the sad truth that those who take irreconcilable stands on important questions that touch the meaning of the eucharistic act cannot in good conscience celebrate together until their differences are reconciled.

With the progress of ecumenical dialogue, there is, however, a growing realization on the part of Christians everywhere that many doctrinal differences which were supposed to divide Christian communions in the past are not so much differences of faith as differences in the formulation of a common eucharistic belief. Lutheran theology, for example, was originally suspicious of a sacrificial interpretation of the eucharist. That suspicion was rooted in part in the fear that the mass might be misunderstood as a substitute for Golgotha or as meritorious in its own right. Since the reformation, however, Lutheran theology has made significant advances toward incorporating sacrificial imagery into its theological understanding of the eucharist. This progress was mediated in large measure by reflection on Jesus as the *ebed Yahweh*, the suffering servant of the Lord. At the same time, Catholic theology has moved from a dominantly sacrificial, objectivistic eucharistic theology to one which insists on the fiducial, communal, and ecclesial aspects of liturgical piety. Another area of convergence between the two traditions has been insistence on Jesus' active presence in the total act of eucharistic worship. Catholic-Anglican dialogue has already produced official accord in eucharistic doctrine. And there are signs of significant progress in the question of Anglican orders.[3] But despite recent ecumenical progress, one still encounters areas in which Christians remain seemingly entrenched in irreconcilable eucharistic doctrines, especially when it comes to the question of the real presence of Jesus in the eucharist. We shall return to this problem in a different context.

2. The fact that the eucharistic act is a public act of covenant worship which engages the faith of the Church universal links eucharistic worship to the sacraments of community initiation. For in the eucharist the faith that is professed in Christian initiation is officially and publicly reaffirmed. As we have seen, both baptism and confirmation demand a covenant commitment to the God who has revealed Himself in Jesus and the Spirit. But as we have also seen, the orientation of one's faith commitment in each of these sacraments differs. In baptism, one assents in faith to Jesus as Spirit-baptiser and as author of the Adamic reversal; and one assents as well to a lifetime of openness to growth in the gifts of sanctification through an appropriate response to the service gifts which are operative in the Church universal. By confirmation, whatever ritual form it takes, one commits oneself to a lifetime of willingness to follow whatever personal call to the active service of others in Christ's name the Spirit may choose to give. Both commitments are, moreover, integral to the Christian covenant of initiation. Neither is optional.

As the public reaffirmation of both of these commitments, the eucharist is simultaneously a personal and an ecclesial act. In it one reaffirms one's desire to grow in the mind of Jesus by openness to the voice and the action of the Spirit as He comes to experiential visibility in the charismatic activity of one's covenant brethren. And in the same act one affirms one's personal consent to whatever summons to ecclesial service the Spirit may choose to give.

The only community in which the eucharist can be authentically celebrated is, therefore, a charismatic community. Hence, to the extent that any Christian community celebrates the eucharist without repenting truly and actively of its failure to respond to the gifts of sanctification and to all of the gifts of service, to that extent it transforms the eucharistic action from an act of blessing to an act of divine judgment. The sacraments effect what they signify. If they signify hypocrisy, that is what they effect. Moreover, there can be no doubt but that ordained apostolic leaders have the responsibility of forbidding a seriously hypocritical celebration of a eucharistic covenant renewal.

Eucharistic worship and charismatic worship are not, then, opposed to one another. Rather, they remain lopsided and incomplete in isolation from one another. By the same token, sound liturgical renewal is possible only through the integration of charismatic and sacramental worship. Such integration can take place in a variety of ways. In informal celebrations of the eucharist, the prayer meeting can function as the liturgy of the word, provided the basic elements which are present in the liturgy of the word are present in the prayer meeting itself; confession of sins, praise of God, meditation on his word, and kerygmatic proclamation of the good news. In more formal celebrations of the eucharist, spontaneous charismatic prayer can form an appropriate liturgical response to the readings. And it is an ideal prayer for the celebration of God's presence in the community after communion. Moreover, shared, spontaneous worship at major charismatic renewal conferences has shown that it is possible even for thousands of people to worship together in the Spirit. In very large gatherings, however, this can ordinarily be more easily accomplished if selected individuals with tested charismatic word ministries are allowed to minister publicly to the assembly at the time of spontaneous prayer.

For ordained apostolic leaders to refuse to minister pastorally and eucharistically to charismatic prayer groups when such ministry is both possible and needed is, therefore, genuinely irresponsible. No ordained apostolic leader has the right to circumscribe ministry to others on the basis of personal ambition or esthetic preference. The ultimate criterion should be the call of God and the concrete needs of God's people.

By the same token, any eucharistic community which resists the integration of eucharistic and charismatic worship courts serious religious inauthenticity. Sterile eucharists celebrated in communities which give little sign of growth in the gifts of sanctification and of service transform into an exercise of rubrical formalism what ought to be a proclamation in joy of the shared acceptance of God's forgiveness and love. At the same time, charismatic communities which fail to acknowledge the centrality and importance of eucharistic worship must come to terms with the serious inauthenticities which mar their approach to community prayer.

3. The reappropriation of the charismatic basis for eucharistic worship also provides a speculative context in which unnecessary and fallacious liturgical antinomies can be avoided:

a. It is, for example, misleading to tell people that they must come to the eucharist seeking to celebrate the resurrection of Jesus rather than to recall His death on Calvary. It is misleading because eucharistic prayer seeks to do both. To celebrate Jesus' resurrection is to celebrate His complete pneumatic transformation. That transformation revealed Him fully as Spirit-baptiser; for by it He was empowered to breathe His Pentecostal Spirit into the Church. The sign that Jesus is risen is, therefore, that the Christian community is in fact being visibly transformed by the power and the anointing of the Spirit. To celebrate the resurrection of Jesus is, therefore, to celebrate the Spirit's active charismatic presence in the community.

But the Spirit is charismatically present by His gifts of sanctification and of service. Through the active service of the service gifts, He teaches the community to put on the mind of Jesus. At the same time, the Christian community cannot put on the mind of Jesus without entering into His atoning sacrifice. For to put on the mind of Jesus is to commit oneself to living in a faith-dependence that comes to expression in gratuitous sharing, unrestricted and atoning love, and mutual service in worship. To put on the mind of Jesus is to enter into His *kenosis*, to say "yes" to dying for others as Jesus died for us, if that is what is required to express to them love and forgiveness in God's name. To enter into Jesus' *kenosis* is, however, to enter into His pneumatic transformation in a death which culminated in the revelation of His glory on Easter.

What a sound theology of charism reveals, therefore, is that it is theological nonsense to attempt to dissociate Jesus' death from His resurrection within the act of eucharistic recall. In the eucharist, one blesses God for the Calvary/Easter/Pentecost event as a unified salvific process. There are three distinguishable phases in the divine relevatory act of redemption. But though distinguishable, each phase remains unintelligible in isolation from the others.

b. A sound theology of gift also reveals, therefore, the folly of interpreting the eucharist as an act of blessing rather than as a sacrificial act. As a Christian, I cannot bless God and mean it without renewing my total covenant commitment. I cannot renew my covenant commitment to God without professing openness to the gifts of sanctification. And I cannot be authentically open to the gifts of sanctification without entering into the atonement of Jesus, the suffering servant of God.

That atonement is, however, adequately understood in Biblical terms rather than in the categories of medieval theology. Most medieval theologies of atonement draw their inspiration from Anselm of Canterbury. Anselm transformed the biblical notion of "atonement" into the theological concept "satisfaction." He taught that God cannot simply forgive sin out of love. Instead God's justice must be satisfied either through the punishment of the sinner or through some act which repays God for the dishonor done Him by human transgression. The punishment inflicted on mankind as a consequence of Adam's sin fails to satisfy the divine honor. For nothing short of mankind's victory over Satan and the re-opening of the gates of heaven can restore divine order to a universe disordered by human sinfulness. The Word made flesh, Anselm argued, has in fact offered to God in the name of humankind the satisfaction owed to the divine justice. His submission to the Father was total, and by His death He defeated Satan in the name of all mankind and re-opened the gates of heaven.[4]

As medieval theology developed, Anselm's theology of satisfaction began to take on sinister connotations. Both Abelard and Hugh of St. Victor portrayed the atoning death of Jesus as the price demanded by God's vindictive justice. Alexander of Hales insisted that the satisfaction demanded by divine justice must be proportioned to the Person offended, and therefore must be infinite. The penal character of Jesus' death and the infinity of the satisfaction owed to God were, moreover, basic presuppostions of a Thomistic theology of atonement. But a God who takes infinite satisfaction in exacting from His innocent Son the punishment demanded for every human crime is, to say the least, a God with a peculiar sense of justice. And in the late middle ages Scotus quite correctly repudiated the Anselmian-Thomistic understanding of "satisfaction."[5]

The contemporary rediscovery of a Biblical theology of atonement offers a more satisfying interpretation of the sacrificial meaning of Jesus' death, and therefore of the eucharist itself.

In the New Testament, "atonement" never connotes the vindictive satisfaction of God's anger. Nor does it connote the expiatory suffering demanded by an unflinching sense of divine punitive justice. Moreover, no New Testament writer ever referred to Jesus as a scapegoat.

For the writers of the New Testament, salvific atonement means reconciliation, at-one-ment. We are reconciled to God and to our fellow humans through a divine act which frees us from sin and binds us to God in the name of Jesus and through the anointing of His Spirit. By this act of liberation, God acquires a people for Himself, the New Israel bought back (redeemed) by the blood of the Lamb. But while New Testament writers speak of Jesus' blood as redemptive, they never picture Jesus as paying a blood price *to* anyone: neither to the Father nor to the devil. The redemption He brings is not a basement bargain. It is the historical revelation of a divine forgiveness which had existed from the beginning but which is definitively revealed in Jesus' death, pneumatic transformation, and mediation of the Holy Spirit. For by that act, God reveals His willingness to suffer personally the consequences of human sinfulness, if that is the price which must be paid for reconciliation with men.[6]

Under the impact of exegesis, there has, then, been a growing acceptance of the notion that God created the world from the first with a view to gracing it freely through the incarnation of His Son. The difference made in the salvific process by sin was that mankind chose to murder the incarnate Word rather than to hear His message of love.[7]

Jesus' sacrifice was, then, His obedience to His mission from the Father despite human rejection, despite Calvary. His mission from the Father was to proclaim divine forgiveness. But that proclamation was rendered salvifically efficacious only when He was lifted up in glory on the cross and when, as a consequence, He breathed forth the Spirit of reconciliation into human hearts. For it is by the power of the Spirit that we enter into a relation of adoptive sonship with the Father. The test of openness to the Spirit is, however, freedom to consent to a sinful world with the same forgiving, atoning love as Jesus Himself. It is for this reason that one cannot be truly open to the Spirit without being taken up personally into Jesus' sacrifice.

These insights cast light on a phrase which recurs in Tridentine reflections on the sacrament of reconciliation. The Council speaks more than once of the temporal punishments *(poenae)* due to sin.[8] A sound sacramental theology must exclude from such language any connotation of divine vindictive anger or any image of God which is incompatible with the divine act of forgiveness made visible in Jesus.

In an experiential problematic, every new decision shapes the future by defining the past from which the self must subsequently emerge. One's graceless decisions affect one's immediate physical environment: one's body, by endowing it with tendencies which do not express the mind of Jesus, and one's more remote environment by setting in motion forces that are expressive of anti-Christ.

Just as baptism transforms the residue of "original sin" into "concupiscence," so does repentance and sacramental reconciliation transform the evil consequences of one's past sinful decisions into their "penalty." For as a consequence of reconciliation with God, the penitent comes to experience former sinful actions and their consequences, not with personal approval, but with regret and pain.

The sacrament of reconciliation takes away the "temporal

punishment" due to sin in two ways. God by the direct exercise of His healing power can remove the residue of suffering caused by one's sins. Or He can teach the repentant sinner by the power of His sanctifying Spirit to relate attitudinally to the now painful consequences of personal sinful acts with the atoning forgiveness of Jesus Himself: to suffer lovingly in one's own person the consequences of one's own sins while trusting absolutely in the forgiveness of the Father. A similar process occurs in the eucharistic forgiveness of minor faults.

The reappropriation of a Biblical theology of atonement on the part of eucharistic theologians has also forced a reinterpretation of the meaning of the eucharist as the "unbloody" memorial of the "bloody" sacrifice of Jesus. The tendency of post-Reformation theologians had been to assimilate the sacrifice of the cross to pagan sacrifices of appeasement. Such theories were not infrequently colored by the vindictive image of God encountered in pagan tragic myths of evil. But a re-examination of New Testament theological reflections on the meaning of sacrifice exposed the inadequacy and potential distortion of God's word latent in such theories.

The blood of the new covenant is not the blood of appeasement offered to an angry God. It is the liberating blood of the passover, the covenant blood of divine life, the sprinkled blood of purification and reconciliation.[9] In shedding His blood, Jesus entered into His glory by being wholly transformed in the power of the Spirit. In being so transformed He breathed forth on all who believe, the Spirit Who frees them to say "Abba" and Who draws them willingly into the passover of the Lord. Their "unbloody sacrifice" is their consent in baptism and in each eucharistic act of worship to enter ever more fully into the death and resurrection of the Lord. For to consent actively, personally, and communally to the atonement of Jesus is to enter into His redemptive sacrifice. It is to become by His grace lesser mediators of His Spirit by allowing the same Spirit to transform one charismatically and visibly in a manner analogous to His revelatory transformation of Jesus, His apostles, and first disciples.

Moreover, active consent to the atonement takes personal practical form in consent to one's gift of service. One cannot, then, respond authentically to a service gift without entering into Jesus' atoning sacrifice. Hence, one cannot bless God authentically without positing a sacrifical act.

c. Similarily, the eucharist is not a celebration rather than an acceptance of God's forgiveness. It is a celebration of the forgiveness of God that has come to experiential visibility in Jesus. But that forgiveness is experientally manifest not only in the historical person of Jesus, but in the visible transformation of Christians in His image. As we have seen, however, the experientially visible transformation of believers is mediated by the gifts of sanctification and service.

d. Nor is the eucharist a celebration of the immanent God who is with us rather than the worship of God in His transcendence. As we have seen, transcendence in the broad sense is synonymous with the experience of growth. Religious transcendence is growth in the saving life that comes to us from God. For the Christian, the authentic experience of religious transcendence is mediated by openness to the gifts of the Spirit, to His transforming call. But it is the visible, charismatic transformation of the community in the image of Jesus which also mediates visibly and concretely the immanent presence of God in its midst.

e. Finally, it is misleading to imagine that to affirm the entire eucharistic action as consecratory contradicts belief in the centrality of the consecration within eucharistic worship. To affirm the consecration as central to a total act of worship is not necessarily to focus exclusive attention on the formula of consecration. The misleading tendency of Catholic theologians in the past to engage in such vicious abstractionism was facilitated by the attempt of sacramentologists to use hylomorphic theory to define the canonical essence of each sacrament. There is no need here to insist on the inadequacy of such an approach to the sacraments.

But if the entire eucharistic action is consecratory, it is, as Joseph Powers and others have noted, a sign-act, an act endowed with a specific religious meaning.[10] As a symbolic act of communication, the total eucharistic action has an intelligible structure. Some elements in that structure are more central to its total meaning than others. Rites like the initial confession of sins can be omitted without depriving the action of its central significance.

But the consecration cannot be omitted without depriving the total eucharistic action of its meaning. For the eucharist is an act of blessing which is a public, ecclesial covenant renewal. One cannot bless God for the Calvary/Easter/Pentecost event without solemnly recalling the Calvary/Easter/Pentecost event in a profession of faith that engages the community as such. And the salvific meaning of that event was revealed prophetically by Jesus at the Last Supper. All merely human analogies to sacramental symbolism limp. But to celebrate a "eucharist" without a consecration would be a little bit like performing *Hamlet* while excising from the script any reference to the murder of Hamlet's father and to his ghostly apparition to the protagonist. It would be a performance deprived of those symbolic elements that give it unity and meaning.

4. It should also be clear at this point that a theology of gift provides a speculative context for integrating the fruits of biblical research into eucharistic theology.

A theology of gift provides the eucharistic blessing with its most concrete motivation. For if the eucharist is an act of praise to God for the salvation He has revealed in Christ, it makes no sense to celebrate the eucharist in a community that gives no visible sign of having actually accepted the salvation Jesus brings. But a Christian community will experience conscious, visible, pneumatic transformation to the extent that it is actively open to all of the gifts.

Moreover, it should be clear that a sound theology of the gifts incorporates into itself the fruits of recent exegetical research into the meaning of Jesus' redemptive death of atonement. It gives that exegesis foundational grounding in the shared vision of faith which emerges from growth in the gifts of sanctification. Moreover, it grounds ecclesial growth in the sanctifying gifts in the eucharistic community's shared openness in faith to all of the authentic service gifts operative in the Church universal.

As a consequence, a theology of gift endows a biblical theology of atonement with concrete practical significance. To enter into Jesus' atonement one must experience the kind of dying and rising which comes in the active sharing of one's life. That sharing begins with the sharing of the natural, environmental supports of life. Such sharing includes the sharing of one's own body through acts of service that express the atoning love of God, through sexual expressions of Christian love, through the suffering that accompanies the forgiving acceptance of the consequences of human sin, through laying down one's life, if that is necessary, to convince others of God's love for them.

But the sharing which mediates the atoning love of God extends to His charismatic gifts as well. A pneumatic gift in the broadest sense is any grace given to be shared. In the narrow sense, it is an enabling and enduring call from the Spirit of Jesus which demands an active response in words and deeds of faith.

It is through the sharing of all the gifts, from the gifts of sanctification to the gift of tongues, that the Christian community comes to experience itself consciously and concretely as redeemed. For it is in the course of such sharing that it comes to recognize itself as God's own people, those whom God has claimed in love for himself through the transforming power of his Spirit. Through the activity of the gifts, redemption ceases to be a static essence and becomes a dynamic process in which the believing community acknowledges God's call to reconciliation and knows itself to be divinely summoned in free and gratuitous love to a life of union in the one Spirit of Jesus.

5. An experiential approach to Christian belief also allows for a speculative clarification of the more recent debates over the real presence. In the eucharistic theology which preceded and followed the Second Vatican Council, Catholic theologians manifested growing dissatisfaction with manual formulations of the scholastic explanations of "transubstantiation." It was felt, and correctly so, that Trent's qualified endorsement of the term "transubstantiation" had been used unjustifiably to force Catholic explanations of the real presence into the outdated formulas of Aristotelian hylomorphic theory. Karl Rahner, however, correctly pointed out that in its eucharistic doctrine, Trent had endorsed no single philosophical system, including hylomorphism. He concluded, therefore, that Tridentine doctrine should be understood in common-sense categories rather than in technical philosophical terms. What Trent had taught was that, after the consecration, one is no longer dealing with mere bread and mere wine in the common-sense meaning of those terms.

Rahner's minimalistic reading of Tridentine eucharistic theology found an echo in the attempts of Piet Schoonenberg, Eduard Schillebeeckx, and others to reformulate an explanation of the "real presence" in non-hylomorphic categories. Catholic theologians began to wonder how the reality of the bread is to be grasped, if not as an underlying substance. It was suggested, for example, that after the consecration, the reality of the bread and wine changed from God's viewpoint even though from the standpoint of human experience, it continues to look like bread and wine. But just what such a theory might mean remained obscure.

There was, as a consequence, a movement among Catholic theologians to replace the term "transubstantiation" by the term "transignification" or "transfinalization." The suggested change went beyond semantics. In the case of "transignification," it reflected a shift from a medieval metaphysics of objective principles of being to an existentialist equation of being and meaning. In Heideggerian existentialism, the whole being, or reality, of any entity is its total meaning. To change the meaning of anything is, therefore, to change its reality.

Since, therefore, the symbolic use of bread and wine in a public, eucharistic proclamation of divine salvation endows them with redemptive, salvific meaning they would not otherwise have, their reality is changed as well. They cease to be mere bread and wine and become symbolically and sacramentally the body and blood of the Lord.

The term "transfinalization" connotes a similar problematic. But it associates the term "reality" with "purpose." If "meaning" and "reality" are correlative terms, so are "meaning" and "purpose": for it is in grasping the purpose of anything that we grasp its meaning. The use of bread and wine within the eucharistic act changes their existential purpose by endowing their consumption with salvific meaning. For the proponents of transfinalization, therefore, such a change in purpose and meaning implies of necessity, a change in the reality of the eucharistic species.

In his encyclical *Mysterium fidei*, Pope Paul allowed a certain legitimacy to the terms "transfinalization" and "transignification." But he found them theologically inadequate unless they were supplemented by the term "transubstantiation." He suggested that the term "transubstantiation" express more clearly the reality of the change that takes place in the eucharistic bread and wine. But he did not make use of the traditional term mandatory.

The proponents of "transfinalization" and "transignification" have argued that since the new terms insist upon a change in the reality of the eucharistic bread and wine, the retention of the order term "transubstantiation" is superfluous. So far Rome has made no further statement and seems to be content with the clarifications offered by the revisionists.

In his own evaluation of the controversy, Joseph Powers, S.J., has insisted on the symbolic character of the eucharistic act. He has suggested that the shift in problematic from "substance" to "meaning" becomes more intelligible when one sees the eucharist as a "sign-act." For Jesus' presence in such an act can be adequately understood only as a sign-presence. For Powers, then, the presence of Jesus in the eucharist is both active and symbolic, and symbolic because it is active. The reality of Christ's eucharistic presence is the reality of the saving action He performs in and through the action of the Church at worship in and with Him.[12]

But even with these qualifications, the meaning of the real presence of Jesus in the eucharist remains theologically obscure. An experiential approach to the problem, however, casts some light on the question. A "Cheshire cat" theory of transubstantiation was never endorsed by the Council of Trent. The Council fathers had the opportunity to state that in "transubstantiation" the accidents of the bread and wine are left hanging in the air like the smile of the enigmatic feline. But they refused. Instead, they substituted the term "species" for the term "accidents." In a Tridentine problematic, therefore, the problem of the real presence was posed in terms of "reality" and "appearance" rather than in terms of "substance" and "accidents." In making such a speculative option, Trent merely reaffirmed the basic problematic on which the official pastoral magisterium had insisted more than once in its earlier pronouncements on the eucharist.[13]

At the same time, Trent held that Jesus is somehow mysteriously present in the eucharistic species with a certain "objectivity." For while Trent never spoke of Jesus as "objectively" present in the eucharist, it did affirm that He could be adored in the sacred species.[14] What might such an affirmation imply?

The problem of the real presence can be clarified if one can move toward an experientially adequate account of the meaning of the terms "appearance" and "reality."[15] To do so, one must answer three interrelated questions: (1) What does it mean to "appear"? (2) How is the "reality" of an "appearance" grasped? (3) In what sense is the risen Christ really present in the eucharistic species of bread and wine?

The term "appearance" has more than one meaning. And much of the muddle in the debate over the real presence is a consequence of a failure to distinguish three different senses of the term "appearance." In its first use, "appearance" is synonymous with "self-disclosure." Leaves "appear" on the trees. The actor "appears" on the stage.

In its first use, the term "appearance" is not opposed to reality. It denotes an expressive symbol correctly perceived. It also connotes a focusing of attention within consciousness as well as a certain experiential conspicuousness or prominent quality, about the perceived reality. Hence, in its first meaning, "appearance" is actually opposed to "disappearance," to the absence or cessation of conspicuousness. But only real entities can emerge perceptually in an experience or hide from attentive search. We shall designate this sense of "appearance" as A_1.

The second sense of "appearance" suggests the notion of a "clue" or "hint" of a larger reality. The larger reality is not experienced immediately in its totality; but through what does "appear" (A_1) perceptually in experience, the larger reality becomes capable of inferential disclosure. And in this sense it too "appears." In its second meaning, therefore, "appearance" implies a reality which is only a phase or factual moment in a total intelligible reality, or process. In its second sense, "appearance" is, then, related to "reality" as the intelligible whole of which perceived, factual clues are a part. But in its second use as well an "appearance" is real. An example of such an "appearance" is the appearance of the solar system in the rising of the sun. Or it is the appearance of the guilt or innocence of the accused in the evidence presented at a trial. We shall designate this second sense of appearance as A_2.

Both A_1 and A_2 engage one interpretatively. But in each case a different reality is the focus of interpretative interest. In A_1, what appears perceptually is the focus of interpretative attention. In A_2 it is the larger reality which through inferential illumination renders a mass of unrelated perceptual clues intelligible.

There is, however, a third use of "appearance" which opposes it to reality. We shall designate this third sense of appearance as A_3. "A_3" denotes a "mere appearance." It is this third meaning of "appearance" which is linked with the greatest number of confusions.

Dualistic, metaphysical accounts of human experience define "A_3" as an ontologically inferior mode of being. Platonism, Gnosticism, and the dualistic cosmologies which undergird certain forms of oriental mysticism also use "A_3" in this sense. Another potentially confusing use of "A_3" links it with the operational dualism which is the necessary speculative concomitant of traditional faculty psychology. What "only appears" in experience is relegated to "the lower faculties" of sense. What is "real" in experience is grasped by the "higher spiritual faculties," whose formal object is being.

In the experiential problematic here suggested, neither of these fallacious senses of "A_3" is acceptable. Both senses lead to acquiescence in a misleading philosophical opposition of "spirit" and "matter." Moreover, the second demands the acceptance of an untenable faculty psychology.

In the experiential problematic here proposed, "A_3" is best understood as the indeterminate interpretative status of a reality which one seeks to grasp inferentially. For example, a stick thrust into water "only appears" (A_3) bent because on closer examination it is discovered to be not bent at all. As John Dewey has correctly observed, in such instances: "The hard and fast distinction between the perceptive object as mere appearance and the intelligible object as ultimate reality is thus a projection from a period when methods of inferential inquiry were deficient into a period when methods actually practiced leave no room for the distinctions."[15]

In the classic case of the apparently bent stick what appears (A_1) initially is "something bent." When the initial abduction that the stick itself is bent fails to be subsequently verified, it is replaced by a second inference: namely, that the stick only appeared

(A₃) to be bent. This second inference raises the question of the correct interpretation of what originally appeared (A₁). The mind concludes that what was really bent was not the stick itself, but the light rays which mediate its visual perception. When this third hypothesis is scientifically verified, the mind concludes inferentially that in the original appearance (A₁) of something bent, the bending of the light rays became apparent (A₂).

The theological term "species" used at Trent slurs over these three senses of "appearance." After the consecration, the material elements appear (A₁) to be bread and wine. But once the experienced consequences of eating and drinking the consecrated bread and wine in faith is grasped under the influence of the Spirit it becomes clear that they only appear (A₃) to be bread and wine. For their reception in faith mediates an efficacious encounter with God in a ritual meal of covenant renewal whose experienced salvific effects transcend the experienced effects of eating and drinking ordinary bread and wine. Hence, one can legitimately conclude in faith that as a consequence of its symbolic use in the eucharistic action what appears (A₁) to be bread and wine is only an appearance (A₃) of those natural realities. For their consumption in faith produces experienced salvific effects in the believer in which the saving action of Jesus, the one and only Spirit-baptiser, becomes apparent (A₂). Hence, the total reality which comes to appearance (A₂) in the sacrament of the eucharist can be grasped inferentially only within a religious conversion which mediates a correct interpretative understanding of the experienced consequences of the sacramental eating and drinking of the body and blood of the Lord.

The presence of Jesus in the eucharist is, moreover, efficacious in the three senses of sacramental efficacy discussed in chapter five. For the eucharistic sacramental word is a prophetic word that is efficacious either of salvation or judgment for those who share in the eucharistic action. As a prayer, the eucharist is also "efficacious" in the sense that the graces it calls down upon the community are certainly expressive of the saving mind of God. The prayer of the eucharistic minister remains divinely sanctioned, even though those engaged in the eucharistic act of worship resist the graces God seeks to give them in their act of covenant renewal.

For there is nothing mechanical about the reception of grace in the eucharist or in any other sacramental act. Finally, as the decisive personal renewal of a faith commitment, the eucharistic act is experientially efficacious. Once performed it enters into the permanent definition of the emergent self who partakes in it.

Moreover, whether the sacramental minister or the worshippers (s)he leads actually engage in eucharistic worship worthily or not, the consequences of their act go beyond the mere eating and drinking of bread and wine. Those consequences, being salvific in character, reveal the presence within the eucharistic act of a divine reality that goes beyond the human participants. And that larger reality is experienced as the reality of the tri-personal God who came to experiential visibility in the missions of the Son and of the Spirit.

Since the God who has revealed Himself in Jesus and the Spirit is a personal God, His presence in the Eucharist can be correctly grasped in faith only as a personal presence. In a substance theology, mutual inexistence was the exclusive prerogative of the three divine persons. But as we have also seen, in an experiential problematic, mutual inexistence is also the characteristic of space-time entities to the extent that they function efficaciously in one another's experience. The mutual inexistence of the divine persons is a consequence of their dynamic interrelation within the Godhead. But it entails that where one divine person is efficaciously present all are present. Jesus is present in a eucharistic covenant renewal through the action of the Spirit. His presence is active because it effects the pneumatic transformation of those who believe. Through the efficacious action of the Spirit, the eucharistic community exists in Jesus and Jesus in the community. The modality of Jesus' presence in the presiding celebrant and in the community is, however, a function of their respective calls, or gifts.

Within the act of eucharistic worship, the ordained minister confronts the believing community with apostolic authority. That authority is grounded in the Spirit's call to apostolic ministry and in the community's confirmation of that call in ritual ordination. In confronting the eucharistic community, the celebrant reaffirms the salvific commitment of God embodied in His incarnate Word and in the mission of the Holy Spirit. The ordained eucharistic minister challenges the assembled community to renew its covenant of grace. (S)he does so by re-enacting the prophetic gesture which Jesus used at the Last Supper to explain to His disciples the meaning of His impending death.[16] By that gesture, the eucharistic minister challenges the community to a formal reaffirmation of its covenant of initiation.

Jesus, through the power of the Spirit, is present in the eucharistic community to the extent that their covenant "amen" is an authentic expression of their baptismal faith and of their willingness to grow in the gifts of sanctification and of service. Jesus' presence in an authentic eucharistic action is not a mere appearance (A_3), because in its salvific consequences the reality of God appears (A_2). Hence, as the official pastoral magisterium has insisted, Jesus' presence in the eucharist cannot be explained by "mere metaphor" or "figure of speech," if such terms are intended to exclude the grasp of reality. Nor is Jesus' presence in the eucharistic act a presence of "mere power." For the term "mere power" also dissociates "power" from "reality." Rather, it is in the experience of the power of the Spirit at work in a charismatic, eucharistic community that the reality of God's presence comes to full sacramental visibility.

But to speak of Jesus as "objectively" present in the eucharist is potentially misleading. And the official pastoral magisterium has correctly eschewed using the term as such. For the term "objective" like the term "appearance" is surrounded by fallacious connotations. The term "objective," for example, suggests an absolute gulf between subject and object which is, however, precluded by the fact of mutual inexistence. Sacramental theologians have, to be sure, on more than one occasion projected their inadequate philosophical and epistemological presuppositions into their theories of the real presence. When implemented within eucharistic theology, epistemological dualism divorces Jesus' "altar presence" completely from His presence in the minister and in the worshipping community.

An experiential approach to human growth, however, grounds the "objectivity" present in human experience in the initial and subsequent realms of fact. And there are factual dimensions to Jesus' eucharistic presence. Jesus may, then, be said to be "objectively present" in the eucharistic species, to the extent that one may legitimately use such a term, in the qualified sense that the eucharistic elements, once used within a public act of worship, remain permanently capable of functioning within a Christian faith experience as expressive symbols of God's saving presence inasmuch as they can be used in that sacramental act of covenant renewal which has been traditionally called "holy communion." Jesus remains thus present in the consecrated elements as long as they are capable of being so used. And they will be capable of being so used as long as they are capable of being recognized in faith as the elements employed in a solemn eucharistic covenant renewal, that is, until they deteriorate beyond common-sense recognition. And, needless to say, Jesus as God can be adored in His every revelatory manifestation.

There is another sense, however, in which Jesus can be said to be "objectively present" in the sacred species. For His presence there is not the result of the personal faith of the sacramental worshipper alone. His presence there is a consequence first of all of the events of salvation recalled in eucharistic worship. Those events retain their salvific meaning independently of the personal attitudes of those who are summoned to confront them. The events of salvation are, of course, expressive symbols of divine grace. They are endowed with an historical meaning that is capable of correct or fallacious interpretation.

The Lord's eucharistic presence is also a consequence of a public faith act which engages the Church universal. It is mediated by the presence within the eucharistic action of a minister empowered to confront the community in the name of God and of the Church universal. The presence of God in the eucharistic minister and in the worshipping community is not a consequence of the personal faith of any single worshipping believer. It is the revelatory reality to which the sacramental worshipper ought to respond appropriately in faith.

Jesus' presence in the eucharistic elements is a "sacramental" presence in addition to being a symbolically "objective" one, because it is mediated by an act of covenant worship which is a sacrament in the fullest sense of that term. Jesus may be said to be salvifically present in the power of the Spirit in any act that is graced. But he may be said to be sacramentally present in the strict sense of "sacramental" only in an act which is a sacrament in the strict sense.

The elements of bread and wine are, then, really transformed by their very use in the eucharist. For in an experiential problematic, what a thing is is not defined by some immutuable, subjacent, substantial essence. It is a function of its history and of its experiential consequences. For the history of any entity conditions the dynamic tendencies concretely operative within it.

Through their historical subsumption into the eucharistic action, the bread and wine are, therefore, historically modified by use and in the process really changed into expressive, salvific symbols of the active, pneumatic, personal presence of Jesus. That they are really different comes to experiential visibility in the fact that by their symbolic use in eucharistic worship they become capable of effecting experienced salvific consequences in the lives of believers, consequences that transcend the eating of ordinary bread and wine. Upon those consequences the official pastoral magisterium has been at pains to insist over the centuries. Moreover, the eucharistic species acquire this salvific power simply by being taken up in the eucharistic act. That is to say, they acquire it *ex opere operato*, by the mere positing of the eucharistic act.

The pragmatic test of the authenticity of eucharist worship will, as we have seen, be the charismatic transformation of the worshipping eucharistic community. But when the expected salvific consequences fail to follow from the eating of eucharistic bread and wine, Christ continues to be personally, efficaciously, and pneumatically present in the actions of the eucharistic minister, as long as (s)he is willing to function in faith within the eucharistic act of worship. For every act of faith is the work of the Spirit.

6. We are now in a position to reflect briefly on the relationship between apostolic ministry and eucharistic worship. The seven Christian sacraments may, as we have seen, be defined as official public acts of covenant worship which engage the faith of the Church universal and therefore require the presence of a minister to confront the recipient of the sacrament in the name of God and of the universal Christian community. Within the sacramental act, the minister's function is to challenge the worshipper prophetically

to respond with appropriate faith and love to the salvation offered in Jesus. The act of covenant worship takes on different shades of salvific meaning as a consequence of being performed at different stages in the pneumatic, charismatic, development of a Christian faith experience.

There is, as we have also seen, a certain sacramentality attending any graced action. But it should be clear by now that there can be no ritual sacramental act in the strict sense of that term unless that act engages the Church universal formally and explicitly. But the Church universal cannot be engaged in a ritual act except through the presence within the act of some officially acknowledged spokesman.

That spokesman need not necessarily be an ordained apostolic minister. In extraordinary circumstances anyone may, for example, baptise. In marriage, neither sacramental minister is an ordained priest. And extraordinary ministers of all of the sacraments can be appointed for good reasons.

The presence in the believing community of ordinary and extraordinary sacramental ministers expresses the Christian community's conscious need, born of pastoral experience over the centuries, to exercise discerning control over who speaks officially in the community's name. It is possible that in the earliest days of the Christian community there were fewer restrictions on who was allowed to lead the eucharistic celebration. It is even conceivable that there was a time when any Christian in good standing was acknowledged as the equivalent of what is now called an "ordinary minister" of the eucharist.

But even granted the historical truth of such an hypothesis, once the move would have been made to restrict the official celebration of the eucharist to ordained apostolic leaders, it would have ceased to be possible for just any Christian to celebrate the eucharist sacramentally, unless, of course, the community would change its sacramental discipline. For the sacramental celebration of the eucharist in the strict sense demands a minister who confronts the community in the name of the Church universal. And no one appoints oneself to be a public, official spokesman for an entire believing community, or for any human community for that matter.

The notion, therefore, that any private individual can celebrate a eucharistic covenant renewal without the confirming sanction of the Church universal and without acting in solidarity with
its ordained leaders is indefensible. Equally indefensible is the notion that any local community acting with purely local authority
could generate spontaneously a full-fledged sacramental eucharistic minister from its midst or lend sacramental sanction in the
strictest sense to the eucharistic ministry of such a person. For
only one authorized to speak in the name of the Church universal
can celebrate a sacramental eucharist in the strict sense of that
term. By the same token, however, anyone whose eucharistic ministry would in fact be sanctioned by the Church universal would be
capable of celebrating a sacramental eucharist in the strictest sense
of the term, whether that individual were an ordained apostolic
minister or not. In Roman canonical terms, official authorization
to exercise a eucharistic ministry would insure the "validity" of the
celebration whether the celebrant were validly ordained or not.
Such authorization would, of course, have to be contingent upon
the potential celebrant's willingness to "do as the Church does."
The concrete regulation of such matters lies, of course, with the
Christian community acting in solidarity with its ordained apostolic leaders.

7. The attempt to minister theologically to Christians involved in the charismatic renewal has its rewards. But it is not
without its occasional ironies. Openness to the Spirit tends to generate in Christians a deep thirst for teaching. But the enthusiasm
to learn is not always matched by an equal discrimination in evaluating the materials absorbed.

In my own case, the attempt to exercise a teaching ministry in
charismatic circles has been on the whole deeply gratifying. I have,
however, found myself on occasion the object of both Catholic and
Protestant scorn. Frenetic Catholic voices have accused me of
leading devout Roman charismatics down the primrose path to
Protestant heresy. And resentful Protestant voices have on occasion accused me of trying to foist upon Protestant Christians
sectarian Roman views.

Like Paul, I am content to await judgment on the day of the
Lord, rather than be terribly outdone by the judgments of any

human "day." At the same time, I have become convinced with the bishops at Vatican II that the renewal of all of the churches is contingent upon an integration of the authentic values that have come to characterize their separate traditions.

I realize that not everyone will agree spontaneously with all the theses presented in the preceding pages. Not a few Catholics continue to be inclined to resist the fusion of Catholic and charismatic piety for both political and speculative reasons. Most of the speculative objections center around the fact that openness to the gifts of the Spirit seems to predominate in those Christian communions which have least emphasized sacramental piety in the Catholic mode.

But it would take a blind man or fool not to see that contemporary sacramental piety is shot through with legalism, formalism, and apathy. To argue from the fact that many Christians disregard conscious reflection on the gifts of the Spirit to the fact that such apathy is a religious ideal is to confound an "is" with an "ought." The only way to decide what sacramental piety ought to be is to come to a sound experiential insight into the dynamics of an authentic Christian conversion. If the preceding argument has been sound, that insight reveals that openness to the gifts of the Spirit lies at the heart of all authentic sacramental worship.

Moreover, the mere fact that the gifts of the Spirit can in fact be given outside the sacramental system is of itself no proof that such is their normative mode of reception. There is in fact solid evidence in Scripture that anyone who truly is open to the charismatic anointing of the Spirit is summoned by God to full participation in the sacramental life of the eucharistic community. It is this insight which in Acts is used to justify the baptism, without circumcision, of the first gentile Christians. When the Spirit descended upon Cornelius and his household as He had descended upon the apostles at Pentecost, Peter did not conclude that the event was devoid of sacramental significance. On the contrary, he concluded that the appearance of the gifts was a clear sign from God that he, Peter, could in no way refuse sacramental baptism to the uncircumcised gentiles.

Let anyone, then, who disagrees with the stand outlined in these pages show how one can come to an insight into the meaning of Christian conversion without reflecting on the normative development of a Christian faith experience. Let such a person show how the experiential categories here used suffer from inconsistency or inadequacy.

Then let it be explained how it is possible to consent authentically to God in faith without desiring to be led by the Spirit to put on the mind of Christ in the pneumatic, charismatic community which Jesus founded. Let it be shown how it is possible to grow in such a desire without consenting to be baptized. Let it be demonstrated how it is possible to consent to the graces of baptism without consenting to being sanctified in the image of Jesus. And let proof be offered to show why enduring sensitivity to the Spirit in the process of sanctification can be in no legitimate sense designated as "charismatic."

Let it also be shown how it is possible to grow in sanctity without desiring to serve others in the name of Christ. Let it be explained how it is possible to decide in faith upon the ecclesial service one will render without consenting to a gift of service. And let arguments be formulated to show how consent to one's service gift can be authentic without being an expression of one's willingness to serve within the Church universal in whatever way the Spirit may lead. And let it be explained too why the ritual expression of such a commitment should not be part of Christian initiation.

Let it be shown how one can consent to marriage or orders as a Christian without that consent being a response to a charismatic gift. Let reasons be given why such a decision should be exempt from discernment by the community, acting in solidarity with its leaders. And let it be demonstrated why, if they are not exempt, such acts fail to meet the conditions for a ritual sacrament in the fullest sense of the term.

Let it also be shown that one can exercise an efficacious ministry of preaching without effecting the healing of men in faith. Let it be explained why such a ministry, if authentic and salvific, is not charismatically grounded. And let it be demonstrated why an apostolic ministry of healing fails to endow a charismatic ministry of healing with a salvific significance that is strictly sacramental.

Finally, let it be established how it is possible to reaffirm one's baptismal commitment as a Christian in an act of eucharistic recall and to accept its lived consequences without recommitting oneself to active openness in faith to whatever gifts the Spirit may desire to give.

In other words, let anyone who takes exception to the position outlined in these pages speak to the issues. If (s)he can point out factual inaccuracies, logical inconsistencies, or inductive oversights, I would hope that (s)he would find in me the first to say thanks. But if the preceding argument is sound, then the tendency to dissociate a theology of gift from a theology of sacrament is grounded in something else than an integral, fourfold conversion. In more than one instance, it is symptomatic of ecclesiastical or ecumenical jitters.

In more than one place, charismatic piety continues to be regarded by the hierarchy with fear and suspicion. Sometimes those fears are solidly grounded in the uncritical absorption by charismatics of inauthentic religious attitudes. Sometimes those fears are rooted in irrational and anti-Pentecostal bigotry. A theology which denies any serious connection between the gifts and the sacraments can easily pander to what is irrational in such fears. Moreover, it can create the theological illusion that one can continue to minister sacramentally to others without consciously acknowledging both in theory and in practice the charismatic basis and consequences of one's ministry.

At the same time, the speculative dissociation of the gifts and the sacraments provides Protestant Christians whose traditions are sacramentally impoverished with an easy rationalization for continuing to ignore the sacramental dimension of an authentic, charismatic faith experience.

But the gospel has never been benefited by time-serving theological theories. The word of God is a summons to an ever deeper conversion. And the truth of the matter is that neither Catholic nor Protestant piety in many of their present popular forms is completely acceptable.

If both Catholic and Protestant communions are to grow in authentic openness to the charismatic activity of the Spirit, they must learn to appropriate the genuine values which have been concretely operative in the traditions of other Christians. If, then,

Christians from strong sacramental traditions are in the process of learning from Protestant Pentecostals about the gifts of the Spirit, Protestant Pentecostals may anticipate that they have a few lessons to learn from Christian sacramentalists about the meaning of sacramental piety and about the processes of spiritual growth that follow upon initial conversion.

In point of fact, the Roman Catholic community has scarcely begun to explore the speculative and pastoral implications of sound charismatic piety. One may at present observe two legitimate but divergent tendencies in the Catholic charismatic renewal: a centripetal impulse to form covenant communities as pneumatic service centers for the larger Christian community and a centrifugal impulse to effect the charismatic renewal of all existing Church institutions. Like monasticism and parochial life, both are legitimate ecclesial impulses as long as they do not become closed to one another and to the values that the other seeks to embody.

Nevertheless, it seems clear that unless the Catholic charismatic renewal can effect the transformation of existing Church institutions by opening those laboring within them to all the gifts of the Spirit, the Catholic charismatic renewal will remain on the fringes of ordinary Church life; and its effect upon the majority of Catholics will remain minimal.

One important goal of charismatic piety ought, then, to be the charismatic transformation of every parish. Parish ministry is in many places taking the form of team ministry to a parish that is subdivided into smaller worshipping communities. Charismatic prayer groups are developing a similar team ministry. The day may not be far away, therefore, when the normal Catholic parish will be composed of many small charismatic prayer communities with lay spiritual leadership. The lay leaders of these charismatic sub-communities could function effectively as the members of the parish council and could help keep the pastor abreast of developments in each smaller prayer group. They could also aid the pastor in discerning the movements of the Spirit in the parish as a whole and in each of its subcommunities.

Another important goal of the charismatic renewal ought to be the charismatic transformation of Christian education. For the goal of Christian education must be to lead young people to an integral, fourfold conversion. That process will proceed efficaciously only to the extent that Christian educational institutions become charismatic communities sharing freely with one another the gifts given them by the Lord.

The third goal of charismatic piety ought to be the charismatic renewal of every rectory, seminary, and religious house. For true religious renewal must go beyond workshops, committee meetings, and theological discussions. If, moreover, the preceding analysis has been sound, one cannot train novices and seminarians in authentic sacramental piety unless that training integrates into itself training in charismatic prayer.

But it is also clear at this point that the charismatic renewal will have an impact on the rest of the Church only if charismatics are also willing to face the religious inauthenticities they may have unconsciously imbibed by the practice of a doctrinally shallow form of charismatic piety.

If the preceding analysis is sound, it is necessary to replace the classic Protestant Pentecostal account of conversion and the rhetoric it encourages with a more adequate theology of conversion. More specifically, the fundamentalism and moral rigorism one encounters not infrequently among charismatics must be recognized as symptomatic of a failure to integrate fully intellectual moral, and religious conversion. For both tendencies express the attempt to substitute a specific theological or ethical formulation of belief and Christian practice for the living word of God. The other-worldly, chiliastic tone of charismatic piety leaves it all too frequently insensitive to questions of political and social reform. This failure too must be acknowledged as symptomatic of a deeper failure to integrate religious with moral conversion. The failure of a significant number of Protestant Pentecostals to acknowledge fully the sacramental conscquences of an integrally charismatic faith commitment is yet another potential source of inauthenticity in charismatic prayer groups. So is the simplistic account of healing and of deliverance that one sometimes encounters among charismatic Christians. Finally, the invocation of Scripture to lend pseudo-religious sanction to the socio-economic oppression of women must be abandoned as a fundamentalistic perversion of the word of God.

These ideas have been discussed in the course of the preceding pages. That discussion will have achieved its purpose if it succeeds in evoking fruitful dialogue between Catholic and Protestant and between the charismatic renewal and the Church universal.

Notes

1. Cf. Louis Bouyer, S.J. *Eucharist*, translated by Charles Underhill Quinn (Notre Dame: University of Notre Dame Press, 1966) pp. 30-104.

2. *Sacrosanctum concilium*, 10; see also: Bernard Cooke, "Synoptic Presentation of the Eucharist as a Covenant Sacrifice," *Theological Studies*, XXI (March, 1960) pp. 1-44.

3. Gustaf Aulén, *Eucharist and Sacrifice*, translated by Eric H. Wahlstrom (Philadelphia: Muhlenberg, 1958); Joseph Ratzinger, "Is the Eucharist a Sacrifice?" in *The Sacraments: An Ecumenical Dilemma* (N.Y.: Paulist, 1967) pp. 66-77; Francis Clark, S.J., *Eucharistic Sacrifice in the Reformation* (Oxford: Blackwell, 1967); John C. Kirby, "Eucharistic Liturgy in the Anglican Communion," *Worship*, XLII (October, 1968) pp. 446-486.

4. Cf. J. Patout Burns, S.J. "The Concept of Satisfaction in Medieval Redemption Theory," *Theological Studies*, XXXVI (June, 1975) pp. 285-289.

5. *Ibid.*, 289-304.

6. Stanislaus Lyonnet and Leopold Sabourin, *Sin, Redemption, and Sacrifice* (Rome: Biblical Institute, 1970) pp. 134-164, 183-184.

7. Cf. Karl Rahner, S.J., *Theological Investigations*, IV, pp. 105-120.

8. DS 1713, 1690.

9. Lyonnet and Sabourin, *op. cit.*, pp. 178-181.

10. Joseph Powers, S.J. *Eucharistic Theology* (N.Y.: Herder and Herder, 1967) pp. 154-179; see also Carol Stuhlmueller, C.P., "The Holy Eucharist: Symbol of Christ's Glory," *Worship*, XXXIV (April, 1960) pp.

258-268; "The Holy Eucharist: Symbol of the Passion," *Worship*, XXXIV (March, 1960) pp. 195-205.

11. DS 1636, 1651; Karl Rahner, S.J., "The Presence of Christ in the Sacrament of the Lord's Supper," *Theological Investigations*, IV, pp. 287-311.

12. Cf. Joseph Powers, *op. cit.*, "*Mysterium fidei* and the Theology of the Eucharist," *Worship*, XL (January, 1966) pp. 17-35; Eduard Schillebeeckx, O.P., "Transubstantiation, Transfinalization, and Transignification," *Worship*, XL (June-July, 1966) pp. 324-388, *The Eucharist* (N.Y.: Sheed and Ward, 1968); Piet Schoonenberg, S.J., "The Real Presence in Contemporary Discussion," *Theology Digest* XV (1967) pp. 3-11, "Transubstantiation: How Far is This Doctrine Historically Determined?" in *The Sacraments: An Ecumenical Dilemma* (N.Y.: Paulist, 1967) pp. 78-91; Cyril Vollert, S.J., "The Eucharistic Controversy on Transubstantiation," *Theological Studies*, XXII (September, 1961) pp. 391-422; Jean Galot, S.J., "The Theology of the Eucharistic Presence," *Review for Religious*, XX (July, 1963) pp. 407-429; Austin McGregor, "The Real Presence," Worship, XLI (February, 1967) pp. 99-104.

13. DS 1642, 1653.

14. DS 1639, 1654.

15. The approach to the problem of appearance and reality is in basic accord with the position of John Dewey; cf. John Dewey, "Appearing and Appearance," in *Philosophy and Civilization* (N.Y.: Capricorn, 1963) pp. 56-76.

16. Joachim Jeremias, *The Eucharistic Words of Jesus*, translated by Norman Perrin (N.Y.: Scribner's, 1966).

17. DS 690-700, 1018, 1640-1641.